Local Haunts

Local Haunts

Non-Fiction
2012–24

Adam Scovell

Influx Press
London

Published by Influx Press
Mainyard Studios
58B Alexandra Road
Enfield, EN3 7EH
www.influxpress.com / @InfluxPress
All rights reserved.

Printed and bound in the UK by TJ Books.
Published by Influx Press, London, UK, 2025.

Paperback ISBN: 9781914391460
Ebook ISBN: 9781914391477

Cover design: Flavio Mancini
Text design: Vince Haig

For Laura

'There are no walls or fences. My garden's boundaries are the horizon.'
– Derek Jarman

Contents

Wanders   95

Film & Television   247

Introduction

I have always been drawn to strange, forgotten and uneasy places. I adore locales haunted by ghosts of the culture that I love, by synchronicities between individuals and buildings long since passed; by things ignored by most passers-by. These are what I call my local haunts.

Over the last decade or so of writing, I have not only explored and questioned ideas surrounding the links between place and culture, but have actively sought to visit and photograph places haunted by such culture; determined (though not always successful) to find potential connections between people, the artwork they have made and where they have made it.

While focusing on place as a theme in works of narrative art does have its interest, whether in novels, films, or anything else, I am in hindsight more personally interested in the maps that such idiosyncratic approaches to place chart by chance. Few exercises in creative research can have as profound an effect on the perception of a place as trudging off to find some little-known cultural marker: a location from a film, a street where a playwright lived, the grave of an author.

However, the irony present throughout is that such locality in relation to me personally is through cultural interest rather than genuine geographical connection, as odd as that may seem for people more naturally grounded in the places they're born in. These are locales I feel I have inherited a connection to through the arts rather than by dint of where I was born.

Cities become film sets. Streets become libraries. Fantasy and reality blur.

Throughout the last decade, I have been lucky enough to indulge my interests, whether for my own website (when I was afforded greater freedom by money from an academic grant for a totally unconnected PhD), or for other websites that, too, have shared my interest in either culture coloured by place or places coloured by culture.

In spite of each article reprinted here having had a certain amount of rewriting, editing and new research applied since the original publication, I am still incredibly grateful to my various editors over the years who have given me the chance to carve an admittedly unusual niche for myself while never faltering in their support under the pervasive pressures of our increasingly homogenous clickbait era.

A quick glance through the contents will show that a number of key figures preoccupy me more than most. I make no apology for this, aware that several articles exploring the work of M.R. James, W.G. Sebald and Marguerite Duras may not be of interest to everyone. But I hope the potential maps provided here, through words and photographs, may encourage others to visit these unusual places and, equally, explore the unique and wonderful works they inspired.

This volume is split into three sections which naturally overlap. The opening section explores work dealing with writers. The last explores work in film and television, while the middle bridges the gap between the two, exploring both in a very literal sense. This was somewhat easier than collecting all the articles together that focus on the same writers and filmmakers, or ordering things chronologically. Due to the nature of a few figures, some appear across all three sections. By formatting the articles as such, it should highlight that the relationship between place and culture is a two-way street. One unavoidably informs the other, no matter the medium.

It must be said that, in collating this body of work, which represents a geographical as much as a mental map of the last ten years or so of my life, I am under no illusion that such visits or approaches guarantee any new understanding of a particular book, film or anything else. Nor do I deny that such an interest can be, at times, a lonely one. It is simply a surrendering to my curiosity, and that is all. I cannot pretend that such visits always provide insight, and I am, by my own admission, suspicious of those who do mark such connections with the confident assertion of having discovered some great alchemical secret that other writers and critics may have missed.

However, I am more than happy to approach culture from this direction, simply for my own pleasure. It is rewarding in ways that are difficult to fully explain or convey, and certainly I have found that insight does occasionally arise from such visits, some of which is hopefully present on the pages that follow.

I hope most of all that this book is of interest to those who, like me, share such curiosity in finding, exploring and celebrating culture's own local haunts, wherever they may be.

Off the beaten track we go.

Adam
17/11/23

Literature

The Lonely Ghosts of M.R. James

I was shooting some Super-8 footage early one morning on the shingle beach of Aldeburgh on the Suffolk coast when the mist started to rise. Walking the coastline in order to film a short ode to the master of the English ghost story, M.R. James, and in particular his short story 'A Warning to the Curious', meant ghosts were very much on my mind.

The haze slowly rose with the sun and, stood outside Sluice Cottage (the abandoned building that supposedly found its way into James's story as the previous home of its reclusive, unforgiving spectre William Ager), the path crossed the marsh beyond with far more confidence and fortitude than I had. It was an undeniably unnerving place.

As so often happens on walks into literary works, new realisations became apparent; not simply that James had tapped into a place's genuine eeriness to tell his macabre ghost story, but that the perspective of his stories was *solitary*.

Being alone in that landscape and wandering along the empty shingle beaches, as well as the marshes that seemed to exhale a strange, morbid light, showed how solitude was essential to James and his characters who, for various reasons of naivety, arrogance and greed, stumble into dangers alone, as in a nightmare.

Within the strange, unsettled horror of James's ghost stories, there's a sense of melancholy because of this solitude. The writer, a Victorian out of time and living through the dramatic changes of the Edwardian age, seems an anomaly, settling into safe havens away from the progress of modernity and his own dawning horror at its approach.

Following an almost perfect academic trajectory from Eton to Cambridge as a student, Provost at King's College, and then finally Provost at Eton before his death, James was a writer who turned calmly away from the world around him. Such a withdrawal imbued his work with small joys: of a scholarly academic finding new curios, the pleasures of cobwebbed details. But the inevitable isolation such a life ultimately entailed was present as well.

Though James's scholarly achievements were monumental, and still in some ways unsurpassed, he is better known for his macabre tales, which all but defined the English ghost story as an accursed form in itself. Possessed of unique antiquarian detail, James's prose mixed a dusty sense of the ancient with an unconsciously literary sensibility, creating genuine fear and moments of distilled malevolence.

Yet underneath all of this is a perceptible sadness, the macabre hiding a more earnest loneliness. James structured his ghost stories not simply around the visceral imagery of texts and antiquity, with which he had surrounded himself for the majority of his life, but around a very real frustration: an isolated life that arguably forced the academic to make the most of more ghostly pleasures.

James first presented his haunting stories to the Chit-Chat society of King's College, specifically when winter arrived and Christmas was close. Little could the listeners have known what primal horror awaited them on those early readings. Even in hindsight, the choice of reading aloud – for a society renowned for not being particularly concerned with many things bar trivialities, snuff, claret and social pleasures – still seems unusual in hindsight.

Of course, their success inspired James to eventually publish, writing stories more and more to be read rather than as a minor distraction for his peers during the Christmas period. But there's something in this act, and in the stories themselves moving from social performance to written shorts, that conveys the true solitude of M.R. James; the man on the quiet country path, alone except for the ghosts of other concerns.

Solitude

The loneliness of James's stories is often pervasive. Even when there is more than one person within the scenario leading to a haunting, the figure in question is usually alone or will eventually end up alone for a final ghostly retribution.

Solitude is part of the process of being haunted. Eeriness in such stories is derived from others seeing the act from afar or hearing of it second-hand via word of mouth; shrouded rather than fully present.

James's protagonists – academics, cosmopolitans, meddlers – walk knowingly into this solitude, the company of men gradually fading from memory as if the scenario around them has become too implausible to share.

From James's very first ghost story, 'Canon Alberic's Scrap Book', it's as if characters chase after time alone as much as the antiquarian and archaeological knowledge they desire. Our protagonist in this case, 'a Cambridge man', specifically leaves his colleagues in Toulouse to visit the churches of St. Bertrand de Comminges alone.

These friends 'were less keen archaeologists than himself', and he goes on ahead, such is the character's desire to see the various historic artefacts and architecture of the town. Beneath this simple haze of minor detail lies something more telling: the Cambridge man's mentality. He's not merely on holiday for pleasure, but is driven by needs that even people within his field, his peers and colleagues, fail to fully understand. It's the quiet beginning of all loneliness.

These lone men are tasked with sifting through history, pulling out the occasional object from the slipstream; objects that suggest a receding past that others, supposedly now over the horizon, are still unnervingly in consideration of. This is a task for those in solitude.

Professor Parkin of 'Oh, Whistle, and I'll Come to you, M'Lad' avoiding the offers of golfing games in favour of solitary walks along the coast in search of Knights Templar burial grounds; Wraxall of 'Count Magnus' on his lone walks past the tomb of the haunted count, desiring to see him until his hopes become horrifically realised; or Paxton in 'A Warning to the Curious', the amateur on the same Suffolk coastline I walked who found a cursed Saxon crown but is swept away by longings for the days when its ghostly protector didn't provide him with constant companionship.

It's often said that James's characters are autobiographical, a number of traits being clearly derived from the man's own persona: the academic nature, the fustiness, the fear of the unknown and the modern, even down to the man's own holiday habits, often doubling up as pleasurable research trips to note historical interests, architecture, and sometimes the simple rapture of the landscape. But also within them is a leaning towards solitude, a recognition that, for whatever reason (often read as James's own reality as a non-practising homosexual man in an era when such things were actively legislated against), the country path was only ever wide enough for one; choked by seclusion and the ghosts thinly veiled within it, always following.

Trauma

Trauma is embedded into the soil of James's ghost stories. Sometimes this trauma sets in motion the narrative, but other times it is the finale coming full circle or the climax that befalls the prying protagonists. Trauma blackly manifests through this duality, as an anticipator of a violent reoccurrence and as a grammatical end to the meddling.

This trauma need not always be violent or even result in death, though it more often than not does, especially if it is anticipatory of the narrative arc and essential to the accursed nature of the land.

In 'The Ash Tree', a woman is burned for being a witch. The evidence of Sir Matthew Fell of Castringham – a relative of the later protagonist Sir Richard Fell – condemns the witch to certain death, though not before she curses him and the ash tee that looms outside his bedroom window. The trauma is already interred within the East Anglian land, her body later found under the tree after much demonic turmoil has unfolded. Trauma for James, it could be said, is cyclic.

Equally, in 'Lost Hearts', the ghosts – two children murdered by a deranged alchemist seeking their organs for a potion granting eternal life – are representative of a past trauma and a warning of the impending danger for the young protagonist whose heart will complete the alchemist's bloody ritual in search of immortality.

If the trauma isn't already embedded, then it slowly but certainly appears on the horizon for James's solitary walkers. They sometimes walk after it in curiosity, but soon find their feet retreating on the pebbly beaches and empty country paths.

In 'Oh, Whistle…', this is apparent, though not necessarily violent. The character's trauma is eventually one of a contradictory loss of faith in the rational; his views of the world around him dramatically changed by a fearful encounter with ruffling bed sheets. 'There is really nothing more to tell, but,' so James writes, 'as you may imagine, the Professor's views on certain points are less clear-cut than they used to be.' The change is dramatic, though not necessarily always conducted down a deathly cul-de-sac.

James's most melancholic stories, however, do end in violence, and, especially in his later writing, the trauma related to a supernatural encounter is very often deadly.

This is never more evident than in 'A Warning to the Curious', a story whose structure somewhat resembles 'Oh, Whistle…'and yet features a decidedly more tragic tone. It's impossible to shake off the feeling that, writing after the experiences of seeing many of his students and colleagues killed during the First World War, James's more encompassing sadness is draped over his writing, darkening its hues and removing its original fireside warmth.

In 'A Warning…', a familiar scenario is present: a lonely wanderer searching for a lost, valuable object – the lost crown of Anglia – only to find it guarded by a relentless protector. Yet, unlike with Parkin, there is no moment of consideration for Paxton. His trespass, even when reversed with the crown apologetically returned to the soft soil, cannot be forgiven.

Paxton's death is one of James's most violent and leaves its trace on the narrator far more than others. The narrator describes in stark detail the physical wounds the poor man received: his 'mouth was full of sand and stones, and his teeth and jaws were broken to bits'. He may as well have been the victim of a shredding round from a Vickers gun. But perhaps the most melancholy aspect of the story is detailing the sheer disappearance of the dead man. 'Paxton was so totally without connections that all the inquiries that were subsequently made ended in a No Thoroughfare,' writes James.

The character was so isolated, so beyond the help of anyone, that, even after the vengeful ghost of William Ager has torn his face to smithereens, the trauma pales in comparison to the wider tragedy of a man so acutely alone in the world, even in death.

Sorrow

One of the most famous fragments, oft repeated, from Robert Burton's monumental *The Anatomy of Melancholy* is also apt for James's stories, and perhaps could even describe the author himself. 'He that increaseth wisdom,' wrote Burton, 'increaseth sorrow.' Knowledge comes with the burden of melancholy, a heightened awareness of the world and a more astute understanding of its fallacies and tragedies.

Intellectualism is an increasingly isolating pursuit. Even Albrecht Dürer, when sketching *Melancholia* in 1514, placed the character frowning and forlorn, surrounded by the apparatus of knowledge but decidedly solitary, except for an equally moribund cherub and a dog whose ribs shine through its fur to such an extent that it may actually be dead.

James's figures fit within this model. They are often seeking knowledge through paraphernalia, relics, artefacts and objects of all kinds. Through finding cursed gold, a whistle, a child's heart, or a Saxon crown, the lonely men believe something will be closer and within their grasp.

This knowledge is not always academic, nor is it purely satiating intellectual satisfaction. Somerton of 'The Treasure of Abbott Thomas' can barely hide his greed for the cursed alchemist's gold behind a disintegrating veil of antiquarian curiosity. Again, like 'A Warning…', the ghost is unforgiving, the story perhaps a comment on academic arrogance, even if it was ultimately a last-minute addition for James's first published volume. But the drive towards these things is portrayed with genuine curiosity, one that is really James's more than anyone else's.

It's James who cycles alone to village churches desiring their awnings, who pores over old manuscripts, and catalogues Cambridge University's archive of ancient texts and papers. James is the lone figure in the end, even when surrounded by peers and friends at the crackling fireside. He can't help but seem melancholic, retreading the ghost roads of his memories in solitude, on trips where the only company in the end is the accursed and the unholy.

I was grateful for my lift arriving after hours of filming on the marshes and beaches of Aldeburgh. The feeling of being joined only by those unseen faded with the pale mist as a bright sun came up and brushed it aside. It never receded for James, however; he was always alone in the land. Considering the company that eventually arose to break the silence of his haunted wanderings, perhaps that is for the best.

Published by The Nightjar, 24/01/19

The Synthetic Landscape
of J.G. Ballard

We're living in J.G. Ballard's world, so we're often told. Such is the precision of Ballard's not-so-futuristic predictions that it has become cliché to link our current political, technological, architectural and even social states to the man's writing. But, outside of his great 1970s social dystopias such as *High-Rise* (1975) and *Concrete Island* (1974), as well as his morbid millennial retail-park nightmares of *Millennium People* (2003) and *Kingdom Come* (2006), Ballard's shorter writing has just as much to say about our time as his more famous novels.

This familiarity may be because we have moved on so little from the period of Ballard's most popular writing, but it fails to lessen the effect of reading his work; forever inducing a look up from the page just to check that he's not still about, somehow taking notes as the world beyond his death merges with those he created.

This feeling occurred for me most powerfully a few years back, not in front of a London high-rise or underneath a cavernous motorway as to be expected, but while visiting the ex-weapons testing facility of Orford Ness in Suffolk. Equally, it was not a novel of Ballard's that gave rise to this feeling, but a short story written in 1964: 'The Terminal Beach'.

Ballard's story is tragic and surprisingly emotional, far from his more typical laboratory approach to character and narrative. So often does he toy with his characters' lives that he resembles a mad scientist enjoying cruel experiments unleashed upon animals.

The story concerns a lonely man called Travern who takes refuge on the nuclear testing island of Eniwetok after the death of his wife and son. Similar to a number of Ballard's novels, the story links the decline of the environment to the character's mental state; the nuclear fallout from various tests suffered by the landscape decaying alongside Travern's inner state.

Ballard psychoanalyses his character, not through some deep probing of the past, but by giving a segmented tour of the island and the carcass of its facilities; grief as damnation alley. Travern is rooting around his own cracked mind just as much as he is around the smashed, Geiger-melted concrete. He even hides from a naval search party who represent everything in humanity that he can no longer bear. Solitude in the deadly ruins is better than the companionship of the children of the atom.

'The Terminal Beach' is, in a way, a nuclear ghost story. It's certainly not a naïve 'Ban the Bomb' tract. Travern sees visions of his deceased loved ones visiting his new edgeland territory as his mind disintegrates. They watch him from the dunes, drifting nearer as he reaches a critical mass of instability. Sitting patiently, he waits for them to speak. But there are no voices left in this world, one scarred by the continued need for nuclear weapons.

The ghosts of many atrocities haunt the text, almost cathartically like the silent screams emanating from the calamities barely twenty years old at the time of Ballard's writing. Perhaps this is why, like so much of the writer's work, 'The Terminal Beach' has aged so well. It's not simply because the threat of a nuclear holocaust is still conceivable (and seems to have found an unlikely new, if oversensitive, early warning system today in the form of social media), but because there's an anticipation to the narrative, an acceptance that the testing of such weapons unavoidably suggests their eventual use.

Apocalypse is not a theory for Travern but reality.

The island of the story was a heavy testing site for the United States, who eventually planted a huge concrete deposit there for all sorts of nuclear debris. It's a genuine concrete island, far more disturbing than Ballard's actual *Concrete Island*, that strange edgeland under the Westway from his 1974 novel.

My day at the National Trust terminal beach in Suffolk still stirs my thoughts with both inspiration and fear. It was a filming trip that took me on a visit to this strange coastal zone. The trip certainly reminded me of Ballard's story.

Author Robert Macfarlane helped organise access to some of the famous laboratories on the site to film them, the same laboratories described by W.G. Sebald in *The Rings of Saturn* (1996) as resembling pagodas. These are where Sebald imagined himself 'amidst the remains of our own civilization after its extinction in some future catastrophe'.

In an essay for the *Guardian*, Macfarlane describes Orford Ness as 'a dreamscape co-designed by MR James, JG Ballard and Andrei Tarkovsky'. The Ballardian element referenced here is undoubtedly a nod to 'The Terminal Beach', the likeness between the two places uncanny to experience, even if in differing climes.

The warden of Orford Ness drove us into the heart of this zone on a small electric cart straight out of a science-fiction film. The battered mesh fences, shingle pathways and marshland blurred together as my knuckles turned white from holding onto the deranged vehicle. It was, quite simply, a journey into the terminal beach, albeit one haunted by the potential of nuclear fallout rather than actual half-life hazards like Travern faces.

Ballard writes in his story that the 'series of weapons tests had fused the sand in layers, and the pseudogeological strata condensed the brief epochs, microseconds in duration, of thermonuclear time'. There is more than a passing likeness here, even if Orford Ness was only officially the site for testing the firing mechanisms (and God knows what else). Its shifting shores feel equally scarred and difficult to measure.

Walking and filming around Orford Ness resulted in the same feeling as reading Ballard's story: that of a temporal overlap, like receding and incoming tides briefly meeting to create a vortex. The past is there, haunting with the clanking chains of Cold War paranoia. But, if we are unlucky, so is our future.

Published by Fourth Estate, 29/11/17

Salvaging the Ashes
of H.R. Wakefield

The smell of burning must have taken on a chemical flavour as the documents were piled onto the flames rippling behind the grating. In my mind's eye, I can see a worn-down man, someone who has probably seen more of the world's darkness than he realistically would have liked, stoking the fire. Piles of ephemera are littered 'at his feet: letters yellow with age; typed and handwritten manuscripts telling bizarre tales of the uncanny; even some photographs of the man himself.

He was trying to disappear.

In one sense, it was a burning of his mere identity: an action that suggests, more than anything else, a desire to become a ghost before his time. The vanishing man was Herbert Russell Wakefield, a writer of ghost stories. Judging by the lack of discussion of his work today, he almost succeeded in his task. As with everything in our age of digital eternal return, however, disappearance is only the first step towards reappearance.

Unsurprisingly, considering the denomination of his name, Wakefield wrote a combination of ghost stories and weird fiction. Christian names are a curse to weird fiction writers. Like H.P. Lovecraft, M.R. James and E.F. Benson,

Wakefield wrote short tales of the supernatural, slotted into the everyday lives of his distinctly Edwardian era.

Though writing with similar emphasis on personal terror as the writers he followed – James, Arthur Machen, Algernon Blackwood, et al – his writing soon slipped from the public consciousness, falling rapidly out of print and only reprinted a handful of times after the Second World War. Even a collected volume in the 1970s, when a taste for such stories was rife once more, failed to garner the sort of attention given to reprints of similar writers and their work. Wakefield is notable by his consistent absence, as if his ritualistic burning cursed future attempts to bring him back from the grave.

He was born in Sandgate, Kent, the third child of his clergyman father Henry Wakefield, the eventual Bishop of Birmingham. He went to boarding school in Wiltshire – Marlborough College, to be exact – before, like many Old Marlburians, entering Oxbridge to study History at Oxford's oldest institution, University College. Following in the footsteps of Percy Shelley and C.S. Lewis did little for him, as he spent more time on sports, passing through the college with only a reasonable grade and future expectations.

He took his first steps into publishing soon after graduating, working as secretary to the mogul-esque press baron Alfred Harmsworth, before the First World War brought that career to a halt. Serving in the Royal Scot Fusiliers, he saw action in a number of battles and soon rose to the rank of captain. Certainly, reading the stories he would soon produce, war regularly rears its head as the cause of the disturbed state of his protagonists.

The other pillar of his characters' lives was an equally brutal endeavour: working in the publishing industry.

After a stint in America, coupled with a failed marriage, he found a home in London and worked his way up the ranks at William Collins, eventually becoming a chief editor. His characters are frequently intertwined with publishing and, even more so, in the writing of ghost stories. Because of this, his stories sometimes lapse into something akin to ghostly auto-fiction, spiced up with biting critiques of his industry's smarminess.

By the late 1920s, he'd started work on his ghost stories, publishing *They Return at Evening: a Book of Ghost Stories* in 1928. He would go on to publish several volumes and become a regular name in anthology editions and magazines of weird fiction, producing a vaguely respected body of work that would soon fall into shadow. By the end, he seemed jaded with it all. 'I've written my last ghost story,' he wrote in the introduction to his final volume, *Strayers from Sheol* (1961). 'I believe ghost story writing to be a dying art.'

So what lay behind Wakefield's stories? Where did they share likenesses and differences with his contemporaries? And will his spirit be summoned again from the groaning shelves of dusty libraries, or should he be left to rest with the ashes in his fireplace as he so clearly desired?

Shadows

In an apt crossover between reality and fiction, my one and only volume of Wakefield's stories was gifted to me via a partly fictional character. The fictionally malevolent but assuredly real and incredibly friendly nonagenarian Phyllis Ewans (who inhabited my first novel, *Mothlight* (2019)) left her collection of macabre books to me after she died.

Among them was one dusty volume of Wakefield's stories; an original 1932 edition of *Ghost Stories* printed as part of Jonathan Cape's Florin Series that boasts being 'the right size for all times, and the right price for these times'. That price was 2s net each. In this series, Wakefield shared space with the likes of Flaubert, Hemingway and the Brontës. In his lifetime, at least, his status was assured.

Reading Wakefield in the context of the writers he openly admired can be a strange experience, like coming upon misremembered echoes and even retellings of other works. In many ways, his stories (at least those I've managed to find) fill a gap between the fusty, antiquarian world of M.R. James and the weirder, post-Pinter world of Robert Aickman, all horn-rimmed spectacles and *Play for Today*. Wakefield is a sort of missing link between the two, with one overriding concern that partly accounts for the eventual disappearance of his work: the insufferable social milieu of his characters.

The ordinariness of his stories is double-edged, explaining both their strengths and weaknesses. If P.G. Wodehouse had considered more ghastly matters than the wrong tie or an accidental engagement, perhaps his stories might have resembled Wakefield's to some degree.

A sense of class hierarchy is present from the first tale that opens *Ghost Stories*, 'Messrs. Turkes and Talbot'. Like many of his protagonists, Bob Fanning is the Oxford-educated son of rich parents who decides, almost on a whim, to go into publishing, where he 'spends most of his time yawning over typed garbage'. Some things never really change.

Though Wakefield's characters are not especially malicious, it's hard to feel any sympathy for their experiences.

At times, the violent, unforgiving spirits found in James's work are much missed. In 'Old Grey Beard', one of Wakefield's stranger and more daringly erotic stories, even the image of a sultry, caressing grey beard haunting the dreams of a young woman, April Mariella, cannot distract from her intolerable social surroundings. Ghosts and demons appear a welcome distraction.

The troubled story of April ends in peaceful contemplation and contentment with her marriage to the 'bland and innocent' Mr Peter Raines, who, having recently left Oxford (again), is about to publish a 'slim volume of essays' entitled *Constructive Toryism*. On reading this, I briefly missed the presence of William Ager, the ghost with a decidedly more unforgiving disposition from James's 'A Warning to the Curious' (1925).

Another common occurrence to examine before visiting the more attractive elements of Wakefield's work is his obsession with detailed golfing scenarios. In a number of stories, golfing technique and ability are used to gauge the character for the reader rather than actual characterisation. It's almost impossible to get away from this world; one that is reminiscent, perhaps ironically, of the psychotic narrator in Patrick Hamilton's *Hangover Square* (1941). In a Wakefieldian setting, golfing prowess would have been enough to secure social standing in the circle of Earl's Court fascist acquaintances of Hamilton's George Harvey Bone.

In 'The Red Hand', Wakefield's writerly protagonist considers making one of his own characters left wing because 'Magazine readers hate "Reds" worse than murderers – there were more of 'em.' Couple this with the protagonist of 'Mr Ash's Studio' – who, having written

40,000 words, declares, regarding people he disagrees with, 'as golfers say I "don't want them back"' – this gives us a sense of Wakefield's world, and his lack of insight in contrast to writers such as Hamilton. The latter understood that the banality of the hateful human elements manifesting in Europe then also enjoyed a few occasional rounds on the fairway.

Putting aside golf, the real haunting in these stories isn't the implied spirit or malevolent creature but often the valets, golf caddies and servants drifting at the edges, seeming little more than a nuisance. It's a dated precedent, but one worth opening the discussion of Wakefield's work with, simply to show his period twinge and blind spots. For, from these everyday elements, there arises a more interesting thing: Wakefield's modernity.

Modern Spirits

In trying to summarise Wakefield's stories, the best template I could find was in their likeness to the darker films of Ealing Studios, notably its chief portmanteau horror *Dead of Night* (1945). With an array of short segments of varying quality, they all explore that same Edwardian world, from club performers to tweed-wearing upper-middle-class cads in cottages. If that film's own particular golfing segment, featuring the equally Wakefieldian Charters and Caldecott, represents the lesser aspect of his work, then its incredibly effective final story – involving a cursed ventriloquist's doll – captures the atmosphere of Wakefield's stronger work.

There's little doubt that, despite some passing resemblances to M.R. James's stories, Wakefield's are more defiantly modern. His world has little in common with the fusty, hallowed realms of James's scholarly dons, with Lovecraft's ancient evils or Machen's excavated eeriness. Wakefield is even postmodern in regard to his relationship with James specifically, referencing his stories overtly several times, including in 'Nurse's Story', which has the following exchange between a young child and a nurse:

> 'And you read too many of those ghost books. That James, he gives me the creeps!'
> 'Oh, I love them, Nurse; especially, "Oh whistle and I'll come to you!"'

In a number of stories, Wakefield's strangeness manifests in more than simply postmodern quotation, but uniquely in the presence of that most dreaded of elements for James: sex.

As James wrote in one introduction to a volume of ghost stories, he found writers who brought sex into ghost stories frustrating. 'They drag in sex, too,' he wrote, 'which is a fatal mistake; sex is tiresome enough in novels; in a ghost story, or as the backbone of a ghost story, I have no patience with it.' This may also explain why James was so cautious in praising Wakefield's work.

In the same introduction, James suggested of Wakefield and his volume *They Return at Evening* that the author 'gives us a mixed bag, from which I would remove one or two that leave a nasty taste. Among the residue are some very admirable pieces.' It's impossible not to understand what James is really talking about here, slipping into the same tactile language that Wakefield's more affair-filled, quietly seductive stories use. We know what that residue is.

In 'Mr Ash's Studio', the narrative is overtly sleazy. A writer – of ghost stories, of course – rents a studio in which is housed the painting of a woman regularly covered in bizarre red moths that attack on sight. It turns out later that Mr Ash, the partying artist and previous owner of the studio, was eventually betrayed by the woman in the portrait, who married another man in Surrey. Scandal is suggested as far worse a manifestation than demonic insects.

Equally, many stories have some undercurrent of sexuality; affairs are rife and middle-class, tense and simmering like in David Lean's *Brief Encounter* (1945). Women are sometimes presented as the *femmes fatales* of noir novels: glamorous but deadly, proportioned to the male gaze but ultimately to its downfall. Wakefield's modern acceptance of melodramatic sexuality adds an edge to his stories absent in the work of many of his peers.

Ordinary Dread

Wakefield was not confined to this urbane and modern form of horror. He also ventured into more typical old worlds that other writers of his stripe inhabited. In 'The First Sheath' (1940), the strangeness resides in the almost clichéd, tradition-ridden English village where, as one of the story's narrators suggests, 'there are maypoles, of all indecorous symbols, and beating the bounds, a particularly interesting survival with, originally, a dual function; first they beat the bounds to scare the devils out, and then they beat the small boys that their tears might propitiate the Rain Goddess.'

It's almost the norm for this form of weird fiction to, at some point, paint villages as housing secrets, cults and violence; so much so that Wakefield's stories in this vein, while accomplished, are hardly essential or new.

It's Wakefield's unusual, modern domesticity that frames his originality best. 'The Cairn', for example, follows a pair of interlopers looking to climb a semi-fictionalised escarpment in the Lake District. Despite the locals warning against climbing it when snowy – due in part to some unnamed and suspect creature reminiscent of Maupassant's Horla – an unfortunate climb does take place.

Rather than getting straight to the action or taking time on place and setting (a common feature of the form), Wakefield spends more time sketching the character of the naïve climbers.

The leading man, Pat Seebright, 'made an easy £10,000 a year in his father's stock-broker's firm'. His life is laid out for the reader in all its tedious detail, yet the effect is wonderful. Pat's climbing partner is less successful but, interestingly, Wakefield implies an amorous relationship between them, expressed in part by having the pair fall in love with the same woman as a substitute.

The modern lives of these city slickers are not merely an excuse for their naivety, but often take up the sort of detailed space usually reserved for malicious history, ancient folklore and local superstition. Wakefield finds the modern everyday just as interesting and as suffused with curious detail.

In many of the stories, he doesn't even contend with such rural settings, reaffirming his horror with what could be called urban folklore, or what I've previously termed the urban wyrd.

In 'Used Car', an old American car turns out to be imported from Chicago, and is the final resting place of several gangsters and a double-crossing floozy. The upper-class family of buyers and their driver begin to replay history, lapsing through time slips into the final moments of murder, feeling as if they're being choked.

Outside of self-published 'real' ghost story volumes, and E. Nesbit's 'The Violet Car', the closest thing I've come across to this outlandish but effective story is in hearsay regarding the missing Nigel Kneale-penned episode of the BBC science-fiction anthology series *Out of the Unknown*. *The Chopper* (1971), as Kneale called it, was equally haunted, and an unfortunate Patrick Troughton contended with the spirits of the bike's previous rider. That, however, was in the early 1970s, when such modern quirks had fully established themselves; commonplace items of day-to-day life then normalised enough to be deployed in stranger fictions.

Wakefield wrote 'Used Car' in the early 1930s, before cars were so dominant in public life. It shows, to my eye at least, that he had a unique understanding of stranger day-to-day aspects, and how new technology had the potential to slip into the weird and the terrifying. There are few writers of the post-war years who, because of this, do not owe Wakefield in some way for his Victorian – even Dickensian – capacity for being terrified of (and questioning) the cursed machinery that popped up in the twentieth century.

Salvaging the Ashes

So, what to make of Wakefield's legacy? Though for a time mentioned alongside the writers he admired, and even suggested as being a potential successor to their enjoyable evils, his stories are in far lower standing today. Even writers specialising in exhuming these types of forgotten figures have referred negatively to his work for its seeming mediocrity, often unfairly so. Perhaps there's a uniquely eccentric character to his stories that does not translate well for modern readers.

Wakefield's characters are often artists or writers, and the way they are characterised evokes images of Bloomsbury sets and earlier pre-war bohemia. In his noted classic 'The Red Lodge', an artist takes his family away to help with his work, only to succumb to strange visions and hauntings. The creative process is painful for Wakefield and for his characters. The sheer number of stories involving the publishing industry and struggling writers is too long to list. Yet this is when Wakefield is at his most biting and witty.

In another story, 'The Red Hand', we follow a writer in first person as he returns to the draft of an incomplete ghost story. The way the fable is constructed means it's almost a dramatisation of a real-time edit, far more experimental in quality than other ghost stories of the period. It's only when the dreaded red hand of his narrative finally breaks from his page onto ours that the oddness of the story becomes truly apparent.

Wakefield can't help but allow his criticism of the industry to come through in the story, reminding us, after all, that he was the man who burned as much evidence as possible of his own writing life. Of course, some does still exist, including the occasional photograph. But it appears he was pretty successful in his destructive endeavour. 'He had a conscience. In his dirty little way he was an artist. But never would he write again...' as he suggested in 'The Red Hand'. His honesty and accidental autobiography are almost too sharp to bear.

Reading my old volume of *Ghost Stories* around October, I once again pictured the face in Wakefield's photographs burning behind the grate of a fireplace. Sometimes it's best to honour the wishes of writers and accept their desire for disappearance.

In Wakefield's case, however, I instinctively stretch out a hand in reflex towards the fire, and grab a clump of those still-warm, smouldering ashes; hoping to maybe conjure in a circle of words the standing of a lost, sometimes flawed, but ultimately innovative writer of pleasing terrors.

Published by The Nightjar, 27/12/20

Alan Garner's Remembered Landscapes

Throughout his career, Alan Garner has dedicated many books to questioning the landscape of his native Alderley Edge in Cheshire. Under the guise of the fantastical, at the heart of all Garner's work lies a sense of place dictating the direction of his stories. Alderley is not a mere narrative device so much as an expression of personal experience. Garner not only still lives in the location, but is continually haunted by it.

More than most British writers, Garner has *lived* the places of his books. It's a rare feature in the age of extended travel and a hyper-globalised populace. He has spent most of his life in and around Alderley, predominantly in Congleton under the shadow of the Lovell Telescope of Jodrell Bank. It's a place imbued with strange tales and folklore; where the cosmic and the archaic intertwine with ease.

In particular, Garner has been fixated on the Edge that gives Alderley its name: a stone precipice with sweeping views out over the Cheshire plains, all the way to Manchester when the skies are clear (looking like a Mordorian realm from afar, sitting obtusely on the green plain). From his debut novel *The Weirdstone of Brisingamen* (1960) to his memoir, *Where Shall We Run To?* (2018), place is fixed, not simply to set the scene or to provide a backdrop, but because it defines *everything* in Garner's work.

Garner's prose is carved from rock and wood, giving the impression that it has always been here, and the feeling that he is continuing the tradition of his craftsman heritage. Considering a memoir by Garner is in itself an intriguing proposition, if only because his work has often been drenched in biography and the place that coloured it. Was one really necessary when the man's history is there in between the wizards and time-shifts of his fiction?

On a wall near the house of his birth, his forefather's name is cut into the stone, a signature of a modest masonry achievement and a call from those once there to future ancestors. Garner's prose is the same modest signature etched from the elements; of the land remembered and of the remembering land.

Remembering the Land

Especially in his fiction, Garner places land on par with character. In his novel *The Owl Service* (1967), for example, the majority of the book is taken up either with dialogue or place description; there's very little in between. A good example is this simple but beautiful passage: 'Alison sat in the shade of the Stone of Gronw among the meadowsweet. Clive stood in the river.' This binary allows for a melding of inner and outer worlds, meaning the reader can see quite plainly how place slowly becomes pivotal to the lives of the characters. Rarely do they fail to mention or imply some aspect of their location: the roads, paths, hills, forests, peaks and fields that surround them make up a fair amount of their discussion.

They remember the land even when they wish to forget it.

Susan and Colin of the *Weirdstone* trilogy walk the same paths that Garner walked with his father; around the Edge itself, up to Stormy Point and past the various wells that litter the area. One in particular stands out: the 'Wizard's Well' that's rumoured to be a product of Garner's great-great-grandfather, its carved wizard face specifically. It's the same wizard who would eventually turn up as Cadellin Silverbrow in *The Weirdstone of Brisingamen*.

As Garner wrote in that book:

> Just as they were about to turn for home after a climb from the foot of the Edge, the children came upon a stone trough into which water was dripping from an overhanging cliff, and high in the rock was carved the face of a bearded man...

The passage could easily be from *Where Shall We Run To?* with its detail gleaned from memory.

It's fitting that a similar narrative of wandering with his father found its way into his memoir. If anything is remembered from Garner's past, it's almost always enshrined by place. Even when his emotions are the overriding element being summoned, as in his novel *Red Shift* (1973), they are almost always remembered through (and preserved by) place like an insect in amber.

The Land Remembering

In an essay from *The Voice That Thunders*, Garner writes of the Edge that it 'both stopped, and melted time'. In his fiction and essay writing, the landscapes of Cheshire, Wales and Alderley have potential sentience. If his characters at any point forget the importance of the place around them, then it will do its utmost to remind them.

Alison of *The Owl Service* and her frustration at being stuck on holiday in the Mawddwy Valley is a good example of this, as is Ian in *Thursbitch* (2004), who is reluctant to leave the ailing Sal to the mercy of the temporally permeable Pennines.

Ever since *Red Shift*, temporal shifts have dominated Garner's landscapes, often hinting towards a kind of agency. The three male characters of *Red Shift*, Ian and Sal of *Thursbitch*, and even William Buckley of *Strandloper* (1996) all partake in some unspoken communion with the terrain around them, as if the past filters in and allows access to some deeper truth.

Reading Garner's non-fiction, this is clearly reflective of his own relationship with the land. However, to label the latter as an expression of psychology undermines what is really happening, as it seems so essential to all of his post-*Red Shift* narratives, perhaps even being their key instigator. This is even when, as in these later novels, the elements of place-painting are reduced to an absolute minimum.

Psychology seeks answers. Garner's writing, on the other hand, is pure expression, intuition even.

Place instead haunts through names and language, sometimes so intensely localised, unfamiliar and idiosyncratic to the north-west of England that they seem possessed of incantation as much as geography.

This emphasis on locality feels like a form of remembering, an interaction beyond exploration and normal language. It tells of a dangerous openness to place if unaware or dark of heart.

In another essay, Garner wrote of the Edge that:

> It is physically and emotionally dangerous. No one born to the Edge questions that, and we showed it proper respect.

This respect is not superstitious or even melodramatic. It's simply an acknowledgement of a heightened awareness of place in temporal terms; one that is part of a shared continuity with generations gone by.

The past is not fixed underneath the rock and soil but constantly drifting back and forth as the land remembers, even when we briefly forget.

Published by Fourth Estate, 10/08/18

The Haunted Realms
of *The Owl Service*

I can't remember exactly when I first read Alan Garner's *The Owl Service* (1967). Like its inspiration, *The Mabinogion*, or the Stone of Gronw that sits at the centre of its mystery, it seems to have always been there.

It's an unusual feeling because the novel is not particularly old by standards of literature – it turns fifty on the 21st August 2017 – and yet it *feels* older. It may carry the trappings of a very particular analogue period of the twentieth century – with its 35mm cameras in particular playing a vital role – but Garner's connection to deep, unfolding history allows *The Owl Service* to function very much like a more antiquarian text.

This is, however, in contrary to the actual writing, which is deeply modern in form, experimenting with voice and perspective in ways that still seem daring today. This short novel, award-winning in the arena of children's fiction at least, feels unearthed from the ground and yet constructed through accumulated retellings by modernists at the fireside, every evening's version adding layers of crumbly mystery.

Garner began writing *The Owl Service* after a number of coincidences. The first was being given a dinner service patterned with an owl-and-flower motif; the flowing design effectively portrays owls made of flowers, or perhaps flowers made of owls. The plate was designed by Christopher Dresser, and typically fed into the Cheshire writer's propensity for drawing on his everyday life and surroundings, even when writing and considering narratives of fantasy.

The second coincidence was a trip that Garner took to Bryn Hall in Dinas Mawddwy. The reality of place always takes precedence in Garner's work. The house and surrounding valley seemed a perfect landscape in which to begin a continuation of *The Mabinogion*; the twelfth and thirteenth-century collection of Welsh tales divided into branches of legend, myth and adventure. *The Owl* Service is in itself an archaeology of the branch that concerns Math, son of Mathonwy, telling of a love triangle and the jeopardy that comes from a betrayal.

Garner's narrative follows Alison and her new stepbrother Roger, who are taken to the Welsh valleys by their recently wedded parents, to their holiday cottage which resides deep in the countryside. The house is maintained by a groundskeeper called Huw, a housekeeper called Nancy, and her young son, Gwyn.

When Alison hears a scratching noise in the roof above her bedroom, Gwyn goes to investigate and finds a dinner service covered with a strange design, part owl, part flower. Alison begins to make cut-outs of the flowers, making them into owls before the designs disappear.

Eerie events unfold as the tale of Blodeuwedd from *The Mabinogion*'s branch manifests in the household. Blodeuwedd was at the centre of an ancient love-triangle between Lleu – who had her created for him as a wife out of flowers by the magicians Gwydion and Math – and Gronw, with whom she has an affair and plots to murder Lleu. The triangle and its fallout exert its force over the present-day young trio as the spirit takes hold of Alison.

Photography of the nearby Stone of Gronw, a menhir relic that sits in Afon Bryn Saeth, reveals mysterious figures – a man hurling a spear and another riding a motorbike – highlighting that the love-triangle had previously arisen involving Nancy, Bertram and Huw, the latter turning out to be Gwyn's father.

Garner's novel defies simple description. If it's fantasy, it's hardly told in a typically fantastical way. With the writing split between pages of dialogue and pages of place description, it feels experimental in such a binary; the fragmented nature between the people and the landscape overlapping until the eventual finale, where the characters are forced to defy the branch's narrative in order to save Alison.

I remember my first impression of the novel, whenever that may have been formed, being one largely built of landscape. I had failed to remember, on rereading later in life, just how fantastical and ghostly its odder moments really are. But the landscape remained at the forefront.

Instead of conjuring memories of figures appearing in photographs or ghostly talons scratching faces, the novel was about hills, flowers and rivers. The core theme of place retaining a trace of the past is a key motif of folk horror, especially when that place is explored rigorously, and Garner's novel is a fine example.

I feel these landscapes more so than others presented in most fiction, even by Garner. There is a sense of Garner continuing on from the tradition of the *Gawain* poet or *The*

Mabinogion's authors, that sense of old English and Welsh that is essentially normal to the place names I grew up surrounded by on The Wirral, even if alien to the majority of others.

Even North Wales is, in a sense, part of my childhood, and so to be confronted by such landscapes, places that had simply not been present in my reading up to then, was a shock. I felt the floor drop in later years when I found out that the subsequent television adaptation in 1969 by Granada had actually used a house in Bromborough – Poulton Hall, to be precise – for filming due to Bryn Hall denying permission.

I lived not all that far from Poulton Hall – the house of author Roger Lancelyn Green, which lies adjacent to the site where the Battle of Brunanbruh is supposed to have occurred – and it further cemented the idea in my mind that Garner was the only writer I'd come across who was fluent in the sort of places that were mine.

Approaching fifty and with a huge burst of fashionable and critical acclaim (it usually takes a few decades for academia, the literary press and the non-children's end of literary prizes to catch up) in recent years, the novel defies so much labelling. Even I rarely bother calling it folk horror these days.

The Owl Service is genreless and peerless (even in the work of Garner's contemporary, Susan Cooper) because it's so stubbornly fixed, so unafraid of how people express themselves and how, ultimately, we're at the mercy of our history interred in our landscapes.

Garner's novel does not try to learn from history or its landscapes, as is the intellectual distance so often enforced on the subjects in fictional forms. It instead embodies them totally.

It is alive.

Published by Celluloid Wicker Man, 07/08/17

Marguerite Duras's Sea View

Marguerite Duras lived in a little flat in what was once the Hôtel des Roches Noires in Trouville on the Normandy coast. She spent long periods of time there, staying from 1963 to 1996. She would regularly stare out of the window towards the horizon line, or at least was often photographed doing so.

Though undoubtedly there throughout the seasons, the Trouville coast seen through Duras's eyes – in novels and films – is wintry. Trouville is a winter place for Duras, living the latter part of her life there, before the seasons ultimately ceased their cycle in Apartment 105.

Gustave Flaubert fell in love while staying in the same hotel when he was still a teenager; Claude Monet painted the hotel in 1870, likely on an empty Sunday afternoon; and Marcel Proust stayed there regularly, including on trips with his mother a few doors down in Apartment 110. Balbec of Proust's novel is itself a shadow version of the general area of Cabourg just a little further up the coast.

The hotel is a cultural node on the coastline, and Duras finalises it, drawing all of it together, sometimes unconsciously, sometimes overtly, but especially in her films. The space of the hotel and the winter seascape outside is a defining image of her later works, no longer dominated by the colonial images from her childhood of a stifling Gia-

Dinh, the province that would eventually become Saigon when Cochin China became Vietnam.

I believe this wintry atmosphere comes not just from being in the resort at that time of year, but from seeing with a perspective that's looking back on a life. Duras is refreshing when it comes to reassessing the past as she's far from nostalgic. She is instead a natural post-war progression from Proust's pleasurable nostalgia; a bitter flavour is more dominant than the sweet taste of madeleines.

Duras looks to the war and, most importantly, lost loves with both longing and awareness that the growing gap will become ever larger. Many lost loves, in fact, manifest through this building and the beach outside. She may take some pleasure in reminiscing, as she clearly does in her novel *Yann Andréa Steiner* (1992), but such an act cannot escape the reality that the love was lost, increasingly fading in the past tense. No warmth of memory can remove the ultimate chill of her sorrowful present, the empty rooms of the hotel in Trouville's icy winters are haunted by silence and a lack of voices.

Yann Andréa Steiner is an interesting novel because of this use of the location. The love burgeoning between the much older Duras and the twenty-eight-year-old Steiner feels a brief interlude to the isolation of the coastline. There's something knowing about Duras's exploration of the unusual affair, not least in how precarious it was.

Steiner himself was more of a fan than a lover, one who became romantically involved after he met the writer when she introduced her film *India Song* at his university. The events were partly adapted later from Steiner's perspective (and his own diary) into the film *Cet Amour-là* (2003), but the film lacks the integrity of the book, and it fails to capture Trouville's (and Duras's) oncoming winter.

In her novel, Duras even touches on past frustrations embedded into the hotel and the coastline, specifically addressing Proust and his overwhelming jealousy over questionable relations that his lover, Albertine, may or may not have been having with another woman.

She wrote that 'these slow evenings, you remember, when they were dancing in front of him, the two naughty young girls, he, tortured by the desire of them who were on the verge of losing their lives and who cried there, on the sofa in the large living room with sea view'.

Desire is a burden in Trouville.

Fittingly, when Chantal Akerman adapted Proust's *The Captive* (*La Captive*) in 2000, the film ends on the coast at a hotel in winter, with the characters both ending up in the water, one disappearing permanently under the waves. The film fails to convey the complex array of emotions of the novel, however, instead basking in a simplistic, cold distance.

Duras herself would document the hotel most effectively in her film work, filming features and shorts back-to-back there, and then reconfiguring their themes with differing voice-overs. This is most apparent in a pair of films: the feature film *Agatha and the Limitless Readings* (1981), and the shorter *The Atlantic Man* (1981). Both have slow, roving eyes that follow wordless characters, communicating like ghosts through various voice-overs. The performers may just as well not be in the same room, such is the cold disparity between them. Lovers recount times when they were closer, wandering past each other as if deceased and floating to some wintry beyond.

Duras allows herself to be part of these films and their narratives as an all-seeing presence. This is her lonely realm. In the long mirrors of the hotel, her camera and her image appear, not caring about any potential break in continuity of the filmic world. How can there be, when these films are so personal, when her own voice often tells of what she's trying to achieve in photographing these actors wandering around her memories and home?

The rooms are large and empty, where writers and artists once sought and lost their various loves. Only the breeze now rattles the shutters. Duras's work is a haunting, an inability to fully lock the past away by itself. Instead, she locks herself within it, drifting through these cold reflections like her camera does in the building's vast mirrors. As she suggests in her own voice-over, 'The camera will now capture your reappearance, in the mirror parallel to that which it sees itself.'

Despair was infinite for Duras.

Published by Celluloid Wicker Man, 17/09/19

Marcel Proust Turns Away

Marcel Proust turns away. His head is straight but not quite obscured. It could be considered a photograph in profile if not for the angle of his body, crumpled and creating the illusion of multiple positions. His hand weakly grips his lapel, a reaction of solid determination not to let memories break him.

I'm on my third volume of Proust's *In Search of Lost Time* or *Remembrance of Things Past* depending on the translation (À la recherché du temps perdu), and already I feel compelled to write and discuss its moods, places and memories.

Though resisting reading him for a brief time, coming across a particular portrait of the writer turning away crumbled the last of any resistance I had. For there, in one photo, was much of the material I've read so far, yet condensed; over a thousand pages, in fact, seemingly shot through the prism of this one very particular image. Within it, I feel that what Proust saw and scribbled down when lying in bed is captured, like a permanent zoetrope of lost loves, social calamities and artistic endeavours.

So far, Proust has been sent back into his memories. As soon as this action took place – that temporal sway backwards and forwards, between mistakes and hindsight – I imagined the writer looking up and away. I couldn't place what it was specifically that he was turning away from, but there was a sense that looking back meant something was put aside; as if one door opened only if willing to close another. It wasn't the present that was closed off, for the present provided the hindsight afforded which makes the novel astounding and wise. But something was lost, sealed away, undeniably.

Much is said about wisdom, as if wisdom has some tangible currency, but it genuinely is the best way to describe what is on Proust's pages. The writer not only accepts his past errors – so far, his faith in a high society that simply bores him with its ineffectuality seems to be his chief error – but positively dives into them and scours them for detail. He must convince himself that his search for any sort of meaning in existence doesn't lie in the great pompous salons of Paris or the paranoid relationships he struck up with potential lovers.

Proust is looking back and, by doing so, has turned away from the present places. I do feel a kinship with the man in this sense; in fact much of my work seems to be a similar turn, albeit one expressed by walks and odysseys to nowhere.

The photograph, and photography in general, is a fitting medium for the writer. The best editions of the book understand this sense of hazy memory and make use of it in their design (the recent Penguin Modern Classics editions, for example, have covers littered with suitably sepia photographs) while the worst, intimidated by the scope of the work, vie for easy abstraction instead (the previous Vintage editions use tacky cartoon flowers). But photography (and this photograph in particular) understands the necessity and desire to keep memory alive. To turn away briefly back into the grain, the fading light even, is a shared strength of photography and Proust's writing.

Which direction is Proust really looking, then? For philosophers such as Gilles Deleuze, it's all-encompassing, neither backwards nor forwards, simply a wider, fuller breadth of perception. Madeleines are 'redundant' according to Deleuze. Proust can only turn in circles rather than look back and away. But the photograph that sparked my interest shows him turning *away*; not quite fully, but not facing the lens either. He looks wherever his curiosity takes him.

There are other photos of the writer, of course. Plenty, in fact, of the young man smiling towards the camera, posing with family, or enjoying a Normandy view. There's even some apparent (but much debated) film footage of him circling online. But I return to this photo, its decorated chair, its elegance and simplicity, and wonder what the man could see; whether his vision is a temporal 360-degree curve that renders his angle inconsequential, or something deeper. We, the viewer and the reader, can recognise its turn away, but memories tend to possess mirrored walls curving down to the ground.

All may potentially be perceived, whether we like it or not.

Perhaps, then, it's ultimately the reader that Proust is turning away from. It's not a negative action or one done in haste. He's instead enmeshed in the problems of this wider perception of which the reader is only a small fraction.

'Do not regard me,' he is saying, 'look to that and to this and beyond to all.' This may seem ironic considering the writer's desire to somehow help his readers, fulfilling the role that his father, the distanced medical man, never quite satisfied. Proust is signalling our direction of interest and that's enough. This lone action opens up *everything*.

At first, we feel to be looking back with him over his shoulders, a sleight-of-hand distraction for what seems a back-and-forth wander through the memories of one man. But the real memory, the all-encompassing one, is in the act of writing itself; in a musky bed, surrounded by scrolls of text in which everything can and will be present. For that's life in hindsight, whether looked directly in the eye or turned ever so slightly away from, in remembrance.

Published by Celluloid Wicker Man, 23/07/18

A Wander with Georges Perec

What can Georges Perec see out of the window? He's sat as usual in Café de la Mairie, 8 place Saint-Sulpice in the 6th Arrondissment, hunched over his favourite table by the window. More important is the fact that he's looking outside.

Life in the Latin Quarter is passing by as always; it never really stops, merely lulls. On his small, plastic-coated table, he has a pad and pencil bought from a tabac on the rue de Seine – a pencil which has had to be sharpened twice into the ashtray due to the cheap quality of the lead – a box of matches bought along with his second packet of Gauloises, which he's now regretting smoking too quickly. And finally, the empty coffee cup which contained his third espresso of the morning and which, after two previous cups, is starting to taste incredibly bitter.

Perec was part of the area's rhythm when walking there, wandering from another usual spot, perhaps Le Mabillion on boulevard Saint-Germain, to here; presenting a slightly different angle from which to watch the world turn. But now he is frozen out of the moment, and, on this occasion, the world is not turning so quickly. Passers-by are not to be seen in regular bursts but only on occasions. It's early morning; the Parisians are not performing yet.

Perec has already published his short book *An Attempt at Exhausting a Place in Paris* and has no further desire to capture the things often taken for granted by others. He's simply back to capturing the main melody rather than the grace notes, grace notes that were largely the coming and going of buses. But he can't hear anything new. Paris is not awake enough. And so he begins to see other things.

Not the occasional car, or morning wanderer, nor even the local cat that belongs to a tenant in the flat above Café de la Mairie; none of these things enrapture him that morning. Instead, he begins to look through another window, one in his memory. He stares out into the Latin Quarter and sees a young man in a beige trench coat. The man has curly hair but it's cut short enough to sit firmly on his head in tight little knots. He's wearing a maroon jumper, white shirt and tie, probably wandering for the sake of it. Under his arm are several folded newspapers, though they will probably not be read until much later, when back at the flat in Belleville.

Perec watches this man cross the road and out of sight. Yet his eyes follow him round corners, through the window of his memory. The young man is on his usual walk in between working, trying to be a writer in between his archivist day job. Perec's eyes are glazed over, and the patron assumes that the writer, now successful since the publication of his last novel, is merely collecting more visual ephemera for his latest work. But Perec's eyes are keen and occupied, mapping the steps of the young man, first backwards to before he crossed the road and then forwards to where he was going.

The young man stops further down the boulevard Saint-Germain, where he grabs the bundle of newspapers he plans to read later on. He browses briefly through several editions, including *Le Monde*, *Le Figaro* and *France-Soir* before settling on the former two, rolling them up like a patisserie and walking on. He comes to a halt at the road with the slow pedestrian crossing; it is a busier street for the young man than it is for Perec sat in the café.

The young man, seemingly living his job as an archivist, is obsessive in collecting, amassing, hoarding. This applies most to books, so Perec remembers with a brief draw on his last Gauloises, disintegrating into nothing in the ashtray alongside the pencil sharpenings.

The young man is drawn to the spinning stalls of cheap paperbacks outside a shop on boulevard Saint-Michele. The designs are a flurry of colours and names: Boileau-Narcejac, Raymond Chandler, Jim Thompson, men with guns, an assortment of shady rooms but with bright, block colours for shadows. Reams of *Série Noire*.

There are too many to buy, the young man feels, but he knows that he can't resist. There are still some francs in his left coat pocket, along with a string of paperclips strung together, the torn piece of a cigarette packet upon which is written a number he is supposed to phone later, and a single glove taken in haste for walking on a crisp winter's day, now rendered useless by its solitude. He opts for *Sur un air de navaja* as he is yet to read about Philip Marlowe's old age.

More wandering; that day is longer than Perec remembered. Did he really walk so much only a decade or so before? His lungs couldn't stand it today, heavy with choking tar.

The young man is insatiable, the Seine drawing nearer with more stalls of books to pick over, glance at, browse, peruse, buy, not buy, haggle, put back, return to later, hide by turning the cover the wrong way round. He pockets a spent Métro ticket, used by the previous owner as a bookmark from one volume.

Little things matter. Little things are important.

He's in the *famous shop*. Everything is in English but it doesn't matter. There's still the cover art to admire; there's still the sheer aesthetic of words which he can probably just about get by understanding. All letters are drawings in the end.

More books, more paraphernalia to drag back to the flat and his own archive in the making. Perec's eyes wander in reverse around the many corners he has impossibly watched the young man walk around, and back through the Latin Quarter.

Madame Auclair is walking her small dog down rue de Buci. The street sweeper who never moves from near Odéon Métro station is looking mournful. The Bréon brothers, having skipped school yet again, are fighting in the patch of land outside Musée de Cluny, ruining their already torn clothes, much to the later dismay of their father.

Perec finally returns to the Café de la Mairie and the present.

Another espresso is on its way, housed on a shining silver platter, as he returns to the window. Traffic has picked up, people are walking, cars are beeping angrily and there is much to see.

He gives a last thought to the young man, walking on that cold winter's day some decades ago; walking, not because there was somewhere to be, but, so he thought, because *everywhere* was a destination. There was no alternative; he had things he needed to escape.

His pencil begins scrawling, finding its own paths on the paper; more routes for others to follow, sooner or later.

Published by Celluloid Wicker Man, 15/01/18

Georges Perec Escapes

When Georges Perec was eleven, he decided to wander. In fact, *escape* is perhaps a better description; a jailbreak from his aunt's house on rue de l'Assomption, to be exact.

He wandered Paris with who knows what planned. It was such a defining experience for the writer that he later wrote an essay about the feeling of release and the places he encountered on this lost meander called *Les Lieux d'une Fugue*, later published posthumously in the volume *Je Suis né* in 1990. The text was translated as *The Scene of a Flight* in the more recent Penguin volume *Species of Space and Other Pieces*; but, most intriguingly, the text was turned into a short film by Perec himself in 1978, only a few years before he died.

This forty-minute film by Perec contains the majority of the text and finds the author behind the camera, something he was clearly itching to explore at that point in his career. That same year, he was filmed by a television crew stating such a desire for cinema while on set for Alain Corneau's brutal film *Série Noire*, his screenplay an adaptation of Jim Thompson's *A Hell of a Woman*. The potential speed and money in cinema admittedly played into his growing love for working in the medium as opposed to novels (he had, after all, just finished work on the huge *Life: A User's Manual*).

Perec's film was funded by the Institut national de l'audiovisuel, and Perec seems to have been given full freedom to explore a visual response to his own text. Its experimental, essayistic nature is not unlike Alain Resnais's early documentary films. The cinematic medium also allowed the writer a chance to experiment with the audio-visual potential of a fugue itself, intertwining exploration of place, excavation of memory and voice-over with the music of Schumann.

The writer's story is a melancholy one, being that of an orphan lost in the city. He has little money to enact his plan of escape, spending most of it on some milk-bread and a comic book. The essay (and the film) opens with plans to sell a stamp collection, the detail belying Perec's typical collector's sense of thinking; something that can't easily be faked.

However, all is not well. The stamp collectors usually sat at the market, trading in their small, travelled wares, are absent on the day of the escape.

Perec beautifully captures that early morning hum of a city slowly waking up. People are absent, with the exception of the cleaners. Paris is collectively yawning awake.

That lonely day all those years back scarred the writer, though the account is more complicated because nothing necessarily bad happens to him; the day merely revealed something to the author about himself.

Perec renders the telling of his film in a visually innovative way. Though the journey he recounts is hectic and upsetting for his younger self (all voiced by Jean-Pierre Melville discovery Marcel Cuvelier), the camera is achingly slow and patient, determined to map every detail of the revisited places. It's a kind of conjuration of the past, a ritual in honour of his memories.

The film becomes even more of an excavation than the original text. Perec is at pains to show how difficult this experience was for him to revisit. 'And he remained trembling for a long moment,' he wrote, 'before the blank page (and I remained trembling for a long moment, before the blank page).'

In the film, he begins with a doorway, tracking slowly back. Every element is noted by the camera with an ease I imagine the writer was envious of. His pages and pages of text mapping the perception of even the simplest place is swapped for a single, smooth visual that does the same thing more efficiently. The rest of the film contains similar patient qualities, as if Perec is daring himself to revisit an experience that really terrified and shaped him in ways that are only hinted at; undercurrents that sit between each sentence of his prose.

The day also has a clear lineage with his future creativity. His obsession with objects and paraphernalia of all kinds seems an extension of his childhood self here; only, instead of being disappointed by the lack of stamp sellers on the Champs-Élysées, he creates his own worlds: the everyday scenario is collected, marked, catalogued, maintained, itemised and retained for future trading with his readers. There will always be people around him to show his curios to, thankfully.

What was Perec really running away from that day? Loneliness? The tedium of school for a meandering mind? A family history decimated by the Holocaust? It could even have been simply his aunt. But really it feels most likely to be the loss of his parents, especially his mother, and the sense of dislocation allowing him to drift all over Paris in a way someone like Guy Debord could never quite match in earnest; running without destination and with home only present in the official sense, not in the emotional sense. It was the latter that mattered. And, for Perec, it was utterly absent.

Published by Celluloid Wicker Man, 14/05/18

Wandering Through with Robert Walser

I savour Robert Walser's fragmentary work. It's currently a wonderful period for the Swiss writer's prose, not least because much of it is so carefully and lovingly translated; no longer merely a rare curiosity thanks to the odd translation from years previous going for absurd sums online.

The formal qualities of his short snippets and microfictions especially draw me to his unusually optimistic depression, his meandering playfulness and his everyday enchantment. A particular favourite of all these fragments is the humble one-page short 'A Little Ramble'.

The story is from 1914 and pops up in the writer's most productive period, wedged between a variety of projects and jobs while the toil of typing slowly eroded his mental stability. First read in the recently published collected volume *The Walk*, this short vignette detailing a gentle wander in the Swiss mountains was the first of his writing I encountered that dealt with the relationship to landscape; something that crops up again and again in his work.

Walser's sketches are almost always in the first person, the sort of fragmentary rambles of a meanderer unable to contain their inner monologue. 'A Little Ramble' is the blueprint for much of Walser's work in this form, especially

The Walk itself, which is an urban, lengthier exploration of this wandering ideal. The piece here is barely a few hundred words in length but there's much to explore within it.

He opens with setting the scene, a reminiscence of a walk in the mountains earlier in the day. The descriptions are fleeting but almost surreal in choice. The weather and the region are 'damp' and 'gray', but the road is strangely 'soft' and 'very clean'. It's the sort of oddness of description that would not feel out of place coming from the character of a 1960s Richard Lester film.

His walk is a pleasurable one, following the road until he comes across carts and other wanderers, and finally pleasant views out onto a small village, noting the change in perspective that different parts of the road provide of the mountain vista.

Susan Sontag writes of a quietly rebellious quality in Walser's work: 'The moral core of Walser's art is the refusal of power; of domination. I'm ordinary – that is, nobody – declares the characteristic Walser persona.' This rebellious streak comes from a supposed disappearance act, sinking into the everyday. Being a 'nobody' is quietly radical, especially in this age of attention-obsessed writers-as-celebrities culture.

'Nobodiness' is a quietly ironic mechanism, where such obsessive focus on one particular perspective occults and veils that person's presence. Walser becomes a spectre of his own story, perceiving everything all at once and trying to cognise it, even going so far as to relate how his experiences make him feel. He's always disappearing in between his sentences.

It feels as if Walser's act of writing is clinging to existence; that his sensitivity to everything around him somehow constitutes an outer shell for his bodily character and nothing more. There is, however, sadness to this realisation. The inner Walser is still hidden, perhaps because it has to be: an unhappy character whose release would result in something more tragic.

Walser's ramble continues, anthropomorphising everything around him, taking comfort in the company of things. The road is 'snuggled up splendidly to the mountain', while 'gray clouds lay on the mountains as though that were their resting place'. This act could be ascribed as a phenomenological approach to the perception of the world, if so academically inclined and you didn't get out much. It tells us less about the actual lay of the land, however, than it does the loneliness of the narrator who sees it. Even if Walser (or his character) meets people, they are merely fleeting in interest.

The roads and the mountains seem more alive to him than the 'young wanderers' he meets on this particular walk. He sees a village in the distance, hearing music and noticing the dwellings hiding under the cliffs. He looks on this sense of community as an outsider, the lonely man of the mountain looking towards the civilisation he's increasingly losing the ability (and the sheer will) to be a part of.

W.G. Sebald writes of this characteristic in his essay on Walser, 'Le Promeneur Solitaire' (a title itself that highlights the point in question), suggesting that:

> It is enough for us to understand that, in the end, Walser simply could not go on, and... had to resort to keeping people at arm's length with a sort of anarchic politeness, becoming refractory

and abusive, making scenes in public and believing that the bourgeois city of Berne, of all places, was a city of ghostly gesticulators, executing rapid hand movements directly in front of his face expressly in order to discombobulate him and to dismiss him out of hand as one who simply does not count.

This has profoundly negative effects on Walser as a person, eventually finding his lonely way along the path to the psychiatric institute where he would die in the snow (on a walk, of course).

It's ultimately impossible to disconnect this tragic aspect of Walser's personality with the wonderful effects in his writing. His distance from society imbues his curiosity with a tactile sense of wonder and enchantment; where the softness of a road can lead to the profoundest of pleasures; or where even the distance from the society he is increasingly suspicious of can still merit some pleasure when observed from the right distance.

'A Little Ramble' concludes on a Walserian mission statement if ever there was one. He writes: 'We don't need to see anything out of the ordinary. We already see so much.' If ever there was an admission of both the melancholy of the man's evolving situation and the exact belief driving his brilliant work, it is this observation; made by the lonely walker on that soft, clean road, winding like a smooth, white stream through the Swiss mountains.

Published by Celluloid Wicker Man, 27/11/17

Piecing Together Robert Walser

Chance played a huge role in the writing of Robert Walser. I can picture his slow meanderings around towns and valleys, spotting something that fired his brief need to write before getting distracted once more by something else entirely.

I can envision him excited by the way sunlight reflects off a lake's water, astonished by the fustiness of a suited man coming out of a bank, infatuated by a woman's lavish attire sending him into romantic daydreams. He was, surprisingly perhaps, a bit of a Lothario in that latter regard.

Walser chanced upon small, beautiful details, and artist Tacita Dean did the same in her collage work inspired by him, *Berlin and the Artist* (2012). To coincide with an exhibition in New York inspired by the writer, Dean was commissioned for a piece and chose the subject of Walser's time in Berlin as her particular angle, the title a nod to a story by the author.

Walser lodged in Berlin with his brother Karl while there, a noted illustrator whose work can be seen in a number of Walser compendiums, in particular on the covers of the latest New York Review of Books editions. Using found objects such as illustrations, photographs and postcards, *Berlin and the Artist* replicates such Walser-esque chance encounters while finding its own particular stories in the lost and the found.

Dean set some parameters for these works. Rummaging through markets in Berlin, the objects she found and used were roughly from the same period that Walser was living and working in. She even came across new work by an illustrator called Martin Stekker, who she considers may have possibly met Walser through his brother's creative circles. In an interview for *Frieze*, she told of the discovery:

> Very strangely, we came upon hundreds of pencil drawings by an artist called Martin Stekker. It was a remarkable discovery: Berlin observations from a century ago... Well, they were beautiful and I knew I was working on this project, and Walser was already on my mind. I later researched Stekker to find only one reference to him on the internet and discovered he was born in the same year as Walser. Just after that I bought another newly translated collection of Walser's writing, *Berlin Stories* (2012), where I read *Berlin and the Artist*. Immediately I saw a connection between Stekker's drawings and Walser's stories, both observations of Berlin life from the same time.

A Walserian coincidence if ever there was one. The layering of history and chance perfectly embodies the writer's work.

On an aesthetic level, such themes are expressed with equal effectiveness in the work. In one of the collages, a sketch shows a man kneeling (perhaps even praying) while his arms complete the circle of another drawing. These objects are both self-contained yet in communication with each other, aiding the effect of browsing through someone's memories. In another of the collages, two separate photographs show a man writing at a desk. It's a different man in each photo, and a different desk, but the pair work well together.

Even if such a form automatically contains some askance of meaning, it's not necessarily the point of the work; though meanings certainly appear. The objects are connected by a blank, withered looking card as their shared background, but separated into a number of different frames so that the context of each little collection remains precise and clear.

If such pictures had found their way onto one large canvas, the chaos of the endless connections between the images would still have been fitting: an expression of urban humdrum.

Walser's own satire of bureaucratic order simultaneously doffed a cap to it and whispered curses upon it when its back was turned. I imagine making the work was rather like the process of finding Walser's infamous microscripts and turning them into cognisable books for people to read. These are images to be read as well as seen.

Walser's writing was a rebellion founded in taking notice of things, acknowledging the forgotten and the taken-for-granted debris that slip by every day in our rush to sit behind a desk.

In *Berlin and the Artist*, Dean harnesses that same curiosity in collating ephemera, assumed to be lost (or given no thought at all), lifting it out of the white noise of history. In doing so, she not only creates a work in the spirit of Walser but also a work that revels in that same sense of serendipity.

Published by Celluloid Wicker Man, 25/06/18

The Glacial Depressions
of Adalbert Stifter

Reading Adalbert Stifter is like considering the sadness of a lone walker on the winding paths of a mountain. The Bohemian-Austrian writer, noted equally for being an accomplished painter and wanderer, managed the unusual feat of linking inner emotion to daunting outer landscapes. The terror, fear, happiness and melancholy felt by his characters often connected to the mountains, lakes and forests around them; the landscape sketched with lucidity and detail.

Rarely is this landscape of a simple picture-postcard vision; instead, it is more a reflection of the melancholy search for solace in the physical world. Such landscapes have distracting, hopeful qualities, drawing the eye away from a growing despair. Depression shadows the crags and tarns of Stifter's work.

Rather like Stifter himself, his characters are solitary, and face dangers and trials alone. Society is often distanced and out of reach. In Stifter's time, this society had been marked by violent uprising, the famous revolutions of 1848 forcing a change of city and circumstance upon the writer. He soon succumbed to depression, one that resembled a persistent haunting of past failures, having struggled for a large period to sustain himself through his work. Fame suddenly came almost overnight with the success of his story 'Der Condor'. Even after gaining the respect of the academic establishment, from which he received a number of awards, however, the darkness within was unrelenting.

Though incredibly ill at the time, his death was ultimately self-inflicted. In Linz, he took a razor to his own throat, dying a few days later. His prose and painting were, however, hopeful acts, as if he was searching for the things that mattered and made life fizz with sensory pleasure away from his own heavy sorrow.

Within this pleasure, there's still sadness; a loneliness of ice and snow. He witnessed society with stinging clarity, yet he was always marred by his own inability to reach it. No matter how picturesque, Stifter's work is glacial; it knows that better things lie behind the ice – the warmth of a simple meal, the view of a mountain range, the longing for a loved one – but it can't cut through the sheet that separates them.

Behind the Ice

Ice travels slowly but accumulatively, just like depression; a constant grind that cuts valleys into stone and rock. Stifter's writing, for a number of reasons, has similar qualities. This doesn't mean that it's cold or devoid of human warmth. On the contrary, his prose is littered with human moments that are deeply affecting and poignant. But, in front of all his words lies a sheet of ice, digging into the ground of his characters, preventing the sharing of their joy.

In some ways this could be read as shame; he can't be critical of the worlds he creates because of his precarious situation, caused in part by the death of his father, whom he was somewhat dependant on financially.

In his short novella *Rock Crystal* (1845), but also elsewhere, writing is not superfluous but precise in its make-up. There are reasons for his strange contrast between intense detail of landscape and a more general sketching of event and narrative. The reader is never quite *with* the characters, as if venturing more earnestly into their world would mean having to take into account wider problems. It's a clear product of anxiety as much as anything else.

Stifter is almost entombing the children from the narrative of *Rock Crystal*, though this process occurs in the prose before it actually catches up with the pair via snow and ice. As Thomas Mann once wrote of this work, 'behind the quiet, inward exactitude of his descriptions of Nature in particular there is at work a predilection for the excessive, the elemental and the catastrophic, the pathological'.

Rock Crystal opens in this way with pages detailing the land as much as the people who inhabit it, with their shadowy forests and rocky outcrops. *The Bachelors* (1850) is similar in that all the activity of the protagonist is relayed in relation to the physical rather than emotional world around him. We can read the drama, but the inner turmoil of the teller is kept locked in the deep freeze, away from the warmth of the world.

Frosted Imprints

A sense of reduction comes in Stifter's writing from knowing what key notes are required for the creation of place. In *The Bachelors*, a perfect example of German *Bildungsroman* –

those novels following the formative moral and philosophical years of a young character – the mountains 'also took on a more beautiful blue, the brighter and more shimmering the evening light painted the greenery of the trees onto their sides'. Here is a simple sketch, but one which is built with an eccentric eye for detail.

The typical features of the mountains are assumed in the mind of the reader, leaving Stifter to concentrate on what makes them enigmatic or, more precisely, what he can elaborate on to distract himself from melancholy. Though he varies in detail from book to book, and even from chapter to chapter, there's the feeling that this unusual hierarchy is something brought over from his dual role as an artist.

As Hannah Arendt wrote of Stifter, he 'became the greatest landscape painter of literature', a reference specifically to his writing but also acknowledging his interest in landscape imagery more generally.

Stifter's paintings coexist neatly alongside his prose. Both inhabit some sense of escape from the self. The cover of the Pushkin Press edition of *The Bachelors* uses his painting *The King Lake with the Waltzman* (1837), painted a decade or so before the book was first published. One of the reasons why this works for the novel is because of an explicit narrative link. Just like in the painting, there is a boat journey across a vast lake to the house of an obtuse and eccentric relative. The journey is solitary in nature, and the character will be trapped there for a time, but the key is that the painting fleetingly reflects that narrative moment, even if born of some other creative desire.

Stifter's paintings reflect a general relationship in his prose between travellers and the landscape. People always lie in the shadow of the land. They're often inconsequential, threatened by engulfment. If his characters were not already open of heart, it would be easy to read that such modesty was a reaction to simply being in those dominating surroundings. Though naivety and arrogance do define some of his characters, modesty is all that's left as an option when confronting the vast Swiss wilderness. It seems more than a slight projection by Stifter; an honest reflection on his own loneliness.

Glacial Depressions

If visual essence plays some role in Stifter's work, then it must be said how, on occasion, visual emphasis does not always do him justice. In the early 1900s, the Czech writer and artist Ernst Kutzer realised a number of Stifter's stories in paintings designed for postcards.

Though possessing their own qualities, not least in the almost folkloric interpretation of such stories, they show how, with a less careful eye, the transcendent – that hopeful element challenging the depression – can be clumsily removed from Stifter's stories. In between the simplicity lies something beyond words and expression, often created via the unspoken emotions of characters and amplified by the daunting nature of their surroundings.

Kutzer's drawings, on the other hand, are fireside retellings almost in the vein of fairytales. His postcard of *Rock Crystal*, for example, shows the two children of the narrative lost on their adventure in a way not unlike an early Disney animation. It simply becomes another Christmas yarn, though still a pleasant one. In the same story, Stifter wrote:

> The cloudbanks had dropped behind the mountains on every side and bending low about the children, the arch of heaven was an even blue, so dark it was almost black, spangled with stars blazing in countless array, and through their midst a broad luminous band was woven, pale as milk, which the children had indeed seen from the valley, but never before so distinctly.

This is roughly at the same point in the story as the drawing, but the philosophies on show starkly contrast one another. The heavenly and the cosmic are the only comforts left to the children as they fear the worst for their situation. There are good reasons why Friedrich Nietzsche described Stifter's novel *Indian Summer* (1857) as being one of the few German novels to still contain 'magic'. By fighting against his own inner melancholy, Stifter's writing invoked powerful, almost incantatory elementals, though only by retaining an impressionism in his prose.

Inner and outer worlds extraordinarily come together, providing hope to the lost. Only via a reduction of an overly leading narrative would such a feat be possible in a purely visual work.

Stifter, of course, managed this in both painting and literature as it was characteristic of his own creative eye, whereas Kutzer was simply responding to the original call. It is, however, worth stating that Kutzer's illustrations for the postcards representing the novel *Brigitta* (1847) present an irresistible contrast between the beckoning landscape and genteel fashion; adding the scratchy, humble detail absent from more Romantic infusions found in work by the likes of Caspar David Friedrich and others.

A similar problem is present in the various film adaptations of *Rock Crystal*. In Harald Reinl's 1949 adaptation of *Bergkristall*, some effective black-and-white photography can't save the film from the heaviness of a literal adaptation, removing its general melancholic tinge.

Every aspect of traditional narrative filmmaking works in contrary to Stifter's purer aims, labouring them with grounded meaning and emotional guidance via performance and music. It would take a filmmaking style more akin to the likes of Robert Bresson or Yasujirō Ozu to do justice to Stifter's prose and the depression which etched it.

As W.H. Auden wrote of *Rock Crystal*, it was a near miracle that Stifter avoided melodrama in his story. 'What might so easily have been a tear-jerking melodrama,' he wrote, 'becomes in his hands a quiet and beautiful parable about the relation of people to places, of man to nature.' What is still ultimately a story of loss – of innocence towards the dangers of the world – feels far more like an adventure when filmed, with sharp-jawed heroes saving the children. It's as far from the reality of Stifter's delicate worlds as an echo of his work ever strayed.

Ultimately, Stifter was an artist of sorrowful precision, escaping such sentiments by concentrating on the hopeful. His work cannot help but express what he's clearly trying his utmost to contain and even avoid: his frustrations. His is a prose of quiet wonder and amazement at the infinite detail found in people and in places, but it's still distanced, as if written on an island in the middle of a lake, studying village life from the shoreline rather than the streets.

In *The Bachelors*, Stifter writes of a treacherous mountain lake and a previous attempt to traverse it when frozen. His character details it. 'Well over a hundred years have gone by since then,' he says, 'and it seldom happens that the lake is completely covered over with an ice sheet.' There may have once been some bridge back to the land and to the warmth of everyday life, but such things are transient and short-lived when alone with the world.

Published by The Nightjar, 25/09/18

Thomas Bernhard's
Memorial Dungeons

In 1965, Thomas Bernhard bought a house. It was bought between the writing of several works, including *Watten* (1964) and his second novel, *Gargoyles* (1967). The house is not really house in the ordinary sense, but a collection of farmhouses known in German as *Vierkanthof*.

The set of buildings is adjacent to the road of Obernathal in Ohlsdorf near the river Traun, which winds down the valleys to Lake Traunsee in Gmunden. Bernhard converted the buildings variously over the years and occupied them during his most prolific period of writing. Many interviews now associated with the man were conducted there, and simply searching for pictures of him often brings up images of his house.

One suggestion he made was that this house, with its array of rooms and land, was a perfect place to build his 'memorial dungeons'; a phrase I'm still taken with today, as it seems emblematic of the writing process more generally. In fact, Bernhard's *Vierkanthof* really reflects his own writing process back upon him, somewhat explaining his deathly isolation in the building. The reflection was only for one person.

Once housed in the building, Bernhard would write the following in *Gargoyles*:

The empty rooms always had a terribly depressing effect upon my father when he considered, he said, that the person who dwelt in them had to fill them solely with his own fantasies, with fantastic objects, in order not to go out of his mind.

The writer here is earnestly detailing his own process, showcasing the construction of the memorial dungeon.

Such empty spaces are filled with his writing in ways that are clearly discernible: repetitions bouncing off the walls, voices manically filling the silence left open by the absence of others, intensive detail of what happens in the lives of people from outside the four walls of a room, the landscape sketched from distanced views as if seen from a window. Bernhard's walls are one of the many restrictions he placed on his own writing, resulting in his easily recognised style of circular patterns.

I found some photographs of the rooms in Bernhard's *Vierkanthof* online last year, which is what sparked my need to write about the *Bernhardhaus*. I was worried that the only way to see photos when initially searching for pictures would be in digital form, some holiday photos taken on a phone for a travel blog or something similar. Instead, the photographer of the images I found, who now most likely works for the museum that is housed in the building today, very much captured the tone of Bernhard's prose in all their austere precision.

The first photo I saw was of Bernhard's writing desk, but not a photo that actually revealed the desk's function. A green tint hangs over the empty room, heightened by even greener curtains which drape down to the floor. There appear to be three textures: wood (of the floor and furniture), tiled stone (of the floor below the fireplace), and the general stone of the whitewashed walls. The room in the photo is pristine in its mathematical solitude.

The second photo was actually of the desk itself, revealing the function hidden in the previous photo. Among the paraphernalia there is a notepad and pen, a blotting pad, a clock, a handful of trinkets and three photos which appear to be of Bernhard himself.

On the wall there sits an old manuscript, likely from *Schedelsche Weltchronik* by Schedel. The neatness, which I'd wager to be exactly as it was when Bernhard lived and worked there and not enforced by its museum status, is perfectly logical, like the progression of a sonata form.

The kitchen is just as bare but beautifully so, renovated for absence in many regards, its huge size reduced to irony considering its singular occupant. Bernhard inverted the original principle of the building deliberately; the communities that thrived in such properties banished with a detached sense of purpose, leaving the lone man to sit in a physical embellishment of his own skull and the thoughts that whirled around it.

Photographs of the outside of the building are slightly more unusual. Most of them appear to have been taken in spring, the blossom still quivering on the trees. Yet the building itself looks incredibly official, even daunting, rather than homely. In many regards, it's almost factory-like, designed for cold production.

There is, of course, no reasoning to any of this. Bernhard wrote in a room in a house, and that is that. He successfully created his memorial dungeon, the empty space where his ideas lay cannibalising themselves until their form was finally pure. There's little else to express, but perhaps I'm being too much like one of his characters, too determined to let things lie when there are great undercurrents rumbling beneath.

I come back once again to the man's own words, this time from his novel *Concrete* (1982): 'Everything is what it is,' he wrote, 'that's all.'

There's no meaning. There's no reading. The rooms just are. And that is *all*.

Published by Celluloid Wicker Man, 29/01/18

The Photography of W.G. Sebald

'Tiny details imperceptible to us decide everything!' So suggests one of W.G. Sebald's characters in his novel *Vertigo* (1990). It seems as apt a statement as any to introduce the writer's work. In a brief but successful literary career, the German-born, East Anglia-based writer quickly rose to prominence, influencing an array of writers and artists.

With what would have been his seventy-fifth birthday on the 18th of May this year, two exhibitions in Norwich – *Lines of Sight: W.G. Sebald's East Anglia* at Norwich Castle, and *W.G. Sebald: Far Away – But From Where?* at The Sainsbury Centre – shine a light on his complex and deeply layered work. Yet what do these exhibitions say about Sebald as a writer, not simply in terms of the process of writing with the inclusion of photography (a practice that marked his four main novels), but in regard to the resonances and themes of his work today?

Winfried Georg Maximilian Sebald, or Max to his friends, was born in the Bavarian Alps in 1944. He studied English and German literature in Germany and Switzerland. In the mid-1960s he travelled to England, where he first taught at the University of Manchester. Aside from a handful of brief stints abroad, he settled firmly in Norfolk, working his way up the academic ladder at the University of East Anglia. He became a professor and the chair of European Literature, as well as founding the pivotal British Centre for Literary Translation. There's a reason why their yearly lecture is named in his honour.

Though publishing late in life, Sebald's writing career was unprecedented in its rise. His first novel, *Vertigo*, was published in German in 1990, though it was not translated into English until almost a decade later. It was followed in German by *The Emigrants* (1992) and *The Rings of Saturn* (1995), whose eventual English translations in 1996 and 1998 respectively garnered critical appreciation. *The Rings of Saturn* won the *LA Times* Book Prize and Sebald quickly found himself revered, seemingly much to his own horror.

In spite of publications of previous essays and poetry collections since, Sebald's literary life was arguably bookended by *Austerlitz* (2001), his first book to be published initially in English before a German translation, and with a sizeable book deal this time around.

During this time, Sebald's rise in the literary pantheon had been unparalleled, and so his early death from an aneurism while driving in Norfolk on the 14th of December 2001 cut short a career that clearly had a great deal still to give. Even Horace Engdah, the previous secretary of the Swedish Academy, put his name forward as a potential candidate for the Nobel Prize had he lived; a startling placement for a writer of only four novels.

There's no doubt, then, as to the power of Sebald's work, which is a stark mixture of meandering travelogue, archaeologies of history and dissections of melancholy, as well as rich and detailed character portraits matched in atmosphere by the grainy photographs and seemingly inconsequential ephemera that litter the pages.

It is this backlog of information that sometimes makes discussing Sebald's work difficult. Not only has a veritable cottage industry quickly assembled in discussing and analysing his books, especially in academia which, like Saturn, enjoys devouring its own young, but an aura surrounds his writing which it is a little too easy to become possessed by. I have certainly been guilty of this in the past.

It's with this admission in mind that I found the two exhibitions to earnestly show a more tangible, practical way to understand the man and his work. They highlight two key aspects to it: the ability to uncover the darker elements of our shared past, which constantly threatens to repeat; and why his engagement with walking and place was dramatically different to the images typically, and often unfairly, associated with such perambulatory forms of writing.

Wandering After Death

Walking around Norwich Castle's exhibition is very much like following a condensed version of *The Rings of Saturn*. It's arguably the writer's most revered book, built on a long walk around the East Anglian coastline; long enough, in fact, to have hospitalised the writer soon after completing it.

Along with the photographs from the book (and, more intriguingly, those that didn't make the cut), various objects mentioned and shown in its pages have been sourced to appear within the four walls of the exhibition. This sense of meandering, especially in *The Rings of Saturn*, has often seen

Sebald wrongly associated with other lone walker writers, flâneurs and new psychogeographers in particular; as if he was merely another voice following in a much practised field, at least here in Britain. This exhibition allows for a much deeper engagement with his work.

Sebald was often blasé about the photographs he took during his walks, and, looking at the results on display, it's clear that he was doing himself an injustice. The East Anglian light within them is stunning, the shades and tones rich, the landscapes detailed and the eye perceiving them inescapably curious. Such images were famously photocopied repeatedly to achieve the black-and-white Xerox graininess they are rendered with on the page, so their accomplished nature is surprising to say the least.

The reality of the images and their qualities is intriguing but, more importantly, there is a dark reality behind them. Unlike other such journeyed narratives around Britain's landscapes and cities, there's little desire to add layers of either grubby, performative authenticity or gushing Pastoralism, both seemingly so essential to other books of this form; as if the admiration of such things was new rather than simply another collection of older fetishes. Sebald instead plays upon the banal – for a deeply underrated strain of black humour, it must be said – and the vastness of his places. The melancholy is an effective editing process, if anything removing the clichés.

For me, this means Sebald has more in common with the writers he openly admired such as Robert Walser, Adalbert Stifter or Thomas Bernhard; writers he himself often wrote about and arguably kick-started a wider appreciation of in English language readership.

The Rings of Saturn, for example, has far more in common with the meandering microfictions of Walser than any British walking books, fiction or non-fiction. The book also has more in common with Stifter's *The Bachelors* (1852) – with its detailed landscapes seen with a mixture of darkness and practicality – than any novel wandering the endlessly trekked Lea Valley or the like.

His eye builds contrasts with a reality that plagued the picturesque. The stark renderings of place and atmosphere lure the reader in until close enough to see the horror behind the history, usually derived from the Second World War. This contrast also makes the syntax of his writing compelling and antiquarian, with far more in common with older European essayists than twentieth-century British non-fiction writers. His work is thankfully devoid of the forced poeticism and poignancy seemingly now obligatory in new nature writing and landscape writing in particular. Sebald's flowing sentences, by contrast, are seemingly taken out of time.

Of course, not everyone has been satisfied with Sebald's vision of the East Anglian landscape, even though it was by no means the only place he wrote about in such detail. Naturalist and writer Richard Mabey and the cultural theorist Mark Fisher were both dissatisfied with Sebald's representation of Suffolk. Yet both their criticisms, in their differing ways, can be explained, and arguably undermined by their context.

There's firstly the obvious aspect of Sebald's work still ultimately being fictional. It's rather like being frustrated at Émile Zola for his representations of rural France, or at Raymond Chandler for his seedy portrayals of California.

That same stretch of coastline that Sebald found barren and melancholy is a haven for wildlife and a resort for birdwatchers that flock regularly to many sites there. Minsmere in particular stands out as an obvious omission from the novel, housed between two of Sebald's pivotal markers in *The Rings of Saturn*: Sizewell Nuclear Power Station and the crumbling village of Dunwich. A Mabey-esque wanderer would probably have found several books' worth of excitement and joy at the wildlife on display in just that spot. Sebald questions a place that has provided Mabey with pleasure and inspiration; his criticism is, therefore, undermined by clearly being taken rather personally.

Fisher is slightly different, though there is likely some overlap with Mabey's criticisms. The landscape in question was, instead, a place of solace and personal happiness throughout his life, a refuge from the increasingly stressful academic and digital world; an escape from Goldsmiths University and all of its platitudinous hypocrisy and middle-class faux-authoritarianism. It was also the subject of a devoted sound project of his: *On Vanishing Land* (2019) with Justin Barton. For Fisher, the problem was how a writer could *not* find within the various beautiful vistas and flat, never-ending horizon lines a sense of comfort; a chance to rebuild the walls constantly knocked down by depression.

'The landscape functions as a thin conceit...' Fisher wrote critically of Sebald's portrayal. Fisher did, however, express a potential change in view of the writer's work in a review of Grant Gee's documentary *Patience (After Sebald)* (2012). His overarching criticisms seem to be born more of reactions to Sebald's work and the general machinations of the publishing industry to create and portray 'great literature' than anything else.

Whether such rehabilitation occurred in Fisher's eyes is sadly a question that will remain unanswered. Again, though, the context of Sebald is worth noting: the eyes from another continent avoiding all forms of nostalgia, the discipline to stick to a form, partly autobiographical, partly in character with the narrators of his books.

All of these aspects explain the differing views of the landscape, as much a fictional character in Sebald's work as any person (the photographs here are good evidence of this), and also attest as to why Sebald is so different from the more typical perambulatory writers, arguably for the better.

The Veil

With some suggesting that Sebald inaccurately sketched places, bending them to suit his own needs, it's unsurprising to find the most intriguing aspect of the exhibitions, and Sebald's writing as a whole, is the sense of trickery that lies behind it; its mixture of fact and fiction, its narrator a shadow-self of the writer, its history real and yet its figures semi-fictionalised.

Of course, such sleight-of-hand manoeuvres are clear when properly dissecting his work, whether walking around the places his ghostly alter egos wandered, or even researching the writers that inspired him.

Such trickery became most apparent when discussing the *Far Away* exhibition with one of its curators. The exhibition was still being installed during my visit to the brutalist campus of the University of East Anglia, and so the conversation tended towards Sebald's photographs rather than the generically pompous abstract artwork also housed in the show.

As in the other exhibition, Sebald's photographs were laid in roughly the order in which they appear in the book, *Austerlitz* in this case, along with many that failed to make the final text. There's a beautiful experimentation within the photos, a moment perceivable in particular where it's obvious that Sebald discovered the panorama setting on his camera and used it until the photos fitted into his schemata for the book (something often assumed to be cropped in the formatting of the photos at a later stage, as in his previous work).

The journeys there are a far more sporadic display than the more linear *Rings of Saturn* walk, traversing locations from East London to Paris, Marienbad to Prague, lending the photos a feeling of flux.

One of the photos caught my eye: of a messy office space supposed to be that of Jacques Austerlitz, the main figure of the novel. I'd seen the photograph scanned and published online several times, its archaic fustiness being typical of Sebald's atmosphere and tone. It had often been falsely attributed as being Sebald's office, as if the dividing line between the narrator and writer was always inescapably paper thin. I was curious, then, to find out more.

'You'd be surprised to learn,' the curator said, 'that it's actually an office of one of Sebald's colleagues.' Even more intriguing, however, was the revelation that said office, so antiquarian and dusty, was actually directly below where we were standing in the Sainsbury Centre at the time. The office was one of the metallic cubicles below us, housed in the incredibly futuristic-looking hangar, which is now home to an array of mostly modernist design work and sculpture.

Sebald describes the office in the following passage in *Austerlitz*:

> Almost every time I went to London in the years that followed, I visited Austerlitz where he worked in Bloomsbury, not far from the British Museum. I would usually spend an hour or so sitting with him in his crowded study, which was like a stockroom of books and papers with hardly any space left for himself, let alone his students, among the stacks piled high on the floor and the overloaded shelves.

The deception is clear in hindsight. Comparing the photograph to the reality of the space, a reality which I would have remained oblivious to had it not been pointed out to me, showed Sebald's true skill and the fictional disjoint in his work; in casting believable veils over reality in order to do justice to very real historical trauma.

With this realisation, the veil was no longer shrouding. And yet what was left in its place was equally as powerful and mysterious: namely, the question of why, knowing the tricks and mechanisms deployed in his work, Sebald's novels still retained a powerful essence of moral truth.

As with so many things connected with the writer, it's likely to remain a mystery, a cobweb seeming to briefly find shape and design before floating back into the ether. But perhaps Sebald's troubling sense of accumulated history contains some semblance of an answer.

The Accumulation of History

Writing this on the day of the European elections, one particular idea of Sebald's feels resonant. The deeply moribund character that occupies even his lightest novels seems to be tracking the root, or source, of their narrators' melancholy. Often in his novels, the site or source of this feeling is located unconsciously in history, though it becomes more complicated than an act of remembrance or haunting. Instead, historical calamities seem to emerge out of vast patterns.

The Sebaldian narrator – whether through walking a landscape (something that happened a lot less than is often assumed) or talking to people he meets on his travels – finds such patterns in history and recognises his inescapable place within them.

This was partly autobiographical as well, stemming from Sebald's own concerns over his father's potential role in the Second World War, hence its lingering power, especially in *The Rings of Saturn* which deals with the fears of what could be called the accumulation of history. Essentially, the realisation is one of growing catastrophe.

The tragedies of yesteryear, whether the world wars, their forewarnings in previous colonial conflicts or the formation of early empires, seem to inescapably accumulate. The mechanisms behind them gain momentum. Such historical events from the past were not something that could be directly learned from positively either, as is so often suggested. Instead, they were merely a preview of a greater calamity ahead. As the writer famously put it, 'We learn from history as much as a rabbit learns from an experiment that's performed upon it.'

The effect this has on Sebald's curatorial eye is there for all to see in his prose, but also in his photographic subjects, too. In the *Lines of Sight* exhibition, his eye roams haphazardly to express this quiet trepidation, marked by memories of previous epochs threatening to repeat in the future.

He finds synchronicity at the Orford Ness weapons testing facility on the Suffolk coastline, the photos almost post-apocalyptic, to the point where the landscape resembles a place hit by the weapons actually researched there (the site was the testing station for the firing mechanisms of a variety of large-scale weaponry, including nuclear warheads).

Further along the coast, Sebald ties this apocalypse to a natural one, an ecological mirror in the form of the lost town of Dunwich, once one of England's largest ports, now mostly fallen under the waves. Ecological catastrophe is present in these photographs as much as man-made catastrophe, the two speaking the same language on some level. But the sense of accumulation is there. It can be felt through something as simple as the image of a Jewish grave in Tower Hamlets Cemetery or an East Anglian cliff falling into the sea; the bones from the Greyfriars Priory intermingling with the pebbles on the beach, as if all the stones were somehow gathered there to acknowledge some mass extinction event.

As the results roll in for the election in the coming days of editing, switching between writing this and watching with banal horror history circling around once again, it feels almost absurd to call Sebald's writing timely. He was merely watching with a wider grasp of such historical momentum; aware of the wheel still turning.

Sebald as a writer knew that fiction could be a useful way to address real echoes from the past and, equally, that such a past benefited from certain freedoms allowed within the form of the novel. Considering his chief subject (albeit almost always addressed indirectly) was the Holocaust, it's unsurprising to find him creating fictional imprints to whisper greater truths. Staring head on, even when armed with a camera, was (and still is) almost unbearable, as the echoes repeat and once more grow louder.

Published by The Quietus, 28/08/19

A Phantom Coincidence
in W.G. Sebald's Poetry

A few years ago, I was sat on a couch in Strasbourg reading essays by Teju Cole from his volume *Known and Strange Things*. It was a dark night and I was alone, glancing up occasionally, as I often did when in my ex-partner's flat, to stare at the city's famous cathedral lit up against the black sky. I was at a point in the book when Cole begins to explore the work of W.G. Sebald – a major influence upon his own writing – when something stuck out.

The essay, titled *'Poetry of the Disregarded'* and published in the *New Yorker* a few years earlier, was about Sebald's often neglected poetry, an essay marking the publication of selected works in the volume *Across the Land and the Water*.

Cole had quoted part of a poem included in the volume from a long, meandering text appropriately titled *'Remembered Triptych of a Journey from Brussels'*. Taking the words totally out of context to make the point that Sebald's poems can be almost baffling in their allusions, the quoted segment was as follows:

Strasbourg Cathedral
bien éclairée. – Between thresholds
lines from Gregorius, the guotesündaere,

from Au near Freiburg, rechtsrheinisch,
not visible from Colmar – Haut Rhin.
Early morning in Basel, printed on
hand-made Rhine-washed lumpy paper
under the supervision of Erasmus of Rotterdam

I remember looking up from this poem and staring at the very cathedral it had just mentioned, noting also that, due to the available flight routes, I had followed the journey mentioned in the poem mere days before, travelling from Basel through Colmar to get to the city. I was even due to visit Freiburg that trip, specifically to photograph Erasmus's house as it was the inspiration for a dance school in a 1970s Italian horror film: Dario Argento's *Suspiria*.

Sebald's work has always had an uncanny aspect, not least because he had the ability to draw upon things that, though seemingly inconsequential, gain meaning at the strangest of times and on a deeply personal level. I used to call this the writer's ability to conjure Phantom Coincidences because, unlike most other writers, he laid subtle, obscure hints, especially in regard to places and buildings, that always eventually managed to find their way underneath the footsteps of many personal realities. What Cole rightly labels as Sebald's 'opacity' is really an element that is always at some stage in the process of being understood rather than a forever hidden enigma.

This Phantom Coincidence has happened to me before with Sebald's writing, finding something uncanny in certain elements of *The Rings of Saturn*, when I later found out that several places – which are visited in the book and which lingered in my thoughts after first reading for no discernible reason – were actually visited in childhood. Memories came flooding back in the strangest of manners. Synchronicity is undeniably one of Sebald's most effective ploys.

Vague memories of getting lost on Dunwich Heath came to mind. But there was something more that came with reading the fragment of the poem rather than the novel, not least in the coincidence that Cole had chosen this specific part. It was rendered even odder considering that the line he begins his quote on does not even start with mentioning the cathedral but with the Banhof von Metz, and a further four lines detailing earlier parts of the trip before this segment of the stanza. It's simply coincidence, but it no doubt lends power to a work when experienced personally. I can't convince you, the reader, of its power until it actually happens to you. Of that, I'm sure.

Cole picks up on Sebald's shift of language and uses this as further proof of the poem's indecipherable qualities. Even in the short quoted section, beside a number of place names from differing countries, the language switches between English, French and German. This is more obviously puzzling with the stanza given its full context:

> Départ quai huit minuit seize
> le train pour Milan via St. Gotthard
> I recognized Luxembourg by the leaves on its trees
> then came industrie chimique near Thionville,
> light above the heavenly vaults,
> Banhnof von Metz…

One of the great pleasures I find in Sebald's writing is this change of language, something that always seems to survive the translation process. It's difficult to describe but, in these place names and words, the Phantom Coincidence is lying most prominently in wait. Of course, Strasbourg being as it is, language and culture is incredibly permeable there in the first place.

It's even the theme of my current novel, *How Pale the Winter Has Made Us*, and the in-betweenness ('liminal' is banned from my vocabulary this year) within its history is incredibly Sebaldian.

Passing between France and Germany throughout various wars, Strasbourg has that same air as Sebald's process, lapsing (especially in its buildings) between the two cultures, making this same change in language highly appropriate for poetry about this small part of Europe. This is before highlighting the original journey I took that was ghosted by Sebald, from the north-west of Switzerland, another element in the mix to ponder and itself a place of amalgamated languages and culture.

Sat on the couch that night, I reread the fragment over and over again, trying to understand why it had had such a great impact on me, and wondering whether it was just tiredness playing tricks. I'd been so deep into research regarding the city that to see it mentioned in a writer's work I so admired was surprisingly affecting. Was it Sebald's Phantom Coincidence, Cole's coincidence in the choice of poem, or simply nothing at all, merely the product of an exhausted mind?

Putting it into words now, it seems rather inane and probably something to do with being in that specific period and place; in other words, impossible to fully describe. But, in that moment, the words jumped out from the essay, the cathedral's lights seemed brighter and warmer than I'd ever seen before. The city and the page, in that brief instance, became one.

Published by Celluloid Wicker Man, 19/02/18

Wanders

A Last Glimpse of Sebald's Land

During the past few months, I've started to map a very particular stretch of Suffolk's coastline. The aim of such an activity has been to produce a trilogy of short films, all exploring the eeriness of this coastal region. Though the trilogy will not be completed until well into 2017, the filming and walking has already been undertaken, and this particular wander details one of the film's walks: trudging from the *Quatermass* vista of Sizewell nuclear power station and its shingly shores, all the way along past Minsmere RSPB reserve towards Dunwich Heath and its beach.

The territory is now arguably defined best by W.G. Sebald in his novel *The Rings of Saturn* (1995). The narrator spends a fair amount of the book discussing his own perambulation along its disintegrating clifftops and beaches. Interestingly, it's one of the most depressive points in the book, and I've often heard criticisms aimed at it for this character; namely, that the impression is largely fictional and the coastline itself is undeniable in its calming beauty.

The day started with being dropped off right outside Sizewell A. The sun was ablaze and, in spite of a nuclear dome looming large over the landscape, there were numerous groups of people about, enjoying the shoreline. The area even has a Sizewell Café, implying the sort of cash-in on some famous monument or attraction more often reserved for somewhere National Trust-esque, only with said attraction being a dystopian-looking nuclear power plant rather than something typically picturesque.

I loaded up with my various filming gear and trudged off alone into the dunes and marram grass. Ironically, the first thing that came to my attention was not the overbearing buildings of the plant itself but two odd structures some way out at sea. The place is clearly a haven for industrial detritus. It wasn't, however, the design of these structures that caught my attention but the sound of screaming emanating unnervingly from their rigging. My ornithologist father later told me that they were flocks of kittiwakes taking shelter there, though my previous memories of the bird had lacked such eerie potential.

After spending some minutes mesmerised by these possessed rigs, I wandered back from the beach and towards the plant. Though several joggers were about, the place quickly seemed distinctly empty. This was made more unnerving by how surveillance-saturated it felt when walking its perimeter. Like Winniden Flats of *Quatermass II* (1957), it was a zone of secrecy; various security cameras keeping a close and careful eye out as I set up my filming equipment and shot Super-8 footage of the alluring dome of Sizewell B and the almost art-deco-looking concrete of neighbouring Sizewell A.

Were they simply making power, or was there a pulsating mass of living sludge writhing beneath the whiteness of the dome? Sebald writes of B's dome that it 'can be seen on moonlit nights shining like a shrine far across the land and sea'. Indeed, the place did produce the feeling of theological worship, a kind of demented pair of cathedrals.

It seemed, as I climbed the slight incline towards the plant, that the gorse, radioactive with its vibrant yellow and coconut aroma, seemed unnaturally prevalent; as if the power station had sprouted its own organic defence beside the more typical wire and mesh.

Alongside the plant, I stopped by a group of concrete cubes to take stock. It was a bad move as my walk had been unknowingly paralleled over the way by a group of roughly forty people with a pack of excited dogs hidden by the dunes. I stood still while various owners attempted to recall several of their companions from around my legs and filming gear. Only the threat of the owners walking back in the direction of the Sizewell Café eventually drew them away, panting excitedly in the endless heat.

This point in the landscape seemed a cut-off, acting as an official designator for the end of a walk. Even people walking on the beach, but not from the group, seemed to stop at this marker and turn back. Henceforth, I was enjoyably alone, pondering going as small pebbles found their way again and again over the back lip of my boots.

The beach was becoming more and more Jamesian as I kept looking back, trying unwisely to find menace in the odd silhouette of a far-away walker. It reminded me of one of my favourite lines from M.R. James's *'Oh, Whistle, and I'll Come to You, M'Lad'*, where its character, Parkins, 'quickly rattled and clashed through the shingle and gained the sand, upon which, but for the groynes which had to be got over every few yards, the going was both good and quiet.'

My walk was the same, and I took great pleasure feeling at the mercy of the landscape. Sadly, it was only to be the sun burning my neck that would later haunt me. This sense of being alone was broken almost instantly when I came upon a strange, man-made monument constructed some way down the beach. It wasn't near enough to the slowly approaching Minsmere nature reserve or to the café back at Sizewell to be within easy reach, and yet there it was, standing like a lost totem to some unknown nuclear god.

I continued on, stopping and starting to keep removing the increasingly jagged and persistent rocks that ventured into my boots. As I rounded the corner of the coast, the atmosphere again changed; people became more prominent until it felt more like a high street. I had finally hit Minsmere Reserve, a Mecca for birdwatchers and general wildlife enthusiasts alike. I'd left my father there on every single day of the three-day trip, such was the draw of the place. No doubt the wildlife there is stunning (on a visit last year, they had even caught a death's-head hawkmoth, which was a first for me), but something felt different to the previous segment of the beach.

The path all of a sudden felt surveyed in a different way. The grassy beachscapes gave way to wooden fences and coach-loads of people carrying equipment of varying sizes along the narrow pathways, some of which made my own filming escapades seem like a pleasure jaunt by comparison. I followed the path along from the reserve quickly and away from its multitude of people, up a gravel track towards the heath.

The faded purple of the heath began and I knew I was then officially in the territory of Dunwich. The pathway instantly recalled Sebald's meander onto this heath, the landscape where he got lost; as if the paths among the heather were sentient and playing tricks on him.

'Shading from pale lilac to the deepest purple,' he wrote of getting lost on the heath, 'it stretched away westward, with a white track curving gently through its midst. Lost in the thoughts that went round in my head incessantly, and numbed by this crazed flowering, I stuck to the sandy path until to my astonishment, not to say horror, I found myself back again at the same tangled thicket from which I had emerged about an hour before…'.

The heath is officially National Trust property now, though unlike some other places owned and procured by the company, this one is desolate and empty. I sat on a bench overlooking the reserve and looked over to the dome of Sizewell B. This was the bench whose view initially inspired the desire to make the film that had brought me back.

I ate there, accompanied only by the occasional rustling lizard in the vegetation (and even a tiger beetle, an insect I hadn't seen for years). The walk with the equipment and in such blistering weather had taken its toll, and I sat on the bench for some time, recovering from the first two thirds of the walk.

Sebald was constantly coming to mind at this point, the heath having great import for the chapter in *The Rings of Saturn*. He found the same omens as I had in its dusty vistas; where the unnatural destruction of place through man-made catastrophe felt palpable. The coastline acts as a portal to other times.

The heath slowly dissolved into forest and, simultaneously, noise began to grow. At first, it had the likeness of white noise, as if an old television had been left on. As I approached the road, I realised it was coming from a particularly loud caravan site, the smell of chips and the sound of screaming children wafting through the forest.

I began to wonder what frame of mind Sebald must have been in to block this out, so contrary was it to his own pessimistic solitude. He was, after all, contemplating the very destruction of civilised society when walking the dunes and its heath. Would such a thought have come so strongly when encountering such a surprisingly lively area? Perhaps the site was yet to be built in 1995, though I doubt it would've made a difference to the resulting book.

While not possessing the atmosphere that Sebald described, it did result in me quickening my pace down an endless road to get away, past houses selling small clumps of vegetables and other home-grown objects out of neatly stacked boxes.

Turning onto the main road, it became clear that it was closed, the traffic being inescapable on my last visit but now enjoyably absent. I followed it along, all the way down to where a large and quite friendly pig is kept in a bit of wooded forest. Here, another road gently meandered off, distinguished by quaint country cottages and a darkening piece of woodland.

Eventually the path led to the woodland growing on the very edge of Dunwich's cliffs. When last visiting, it had become clear that this was the forest featured in Jonathan Miller's adaptation of James's 'Whistle and I'll Come to You...' for BBC Omnibus in 1968. The caravan site is actually where Parkins (Michal Hordern) stays, albeit in the period house that sits at its centre. Though largely filmed up the coast in Norfolk, specifically Waxham, the forest segments and some shingle beach segments were filmed in Dunwich.

An odd concrete bridge hangs over the wooded path, seen briefly in Miller's film, and I walked under it to follow the leafy route all the way to the cliff's edge. Ignoring the paranoid signage of the place, I sat with my legs hanging over the edge. I don't believe in the simplistic ideal of rural enclaves healing weary urban minds but, on this one occasion, it was accurate.

The waves were gently ebbing below and a cooling breeze blew as stones and bones crumbled into the air. I doubled back along the path after spending some time enjoying the view, and was surprised to find an almost perfect holloway; they sprout places. The path wa rabbits and confident on the walk: Greyfriar

This is one of the l original area of Dunv few fields either side ruin acting as an aleph 'Dunwich,' he sugges thousand souls, has di

w
dist
I'd
Destructio
left to reac
during the fina
burning building

air.' Of even more prescience was the so-called last grave; a gravestone standing on the very precipice of the cliff where once a full graveyard stood. A few more dogged winters will eventually drag it down into the sea, though hopefully not before some respected antiquarian has had the chance to excavate a whistle from its collapsing soil.

I walked along the path to a relatively busy car park next to Dunwich beach, wandering back upon myself some way out until the sound of people died away again.

In the distance and around the coast, I could just make out Sizewell once more as its eerie dome jutted out over the peak of the land. I sat quietly and waited for my lift, which as not due for another hour (with added 'Minsmere action time', of course).

brought Sebald's *On the Natural History of* with me, one of the few of his books I had about the destruction of German cities years of the war; ghosts of flames and joining the ghosts of Jamesian bed sheets and Dunwich horrors that were already floating in the ether.

I sat waiting and reading as the tide gently drew the beach's pebbles back and forth, awaiting the future calamity to repeat or, as Sebald described via a quote from Sir Thomas Browne, 'a last glimpse of the land now being lost forever'.

Published by Celluloid Wicker Man, 20/06/16

The Grave of W. G. Sebald

Few writers have produced so many potential maps for literary pilgrimages from so few works as W.G. Sebald. With place occupying an important role in his novels, to the extent that several of them can be walked and explored in detail, the writer unconsciously highlighted places that now sit unusually within what could be called the 'Sebaldian'. Whether it be abandoned weapons testing facilities, gloomy London train stations or East Anglian countryside, the writer marked the atmospheric places he wrote about with such effect that he spawned a popular desire to visit places with a skill that most local tourist boards would be envious of.

Having become enamoured with his work over the last decade, and with his novels explicitly connected to a sense of place, I have since visited a number of Sebald-related sites over the years. From the East Anglian locations walked in *The Rings of Saturn* to the East London haunts that found their way into *Austerlitz* (2001), I have spent a great deal of time walking after Sebald, chiefly out of curiosity rather than under the illusion of gaining greater insight into his work. There's little doubt that, with his mode of writing still ultimately being fictional, following in the footsteps of his narrators is a pastime that generally reveals discrepancies rather than synchronicities between novels and places.

Of all the places marked by the writer, the one I had avoided for so long was his grave. There could be no misreading of this place, no characterisation or editing on the writer's part. It was a depressingly early full stop to what should have been a much longer series of sentences. But, having searched for so many Sebaldian places, sometimes through endless research, other times through trudging the paths he really walked, it felt the right point to end what had been almost a decade of obsession. Aside from a future visit to the île Saint-Pierre, the Swiss island jutting into Lake Biel which could be excused as a trip for connections to Jean-Jacques Rousseau and Robert Walser as much as Sebald, this felt like the last page of his landscape to explore.

Sebald is buried in the churchyard of St Andrew's in Framingham Earl, not far from where he lived in The Rectory at Poringland. The church is a typically East Anglian building, bustling with antiquity and wildlife in equal measure due to the surrounding countryside. Though possessing a beautiful Norman round tower, which must have seemed like a beacon across the fields several hundred years ago, the church has also been argued as containing Saxon heritage, too. In other words, the site is an incredibly old one; suitable as a resting place for a writer so often taken out of time.

The day of the visit was warm and sunny. I was already in Suffolk for the appropriately Sebaldian task of filming at Orford Ness and its laboratories, featured heavily in *The Rings of Saturn*. My father was keen to travel further north after our filming, in search of a great grey shrike that had been blown onto the Norfolk coastline. Before heading in search of the bird, however, he kindly drove me to Framingham Earl to see Sebald's grave. The village's roads were submerged in greenery, turning the A-roads and byways into shadowy holloways. Though a few incredibly large properties littered the area, there was no sign of people. The place was absence made manifest via woods and fields.

We walked around the churchyard for a time, my father looking at the butterflies as I admired the old graves and architecture. Soon, behind its own dark green bush, Sebald's grave came into sight. Made of a jet-black stone, the grave stood out among the mostly lichen-covered neighbours crumbling into the ground, as well as for its variety of mementos: from a vase of flowers to a variety of pebbles carefully placed along the grave's head. Blue damselflies seemed strangely drawn to the spot, hovering and zipping about the air like quicksilver. The insects are fond of his grave.

Having followed this man so often, it felt like the end of the line; not so much the end of the obsession, but certainly its peak, where the admiration could finally retreat into the unconscious. As the Polaroid photo I took developed in the thin darkness between the pages of a Raymond Chandler thriller, it felt that it was finally time to stop following.

Published by Caught by the River, 14/12/19

Alan Garner's Edge

'When I was not confined to the house, I would
spend my days and my nights on the Edge.'
– Alan Garner

On a frosty but sunny January morning, I was steadily
making my way along the M56 towards Macclesfield. I was
on my way to Alderley Edge in Cheshire, the stalking
ground of writer Alan Garner.

In 2015, I had made the same journey in order to make a
film there, quickly zipping between Alderley, Congleton
(where Garner still lives) and Mow Cop further down the M6.

With such haste, I'd been unable to fully explore the Edge on foot properly, in part due to the need to get shots that were at the mercy of the weather and the approaching dusk.

My aim in returning was to properly explore the Edge in relation to Garner's history, and especially in the context of his first novel, *The Weirdstone of Brisingamen* (1960), which maps the area in such detail (as well as providing an actual illustrated map) that reliving Susan and Colin's magical adventure is possible with little difficulty. After all, the subtitle of the book is 'A Tale of Alderley'.

Driving through the town which resides further down the hill, it's clear that the area has changed dramatically since Garner's time. The affluence of the place is all too clear: its local supermarket is Waitrose, its other shops are almost all independent, supercars are parked along the high street, and everyone is dressed impeccably as they push huge designer prams around. This is no longer the realm of the ancient or of working-class characters like Garner's Gowther and Bess Mossock.

The new sheen to the place is, however, quickly lost once on the Macclesfield Road, itself initially lined with large-looking mansions but one that quickly descends into forest and rock. A few minutes hence, and civilisation virtually vanishes; only reappearing like a conjuring trick when the official National Trust car park appears alongside a certain pub.

The Wizard Inn is one of the key points in Garner's story and is the first stop on any Garner-related walk. In *Brisingamen*, Garner writes the following about the pub: 'It was named The Wizard, and above the door was fixed a painted sign which held the children's attention. The painting showed a man dressed like a monk, with long white hair and beard...'

Little has changed on the surface. The building retains the same black and white design, built on the edge of the forest. The sign still hangs proudly above the door, its magical character standing confidently as protector of the area. It's aptly one of the few buildings around whose sense of magic is palpable, its beams bending gently with age and its windows creaking. The only downside is that it's now an upmarket restaurant rather than a pub. Perhaps a local pub is a little too downmarket for the new generation of customers.

My aim was to hit the Edge as soon as possible. The path wound around and through the forest, past several mines which may or may not have housed various groups of aggressive Svarts, Garner's makeshift equivalent of goblins.

The day turned groggy, raining on and off throughout the walk. Instead of veering left straight away towards the forest,

I meandered straight on through a thin path created by barbed wire on either side, fields stretching out as far as they dared. In terms of Garner's map, it was heading towards Clockhouse Wood, though the weather meant that a left turn was soon taken back to the main area.

The path twisted and turned through a battered gate, though the neatness leading up to the Edge's various points began to feel rather unnerving; there was a viewing point and path so unnaturally created that it felt perturbing, though the view itself was excellent. Garner writes of this Edge in *Brisingamen*, describing it as 'high, and sombre, and black'. Further elaborations come from Susan and Colin's reaction to the place:

> Nearer they came to the Edge, until it towered above them, then they turned to the right along a road which kept to the foot of the hill. On one side lay fields, and on the other the steep slopes. The trees came right down to the road, tall beeches which seemed to be whispering to each other in the breeze.

The beeches were whispering as the wind picked up. The view distracted from properly finding the Golden Stone, another Garner site, the muddy track softening underfoot as the day went on. It was aptly refreshing, however, from the bark-chip-laden path of the first view. There was an obvious attempt to make the place a safe retreat for the inhabitants of the suburban sprawl down the hill.

The wildness of the eventual rocky plains of the Edge will never be fully subdued by this neatness, however. The outcrop switches between jagged and smooth stone in a single footstep, allowing a Roman-sentry view onto the Cheshire plains. It's a view that transports temporally as well as physically; the viewer small in both place and time.

Garner developed a unique but emotionally lethal view of this landscape. He wrote that 'for me the Edge both stopped, and melted, time'. But he also wrote in the same essay that the Edge 'is physically and emotionally dangerous. No one born to the Edge questions that, and we showed it proper respect.'

He's evidently not only discussing the dangers of an incorrect footing but of a relationship with the self; places that force us to reflect on our own minuteness and pitiful position in the world. We are tiny. The rock was here before we were born, and will be here once we and Waitrose are dust among the strata. Garner knew this, especially as the rock transcended through his own family, right the way back like a sandstone vein.

With such a view potentially being read as pessimistic to some degree, it's worth restating the sheer beauty of the rolling landscape beyond. Perhaps the surprisingly morbid quality of Garner's vision of this place is partly to do with his attachment to it. 'They were on top of the Edge now,' he wrote in *Brisingamen*, 'and through the gaps in the trees they caught occasionally glimpses of lights twinkling on the plain far below.' It's a description tinged with complex affection.

This aspect of emotional danger doesn't quite fully manifest in *Brisingamen*, but the spellbinding nature of the place certainly does. For example:

> To the north, the Cheshire plain spread before them like a green and yellow patchwork quilt dotted with toy farms and houses. Here the Edge dropped steeply for several hundred feet, while away to their right the country rose in folds and wrinkles until it joined the bulk of the Pennines, which loomed eight miles away through the haze.

The walk continued, though not with the handrail caution of the path. Down through the valley of the stones, little discernible way presented itself. Behind the Edge, a quick stray from the path lead to some eerily abandoned mineshafts, of which the danger became all too obvious. Standing unwisely and irresponsibly over a precipice, the hazardous nature of the place, the same aspect that Garner explored, was briefly felt.

The rain soon returned, and the Edge had ironically found its edge again. The mud clogged the grips of my boots as the gravel path appeared. Past the small, obviously Victorian 'Druid' stone circle and back around into the forest's valley, an unstable path eventually led to Stormy Point and its adjacent Holy Well.

The sound of the water was incredibly pleasant as it dripped and bubbled, in part because it was the history of Garner and the place made manifest; a source. He talks about this well several times in various essays, mentioning that it's where his family gathered both their water and their children's pocket money. 'Our water supply derived from the Holy Well,' he admitted, 'which granted wishes to tourists at weekends, and an income for the children of our family who, on a Monday morning, cleaned out the small change.'

His grandfather even claimed that the well's water was 'a cure for barren women'. I drank some in spite of being neither barren nor a woman, and also as a two fingers up to the prevalent idea of everything outside being contaminated with germs. Have we ever, in our history, been so afraid of the tactile outdoors?

The ground was incredibly loose at this point and it made sense after reading Garner's research of the place:

> Below the well the ground is almost precipitous and is a deep bog, deep enough to strand a child. In it is a rock of unknown size, but of several hundred tons. It is reputed to have fallen from the cliff in the year 1740, and to have shaken all the cottages of the Hough.

The boggy nature was evident and the walk back up the side of the valley was enjoyably slippery, even catching an absent-minded dog walker off balance as he fell off the path and down the side.

The last stop on the walk, which was haphazard enough to sadly not include several other relevant locations such as the West Mine or Thieves Hole, was the Wizard's Well; another natural source of water, it bears a carving of a wizard and an inscription that reads: 'Drink of this and take thy fill for the water falls by the Wizhard's will.' The carving is reputedly one of the many remains of handiwork by Garner's great-great-grandfather, Robert. The well sadly proved too magical for my camera to properly capture it, its overhanging rock swallowing most of the light from above.

I rubbed my hand on the Wizard's mossy beard and then on my own, perhaps for some luck in it growing long and bringing wisdom, though both seemed unlikely. In *Brisingamen*, Colin and Susan also find the Wizard's Well, which provides a clue to Cadellin's presence on the Edge:

> Just as they were about to turn for home after a climb from the foot of the Edge, the children came upon a stone trough into which water was dripping from an overhanging cliff, and high in the rock was carved the face of a bearded man, and underneath was engraved...
> "The wizard again!" said Susan.

The face of the wizard in the stone was the final stop on the walk before the warmth of the inn called us away from the Edge. It wasn't, however, to make for an entirely uplifting end to the walk.

The inn itself, rather than the restaurant, is still functioning in its service of foods for more transient travellers. It's housed in an incredibly old building, more like a barn extension next to the original pub. This outer layer is misleading, however, as, upon entering, the strangest collection of things is presented.

Though the beams creak with age, the fire crackles, and the oak is marked deeply, the inn is really a sentinel enclave of the town. People were sat discussing holidays in Dubai and how to get their second iPad repaired. Radio 1 was at full volume blasting 'Mr Brightside' by The Killers, and there was even a sign on the counter that read 'Have a totally amazeballs day!' It was like entering back into a twisted form of reality, loud and brash, alien to the ancientness of the building and the character of the Edge as a whole.

While sat at a table, a figure came in with a long, grey beard. He was in walking gear rather than a long cloak but, upon witnessing the atmosphere of the café, he sighed, turned and walked back out. It seemed impossibly poignant, even if it was likely because there were no seats available. Perhaps he went back to the gates and to Arthur's sleeping army again, to wait another hundred years to see if things would improve.

The Edge is such a wild place, so full of magic, that it feels like a portal to some Arthurian past. Garner writes that 'Coincidence, error, fantasy or folklore: this is a reality. And for this I care.' My walk on the Edge provided all of these things, though it seemed a reality slipping away, stone by stone, gradually going into hiding under the rocks and trees, lying in wait for a new dawn.

Published by Celluloid Wicker Man, 15/02/16

A Northern *Concrete Island*

'Somewhere in this nexus of concrete and structural steel, this elaborately signalled landscape of traffic indicators and feeder roads, status and consumer goods, Vaughan moved like a messenger in his car...'
– J.G. Ballard

In the dead space around Christmas 2015, I found myself meandering back towards my old secondary school on The Wirral, one of only two things that I still have nightmares about. It wasn't the school that was my destination but the area that surrounds it which, for me, defines a very particular type of landscape, and one that reminds me of a very personal solace.

Walking along Mosslands Drive in Wallasey, an unnervingly straight suburban road whose name and history implies an aptly boggy transience, I began to have flashbacks of what this journey meant to a younger version of myself; forever on the lookout like a preyed-upon herbivore from the more aggressive variety of peers; all keys, chains and Stanley knives.

It was fear that often drove me into the concrete area in question, albeit rebelliously, as it was strictly ordained by various teachers in the school that it was dangerously out of bounds and punishable by detention if caught beyond its frontier. Ironically, it felt safer than the rather flexible boundary of the school with its host of ubiquitous, violent young men.

The place in question follows a footpath initially parallel to the school that provides the strange Ballardian privilege of walking alongside (and then directly underneath) a motorway; the M53, to be precise. This gives rise to an unnerving feeling due to the speeds at which the passing cars hurtle by. The vision of one flying over the edge and towards the walker on the pathway is constant as the noise made from each vehicle's passing is so tremendous.

The New Brighton to Liverpool train also runs underneath the motorway as it stretches out into its various lanes, adding to the screaming white noise. As the path unwinds, it curves inwards and the walker is taken directly underneath the first slip road of the motorway. The noise at this point is always dizzying. Waiting for a passing train is essential for the desired woozy effect of standing within the arteries of both train and motor routes, like a transport synapse in the middle of a paraphrenic collapse.

If anything, it feels like the blood-rush before a fainting spell. Perhaps it's what extinction itself actually sounds like: a motorised vibration rising to the point of unstoppable expiration. 'The traffic drummed over his head, no more than twenty feet away, an unceasing medley of horns and engines...' as Ballard wrote in *Concrete Island* (1974).

At this point, the adjacent underworld beyond seems at first impenetrable due to the razor-wired fences that protect the train track. This illusion is broken when walking further to meet a brutalist bridge which crosses the railway lines and, in the opposite direction, the growing pools of murky water that lead to the radioactive greenery of Bidston Moss.

The area itself, especially when seen from the train on its way towards Birkenhead and Liverpool, allows sights of these flooded areas, recalling The Zone from Andrei

Tarkovsky's film *Stalker* (1979); all submerged train tracks, overgrown fences and debris-littered edgelands. A feeling of distance arises from these artefacts, left by a more industrious, unsparing age, though created without the aid of a crashed meteorite and its subsequent fallout as in Tarkovsky's film. Laziness was its only catalyst here.

Straight ahead of the bridge is a semi-functional business complex ruled over by the DIY warehouse, B&Q. However, it's almost entirely hidden by rustling shrubbery of various forms, adding an amusing impression of desired secrecy to the building. Trudging through a brief mire of mud and rubbish leads, eventually, to what looks like a graveyard of roads. The layout of a ghost road is still remarkably defined, dirtied by road paraphernalia. As Ballard describes his similar landscapes, 'The damp earth was dark with waste oil leaking from the piles of refuse and broken metal drums on the far side of the fence.' It may as well have had further signs detailing 'Please give way, oncoming spectres'. These are Ballard's ghosts as well as mine.

Ballard wrote *Concrete Island* as a response to both his own fetishisms growing around cars and consumerism, and how this new merging of materialism and sexuality had affected the topography of the London motorways and surrounding areas. It follows a man trapped in a space such as this, detailing his growing adaptation to the landscape. I failed to find the punk and tramp inhabitants that Ballard's own Robinson Crusoe, James Maitland, found under the Westway, yet both could be equally sustained by this Northern equivalent.

Ballard himself discussed the ubiquity of these types of spaces in the 1994 introduction to the book:

As we drive across a motorway intersection, through the elaborately signalled landscape that seems to anticipate every possible hazard, we glimpse triangles of waste ground screened off by a steep embankment.

It begs the question as to why they rarely appear in wider British culture. Are they not worthy of creative interest?

The many pillars, which when perceived from lower levels look like forms of uncompromising menhir, are scrawled with colourful graffiti. The whole cavern feels like a theological site designed for unspeakable rites; its emptiness on the day was in juxtaposition to the feeling of its constant but unseen use above by motorists.

Debris is scattered around like the remnants of an invisible warzone. 'Below the overpass, at the eastern end of the island, a wire-mesh fence sealed off the triangle of waste ground from the area beyond, which had become

an unofficial municipal dump,' as Ballard accurately described it.

The motorway's various slip-lanes rise together until the only patch of sky available is a thin sliver, dominated by views of the paranoid signage reminding drivers of all the rules and regulations which may (or may not) prevent them from becoming pulp on the concrete below.

The space feels contradictorily grimy and antiseptic because of its cold, silvery light. The contrast finds a visual cue in the various medicinal litter germinating between the healing, greasy leaves of dock.

The walk under the M53 and its various caverns always produces a huge range of excitements and impressions, though some ineffable sadness does permeate the space; a punctured commercial zone, typical in its production of natural detritus that forces all around it to adapt or perish under its blanket of concrete. As Ballard suggests in an article for issue six of the magazine *Interzone* (1987), '*Homo sapiens* has won his intelligence from the ordeal of surviving an extremely hostile environment.' In this vein, my visit brought back one final memory which tied into a sense of survival.

On walking back with my father from the area some years ago, we came across an extremely angry-looking purple caterpillar of the puss moth. This caterpillar is a daunting and surprisingly aggressive larva, blessed with what looks like the face of a high-level bureaucrat and a whipcord double tail, spending most of its life as a shade of neon green before turning a virulent purple when ready to pupate.

We took it back home and, learning that it built its cocoon from bits of wood, it was supplied with various twigs with which it constructed a suitably Modernist housing to metamorphose within. For months afterwards, I waited to see the moth emerge, famous for its bulky size and intensely fluffy persona. Some months later, after another walk back from the M53 zone, I arrived home to find the wooden cocoon open but, in place of the glam-rock moth, sat a huge parasitic wasp.

The caterpillar had been a living incubator and food supply for the wasp's own larvae. We failed to identify it, as did the entomological department at the Museum of Liverpool, but it seemed an apt conclusion for something lifted from such a space; unforgiving, just like the road near which its mother first laid her eggs within the caterpillar's body.

I sometimes wish my earlier memories of this landscape would equally burst from my own body and simply leave. But, every time I revisit this dirty landscape, I'm glad the graffiti-covered, concrete parasites of my own unhappiness are carried inside me, even if only to ground me.

The motorway spares no illusions as to the true nature of being alive.

Published by Celluloid Wicker Man, 18/01/16

Malcolm Lowry's Peninsula

Malcolm Lowry was a wanderer. An urgent need to keep moving pervades his writing, giving rise to the feeling that he was trying to escape something, the likely culprit being alcohol. Though writing across a number of forms, in particular poetry, Lowry is still most famous for his novel *Under the Volcano*, published originally by Reynal & Hitchcock in 1947. It's a dizzying, heady piece of work, soaked in sweat and cheap spirits. But, almost three quarters of a century on, one aspect sticks out: its brief but regular glimpses into Lowry's youth on the peninsula of The Wirral, England.

As with most artists, filmmakers and writers of all sorts, Lowry's heritage for a long while was falsely attributed to Liverpool, the city overlooking the River Mersey. It has a far stronger cultural pull than the peninsula on the other side, in spite of its unique wealth of culture.

The son of a broker at the Liverpool Cotton Exchange, the desire for journey was embedded from an early age. The irony is that his wandering was deeply driven by his original locality and its role as a port. As Bryan Biggs and Helen Tookey footnote in their introduction to the volume *Malcolm Lowry: from the Mersey to the World* (2009), 'To be strictly accurate, Lowry sailed from the Birkenhead docks. It is Liverpool, however, that stands in his writing as the symbolic "point of departure" and archetypical port.'

Under the Volcano follows a Day of the Dead unfolding in the Mexican town of Cuernavaca, and consul for the government Geoffrey Firmin as he drinks and reminisces his way through it. He's an old soak drifting further and further into a stewed malaise as the hours drift by. His ex-wife Yvonne visits in the naïve hope of rekindling their love. This is, however, not the point of Lowry's work, and what unfolds over twelve chapters is a kaleidoscope of memories, places, politics, people and booze.

Reading *Under the Volcano* for the first time, and unaware of the writer's shared heritage with my own, seeing recognisable places pop up in between the descriptions of Mexican landscapes and other globe-trotting destinations was a shock to the system. I had never seen the place of my own youth put on the page, never mind in a book that was, by the lovely grey spine's admission, a Penguin Modern Classic.

The Wirral itself is not without its own potted literary history, either. Alongside Lowry, it produced the noted philosophical science-fiction writer Olaf Stapledon, one of Stephen King's favourite horror writers Ramsey Campbell, and the popular Pelican Edition historian Roger Lancelyn Green, among others. Lowry, however, dominates in that his ascendance into the canon feels undisputed, and distinctly at odds with a place that is so regularly forgotten, even when drawing maps of Britain.

In spite of his wanderlust (or perhaps that should be *fernweh*), as Biggs and Tookey suggest, Lowry carried The Wirral's geography within, even when far from its moody shores. 'Yet at the same time he retained always in his mind,' they write, 'the psychogeography of his early years by the Mersey: the topography both accurately real and thoroughly symbolic, of his Wirral "Eden" and its dark twin, Liverpool, "that terrible city whose main street is the ocean."'

Having moved from The Wirral a few years ago, I was looking for an excuse to revisit and re-explore, masking my mixed longing for it behind an excuse of work. Lowry's symbolic heritage seemed a fitting cartography to remap. And so I travelled back to the peninsula with a Polaroid camera, determined to find some of the old ghosts that haunted Lowry in his drunken nostalgia.

Lowry lived in several different locations on The Wirral. He was born on the 28th of July 1909 at 13 North Drive in New Brighton. Aside from several early biographies suggesting that Lowry was born in Liverpool, even when finally found to have been from the other side of the river, there was still uncertainty as to where it was and if the original house had survived the intervening years (due to the intensive bombing of the Second World War).

As proved by writer and photographer Colin Dilnot, the original Lowry family home did indeed withstand the Luftwaffe's attentions. Dilnot notes in his essay 'Lowry's Wirral' that 'Although considerable research has been undertaken on Lowry's early life, there still exists inaccuracies in published biographical accounts.' In other words, like many figures of note from The Wirral, they get rounded up to being from Liverpool, if not lost in the ever-shifting denominations of boundaries between the peninsula's various townships; in Lowry's case between the changing demarcation lines of Birkenhead, Wallasey and New Brighton.

Contrary to the lavish images portrayed throughout his work, the house on North Drive is a modest one, and it was only on revisiting it that it brought back memories of a messy eighteenth birthday party held at a house on the other side of the road. The strangeness of the historical and personal clashing will never cease to provoke unusual feelings on visits. Either way, I took my Polaroid photo, the house teeming with skeletal scaffolding, while haunted by images of my teenage self stumbling past Lowry's birthplace; unaware, happy and aptly intoxicated.

New Brighton feels at odds with The Wirral that Lowry portrayed. Culturally at least, its image has an unusual and varying history. It played host to a very young James Fox up to mischief on the beach in the old Ealing film *The Magnet* (1950) by Charles Frend; its handful of surviving art deco street furniture make an appearance in the beautifully shot music video for 'Wonderful Life' by Black; and most (in)famously, its decaying seaside in the 1980s was the subject of Martin Parr's celebrated photographic series *The Last Resort* (1986). The latter work is certainly closer to my own experience growing up there.

Lowry's more famous property is distinctly closer in character to his portrayed childhood in the novel. Only a few years later, his family moved to the mock-Tudor mansion Inglewood, much further into the affluent part of the peninsula in Caldy. The landscapes around the area are also more in keeping with those that arise in the consul's memory. For example, 'On the shore were the remains of an antediluvian forest with ugly black stumps showing, and further up an old sturdy deserted lighthouse... There was a feeling of space and emptiness.' This emptiness is far from the character of New Brighton, closer to the coastal erosion of Caldy Beach or nearby Thurstaston.

Inglewood today is as lavish as it always was, a large, gated property that suggests the luxury often incorrectly attributed to the whole peninsula. Speculation abounds as to this property being of influence as a model for the Taskersons' house in *Under the Volcano*. It certainly has a similar air of elegance and looks easily doused in comforting childhood nostalgia, but, like most interesting writers of place, Lowry was conducting a typically subtle sleight of hand. Not only did he suggest the house in the novel to be in the differing area of Leasowe (a far cry in every way from Caldy), but even this itself was a subterfuge.

Though marked by the heady, strychnine-soaked vistas of Mexico, combined with a general globetrotting, it's The Wirral and its landscape that stands out throughout Lowry's dense prose. It has the feel of a cut gem gleaming among masses of hot jagged rock, even if the peninsula's array of places only bob up from the depths for a brief time.

As the main character is ostensibly from the peninsula, it's unsurprising to find a certain yearning attached to his recollections, undoubtedly mined from Lowry's own experience growing up there. Early on in *Under the Volcano*, the voice drifts back to youthful adventures on the peninsula:

> It was a kind of grown-up, civilized version of Courseulles on the English northwest coast. The Taskersons lived in a comfortable house whose back garden abutted on a beautiful, undulating golf course bounded on the far side by the sea. It looked like the sea; actually it was the estuary, seven miles wide, of a river: white horses westward marked where the real sea began. The Welsh mountains, gaunt and black and cloudy, with occasionally a snow peak to remind Geoff of India, lay across the river.

Comparing The Wirral to Courseulles-sur-Mer feels a sort of tongue-in-cheek dig at the Normandy coast more than praise for Merseyside. But Lowry sketches its geography beautifully, clearly drawing on experience of the area's keynotes. The shadowy ghost of Welsh mountains haunting the horizon is embedded into many a Wirral childhood. Yet, as some scholars and writers have pointed out, not all is as it seems.

Throughout the segment, Lowry discusses the location as being a small place called Leasowe. Having grown up around there, seeing it named was like a stone dropping; conjuring images of stories of my father who regularly had to fend off fights from gangs in Leasowe Estate during his youth. It was also the last place that noted social realist director Alan Clarke lived before he, like Lowry, moved to Canada to embark on his career of decidedly tough films about violent masculinity such as *Scum* (1977), *The Firm* (1989) and *Elephant* (1989). Lowry's description is almost gentle, yet the area receded into notoriety in the post-war years, only recently coming out the other side, back into some sense of suburbia.

It's fitting, then, that scholars have actually found the real location of the novel to be further into the coast rather than Leasowe itself, near the more affluent Hoylake and deeper into the peninsula's decidedly middle-class south side. As Dilnot has pointed out, the reality is that the description from this segment of *Under the Volcano* is really referring to the Royal Liverpool golf course, which also shifts the location of the Taskersons' house (he traces the actual house that inspired the location to Meols). In other words, Lowry was cutting up the peninsula for his own purposes.

Lowry goes on to discuss the golf course in detail, with its apparent 'Hell Bunker', a place of illicit night-time liaisons:

> He had happened with his girl, who bored him, to be crossing the eighth fairway towards Leasowe Drive when both were startled by voices coming from the bunker. Then the moonlight disclosed the bizarre scene from which neither he nor the girl could turn their eyes.

While Leasowe does indeed have its own golf course and lighthouse – two landmarks Lowry namechecks – the fact he placed it much closer to the industrial aspect of the Mersey makes sense considering the variety of other descriptions in relation to its geography and industry. Hoylake is far from industrial.

Still, I decided to photograph the fairway at Leasowe rather than Hoylake in the end. Something didn't seem quite right in breaking the spell of the book by digging behind its illusions. The strange mesh fence and long, gritty dune road is just as Lowry describes, even if ironically using the frame of somewhere else for inspiration. I'll leave others to excavate the reality behind Lowry's inversions of place.

I recall parties held in the nearby Leasowe Castle, a vaguely Gothic venue that sits next to Leasowe's golf course, and how people would end up drunk on the fairway, indulging in clumsy adolescent moments of passion, just as in Lowry's novel. I remember one boy who got lost on the fairway at night after a party and, like Lowry's character, was seemingly so perturbed by what he found there that he refused to speak about it again. Perhaps he found his own Hell Bunker.

Whether the geography was a collage or not, Lowry certainly evoked an atmosphere, a spirit of the place, even, that possesses an unusual continuity today: one especially obvious if you have ever lived on the strange Viking peninsula.

For a long while, Lowry had several memorials, though surprisingly none were situated on Merseyside. His first blue plaque was adorned to the final property where he lived and died in Ripe, East Sussex. A walk dedicated to the man, along with a more detailed plaque and even a replica of his writing shack (created by Ken Lum, albeit as sculpture rather than building), is to be found in North Vancouver, where the writer found himself washed up on the shore of a beach near Maplewood.

Mark Goodall writes in his essay 'Lowrytrek: Towards a Psychogeography of Malcolm Lowry's Wirral' that The Wirral 'can be a place as weird and disturbing as any textual fantasy'. This obvious connection with his work makes the fact that his blue plaque on The Wirral came so late all the stranger, albeit welcome. It sits on the distinctive concrete sea wall of New Brighton, not far from the house where he was born; unveiled in 2019 on what would have been the writer's 110th birthday.

I took my Polaroid photo after wandering down the steep hill from North Drive. The plaque sits next to a car park and a multiplex of supermarkets and restaurants.

Biggs and Tookey conclude that Lowry 'brilliantly transmutes the geography of Liverpool/Wirral into a symbolic structure that recurs throughout his writing'. I wonder if such a symbolic structure would yield the same results had Lowry drifted through the resort today.

I stared out over the river, but no boats were passing; just flecks of invisible sand, lifted on the breeze. The plaque quotes *Under the Volcano* and its beautiful line: 'The smoke of freighters outward bound from Liverpool hung low on the horizon.' It's a fitting tribute, not only because it ties Lowry to the place that haunted him all the way to the bottom of the bottle, but also because the truly important place, the one so often forgotten, was unmistakably there, even if unnamed.

Published by Literary Hub, 06/08/22

Fields and Little People – Arthur Machen's Grave

Arthur Machen was an important writer of weird fiction. Born in Monmouthshire, he eventually travelled to London, where he failed to enter medical school before embarking on a slow career as a journalist and writer. His strange tales of the fantastical, however, are predominantly what he is remembered for today.

His groundbreaking stories possess heady atmospheres that seep into the bones like a chilly fog on autumn evenings. Reason crumbles as Machen's tales unfold, usually concluding with things beyond comprehension. Perhaps uniquely, Machen's writing straddled both urban and rural climes, finding much in both that allowed his unusual eye to seek out menace and intrigue.

As in *The Great God Pan* (1894), one of his most unnerving and adept stories, the urban and the rural are equally apt places for the macabre and the weird. His stories often explore such divides, finding as much phantasmagoria in Welsh woods as in London streets. It was a pleasing surprise, then, to find, on searching out the location of the writer's grave, that Machen was buried in an equally unusual place; one that earnestly mixes a sense of city with countryside.

Machen's grave is situated in Old Amersham, just south of Amersham itself and its station leading to London. The day of my visit was muggy, like a Robert Aickman story, overcast yet stifling. It felt odd to be wandering around somewhere still technically a part of London due to its tube stop, and yet so clearly tipping over into rural Buckinghamshire.

A minute's walk from the official designation of Zone 9 and a deep forest engulfed the sky. As quickly as the trees had stolen the light, however, a bright yellow meadow shone through an arch of branches, revealing the old town, the church spire and the surrounding hills.

Old Amersham is a typical chocolate box village, coloured by the affluence of outer London shires and clearly a place of city commuters. It's not unlike the village Machen's characters imagine in *The Secret Glory* (1900), where 'they savoured of the long, bending, broad village street, the gable ends, the grave fronts of old mellow brickwork, the thatched roofs here and there, the bulging window of the "village shop," the old church...'. Aptly, this place is a projected memory in the segment it appears in, a hopeful vision of escape from the reality of the city encountered by rural inhabitants. Fantasy often plays a role in the construction of such places.

The graveyard in question sits beside a small stream that trickled noisily past the old walls, a perfect place for faeries and the 'Little People' that so often inhabit Machen's stories.

It took a little time to find the grave, housed in the furthest part of the graveyard and looking older and more battered than most of its maintained marble counterparts. Rain arrived as I stepped over the grass to try and confirm if it was, in fact, his grave. Lichen and moss have grown aggressively over the words, resembling liver spots covering aged skin. The lettering has been smoothened and obscured by the seventy or so years of weather.

From anywhere but intensely close up, it could have passed as a blank stone, only vaguely commemorative in shape and more akin to a thin standing-stone protector of Machen's fellow dead than a gravestone. The letters, however, can be felt, his name finally made out by touch rather than sight. The typography was unusual, filled with unnecessary curves as if possessed of some hidden, geometric meaning. Running a finger along the 'H' of his surname felt unwise but pleasurable, with an unusual hoop joining the letter's two pillars.

Machen's grave stayed in my mind's eye, even after walking for miles in search of another nearby literary spot – the house of John Milton – finding myself thumbing the Polaroid photo I'd taken of the stone monument. It slowly developed in my pocket and deepened with hues of green and grey. The grave found its final darkness later on, while as a passenger on the Metropolitan Line as it trundled back into the city.

I half expected some lingering presence to be captured in its grain.

The train's view evolved into mesh and steel as the photograph locked in its colours and the unusual memories of the day. 'We have just begun to navigate a strange region;' as Machen writes poignantly in *The Terror* (1917), 'we must expect to encounter strange adventures, strange perils.'

Published by Caught by the River, 01/11/18

M.R. James's Childhood Ghosts

Some landscapes become unsettled after reading the ghost stories of M.R. James. With an eye for place and detail bringing authenticity to their recreation, James turned rural landscapes into realms where vengeful demons roamed the northern aspects of country churchyards, and cursed whistles lay waiting just under the crumbling earth of burial grounds. Though equally at home in Eton and King's College Cambridge, having been Provost of both, James's heart really lay in the East Anglian landscape; hazy, flat and with endless horizons.

Though such landscapes feature in only a handful of his noted ghost stories – as well as his book detailing his cycling ventures in search of churches there, *Suffolk and Norfolk: A Perambulation of the Two Counties with Notices of their History and their Ancient Buildings* (1933) – such is their effective rendering that it's difficult to envisage his ghosts without first seeing those evocative topographies stretching out into the distance. Horizon lines in James's work are daunting, not in their picturesque beauty or the way the sinking sun brings out the red rage of the sky, but in the constant threat that they may be broken by something. A figure, perhaps? Or something worse?

This was the landscape of James's childhood, arguably one of the key pillars of what would stabilise his ghost stories. As Mark Gatiss suggested in his 2013 documentary *M.R. James: Ghost Writer*, 'The roots of Monty's stories lay in his childhood in England where his fascination with history and the supernatural was shaped.'

Though born in Kent, James's family moved to Suffolk when he was three. James's father Herbert was offered the parish at Great Livermere, which included the grand housing of The Rectory, all from Jane Anne Broke, a relative to Herbert by marriage. James's childhood there was a happy one but also an unusual one, surrounded by extensive images of religious antiquity and isolated by the countryside.

Michael Cox, James's biographer, has suggested that his childhood there was pivotal to the ghost stories. 'The countryside immediately surrounding Livermere Rectory,' he wrote, 'made a lasting impression on Monty.' This is never more obvious in James's output than in his final published ghost story, one that was never collected in previous volumes but instead published in the *London Mercury* periodical in 1936. The story is called 'A Vignette' and is an unusually autobiographical tale, clearly lifted from James's childhood at what is now Livermere Hall.

'You are asked to think of the spacious garden of a country rectory,' he begins:

> adjacent to a park of many acres, and separated there from by a belt of trees of some age which we knew as the Plantation. It is but about thirty or forty yards broad. A closed gate of split oak leads to it from the path encircling the garden, and when you enter it from the side you put your

hand through a square hole cut in it and lift the
hook to pass along to the iron gate which admits
to the park from the plantation...

This is precisely the geography of the rectory.

The tale is poignant as, like in other aspects of James's
work, there's a sense of reality behind it. However, the
difference here is that James's mode feels eerily confessional
rather than simply sticking to the imagery he knew, genuinely
detailing a childhood encounter with the supernatural.

The ghost manifests in one of James's most unusual
depictions, seeming to appear on the other side of the gate;
its description bizarrely sexual in tone, the ghost 'hot' and
'pink'. But the geography of the story is key, the essence of a
child's perception aided by unusual details clearly taken
from memory:

I must not by the way give the impression that the
whole of the Plantation was haunted ground.
There were trees there most admirably devised
for climbing and reading in; there was a wall,
along the top of which you could walk for many
hundred yards and reach a frequented road,
passing farmyard and familiar houses; and once
in the park, which had its own delights of wood
and water, you were well out of range of anything
suspicious – or, if that is too much to say, of
anything that suggested the Plantation gate.

After visiting so many James-related sites over the years
– from his grave in Eton to the Aldeburgh locations that

inspired his story 'A Warning to the Curious' – it felt right to finally visit this haunted childhood home.

Even on a trip venturing around different parts of Suffolk, Great Livermere was out of the way from other destinations, perhaps all destinations, even. Like many East Anglian locations, it's somewhere to go to rather than pass through. With dusk threatening, I wanted to find some of the details that James discussed in his story, the woodlands and the gate in particular, before darkness fell.

The small village was empty of people, the only mark of the locals' presence being a travelling insect circus whose cart sat in a driveway. The light was fading quickly and so I wandered around the moss-covered stone wall of the house and up the drive. The house is now a private mansion, littered with expensive cars, yet still retains an indescribable *something* that makes it more than simply a large and expensive property. The wall was shadowed by trees which extended all the way around the property like a barrier. There was a rusted gate, more organic than metal, though it was not far enough to be the gate of the story.

I remembered that in another documentary on James, Clive Dunn's *A Pleasant Terror* (1995), the spot in question is visited after being photographed by Michael Cox. Behind the house lies the land in question, stretching as far as the eye can see towards the woods and beyond. East Anglian skies forever threaten to drown the land, their constant expanse like an upended sea.

Unlike in the documentary, in which a local points out where the gate was, the land today has been left to grow wild; the wall now protected by a healthy current of nettles and entanglements of bramble and ivy.

I wandered closer but could barely make out the wall, never mind its haunted gap. My eye instead turned to the land as it retreated behind, the sunset fragmenting the sky into a rich array of reds and purples. I crouched down in the squeaky, damp long grass, wondering what I would capture with my Polaroid. The nearby rusted gate, on the other hand, resisted three separate Polaroid photos; some things simply do not want to be photographed.

James's final story feels like an explanation of sorts, a portrait of an event which haunted him for the rest of his life, sparking an interest in the supernatural which, in the dry academic rigour of his later life, required some form of release. If the story is truly autobiographical, then Great

Livermere is arguably the root of his work: a location in which the trees watch on, shrouds hover behind creaking oak gates, and the solitude of the Brecklands is constantly threatened by things unseen.

I walked quickly along the gravel path back to the car as the sun dived low and darkness swept across the fields with unusual agency. I shuffled my feet in the gravel deliberately with each step, in order to hide the sound of any potential crunches of a pair following my own.

Such things have, after all, been known.

Published by Caught by the River, 29/10/19

M.R. James's Final Haunt

M.R. James, the noted antiquarian and celebrated writer of ghost stories, rests quietly today in a graveyard. It's not an oft-visited place, being a little out of the way and adjacent to the crumbling, residential walls of Eton College in Windsor; situated at the point where the town begins to fade into the surrounding meadows along the Thames.

Graveyards featured variously in James's macabre stories, an obvious regular for tales of the supernatural, but if such a place could be said to summarise the writer's eerie atmospheres, it wouldn't be a fictional one of his own creation but the real one he has occupied since his death in 1936 at the age of seventy-three.

James's life was largely without misstep and littered with academic achievement. Born in Goodnestone, Kent, in 1862, the writer grew up in Suffolk under the intellectual influence of his clergyman father. He studied at Temple Grove preparatory school before successfully traversing the well-worn route from Eton to King's College, Cambridge. An unparalleled academic career saw him take the reins as provost of the college in 1905, steering it through some of its most difficult years, before returning to Eton as provost in 1918 until his death.

In spite of his myriad successes, it is James's ghost stories that have guaranteed him posterity, exerting a growing influence on writers, filmmakers and artists of all sorts. Told initially as a diversion for the Chit-Chat Society at King's College, the notoriously effective horrors soon found James published in a much wider realm beyond the dusty manuscripts that occupied much of his time. His first collection, *Ghost Stories of an Antiquary*, was afforded great acclaim, published by Edward Arnold in 1904, followed by several equally celebrated volumes establishing him as the foremost writer of the genre, still arguably unsurpassed.

Fictional dread can be a powerful combatant against the real thing, something I think James understood. His stories read equally as an unconscious release from his own stubbornly repressed feelings and fears.

Autumn's arrival was one that used to fill me with a very particular but powerful horror, one alien to that found in his stories. Initially signalling a return to a school life on Merseyside that I found miserable and hellish, it was James's work many years later that rehabilitated my love for the colder seasons, replacing memories of black mornings and banal schoolboy tyranny with his self-proclaimed 'pleasing terrors'.

As Susan Hill has suggested, writing these stories was cathartic, they were 'his relief from a secret madness in his inner soul'. My own irksome memories were gradually replaced with his tales of malevolent ghosts. If he found solace in writing them, many have certainly shared in it through reading them, even if strange considering their terrifying nature.

James's stories of antiquarians unearthing forgotten horrors are enhanced by the cold's arrival, constructed on some level in collaboration with the darker seasons. His is a catalogue overtly designed to be enjoyed in cosy surroundings, his words leaking in the chilly unknown like a draught through a sash window.

A Jamesian world is one of cursed artefacts, endlessly subsuming landscapes, forgotten manuscripts and tactile beings that punish the curious and intellectually arrogant. In spite of being fantastical curios, his stories are not simply diversions. His strongest moments of horror – a fully formed mouth felt by an unsuspecting hand under a pillow, a Saxon crown's guardian spirit smashing a man's jaw to pieces on a desolate East Anglian beach, an empty bed suddenly revealing a form sitting up and aware – never leave those who experience them, such is their authenticity of recollection. As Ronald Blythe has pointed out, 'none of his ghosts are benign; they are horrible and extremely shocking'.

Since living in London, I've visited James's grave each year at the first instance of rusting leaves and darkening evenings. The journey is undertaken partly in respectful gratitude for rekindling the joy to be found in autumnal pleasures. Yet, the grave's placement is far from the wide-skied, yellow-hued East Anglia that so much of his work evokes; the landscape that, as Professor Darryl Jones has suggested, 'was to inform his stories in a profound way'.

Eton is at least nearer than Suffolk, and his lasting presence there suggests that his adoration for the academic institutions where he embedded himself took precedence over his favourite landscapes. In spite of my small, yearly pilgrimage being one of knowing ritual, however, my visits have never yet failed to unnerve me, albeit in ways that leave me giddy. Fact and fiction excitingly share the world for a time in that graveyard in Eton.

Many of James's ghost stories are natural maps and can be walked. Even the act of reading them simulates a traversing of sorts, such is their detail. They easily inspire journeys for the reader. James was a landscape artist who, more often than not, subverted such journeys into the pastoral. As Robert Macfarlane argues, his vision of landscape 'is never a smooth surface or simple stage-set, there to offer picturesque consolations'.

His very first story, 'Canon Alberic's Scrap-Book', acts almost as an antiquarian tourist itinerary for the small French town of Saint-Bertrand-de-Comminges in the Pyrenees, while his last, posthumously published story, 'A Vignette', recalls the landscapes around his childhood home in Great Livermere. Authenticity is a strange ally to terror in James's fiction, and it comes most of all from the reliance on his personal experiences of place.

His landscapes are lonely, as in 'A Warning to the Curious' where 'there is nothing but the shingle for a long way – not a house, not a human creature, just a spit of land'. It must be said that this isolation is not one that remains undisturbed for long.

Such inconsequential journeys in curious pursuit of antiquities are the writer's quintessential story arc, not least because he was, to paraphrase one of his more unnerving descriptions from 'Canon Alberic's Scrap-Book', writing from the life. He wrote books about venturing in search of such rural antiquity, in particular his notices to East Anglian churches in *Suffolk and Norfolk*, published with the catchy subtitle *A Perambulation of the Two Counties with Notices of their History and their Ancient Buildings*. He was the chief inhabitant of his fictional worlds, as suggested by one of James's great admirers, Ruth Rendell. As she says about his characters, surely 'they are all M.R. James himself, and none the worse for that'.

Searching for his grave becomes a metaphysical irony, being one of the most deeply Jamesian things to do. Either way, James and journeys go hand in hand.

The day I made my pilgrimage this year was an overcast one, heavy with rainy potential. I made my way from Paddington, stopping briefly in Slough, where the passing trains threaten to sweep you away with their great speed. The train from there to Windsor is more like a model novelty of the type found in British seaside resorts that scoot happy children over short but exciting distances.

Windsor itself was typically subdued, like most towns post-COVID, an archaic place full of contradictions and the friction between old and new. Over the Thames and away from Windsor's intimidating castle, the shrinking buildings leading to the college unfurl with ease. A few winding roads later, however, and the town seems imagined, virtually non-existent.

The small church at the heart of the graveyard is today seemingly abandoned, but actually owned by the college. They have yet to do anything with it, though it looks to be used as little more than a Gothic broom-cupboard. Thankfully, this same benign neglect has been applied to the graveyard and its flora. It's a pleasantly untidy place, where the paths struggle against the confidence of plants.

Only if James himself had designed the plot could it have been more in keeping with the sensibilities of his fiction. The gravel crunches loudly underfoot in the surprising quietude, threatening to suggest steps of another in between each silence. Ivy grows over many fallen graves. Moss huddles close to the stones like a green shadow, and the northernmost part is darkened to a shadowy emerald by a small patch of woodland.

On my first visit, I had initially worried that James's grave would be pristine, having read of its restoration some years closer to the millennium. It was to prove a needless concern, for the site is overgrown to the point where actually finding the grave was a challenge, so determined was the briar to swallow it whole. The earth seems particularly hungry around his memorial.

Even today, James's grave resembles vegetation more than stone. I imagine if he does still walk, his image is more akin to a mossy dryad, a figure of intertwined bark in a long, black Etonian gown, than a more typically spectral image. It was this image that troubled me most as I wandered and stumbled alone between the stones and the woods, swearing again and again to register glimpses of movement at the edge of my vision.

Even knowing the location of James's grave failed to help find it this time round. I swear that it moves a few plots between my yearly visits. It appears to shift further and further into the foliage, increasingly protected by a natural barbed wire of bramble. James understood the subtle, unnerving qualities writhing beneath the pastoral, so it's fitting that the small landscape he now inhabits refuses to conform to a polite, picturesque stasis.

Housing malevolent spirits renders his landscapes all-seeing, shifting with violence and menace in response to the writer's variety of fusty, academic interlopers. His current resting place is no different.

It was peaceful sitting among the dead for a time, and I relaxed on a bench there, eating and smoking alone, disturbed only by an occasional plane from Heathrow and the rustling of a blackbird. On a previous visit, a fallen urn next to a more dilapidated bench had revealed a variety of scurrying life and some white eggs, possibly reptilian. Graveyards are always livelier than their morose reputation.

Taking my Polaroid camera along for the journey, I aimed to snap a few photographs of the grave and its watchful surroundings. The dampness of the stones was in retreat from the sun and its slight appearance through the clouds, so I thought it best to take the photographs quickly. The grave actively resisted my first two Polaroid photos, reflecting the light and causing the colours to fade as if taken in harsh sunlight rather than Eton mugginess.

I waited for a time, taking one of James's view over the plot and the determined, spindly fingers of ivy climbing the church wall, before aiming for two more of the grave. I waited patiently for the images to develop, watching a shape form above the grave like a wisp.

Just as in James's 'The Mezzotint', the image seemed to contain something on the approach, summoning presences out of the earth. It was time to leave, pleasantly unnerved once again by this contradictorily quiet and busy place. I couldn't help but glance back as I made my departure, ignoring the undeniable increase in speed of my footfall as something fleeting dared my eyes to look back in nervous curiosity once again. I left the empty graveyard, content for another year, aware that my departure was conducted under an observant gaze.

Published by Literary Hub, 16/12/20

Angela Carter's Vanished Clapham

'The notion that one day the red dawn will indeed break over Clapham,' wrote Angela Carter in a letter to Lorna Sage, 'is the one thing that keeps me going.' From having read several of Carter's works over the years, all of which have had a variety of profound effects upon my own writing, her relationship to London has long intrigued me.

When first on the train down to view flats in London before moving there, *The Passion of New Eve* earned the caveat of being the only book ever to make me faint, my body slumping briefly and embarrassingly against the window of my Virgin train while the main character graphically underwent enforced gender reassignment surgery. I left the book like an unsuspecting IED in a Stockwell book-box several days after finishing it.

South London, in hindsight, is very much Carter's territory, in spite of being born in Eastbourne and travelling widely. She went to Streatham and Clapham High School, enrolling as a journalist at the *Croydon Advertiser* after graduating, before exploring the world. Yet Clapham is where she eventually returned, where she penned her delirious fantasies and where she eventually succumbed to cancer.

I wanted to find the house where this alchemy had taken place, and so a wander up the South Circular was planned. Carter's desired, if naïve, 'red dawn' was not what I was to find at the end of the road.

I struggled initially to find out the full details of Carter's house. Several posts online had mentioned it, but the only clue I really had was the excellent chapter in Iain Sinclair's *London Overground* in which he detailed his visits to her over the years. A few emails later and Iain had confirmed the exact house, so I started my four-or-so-mile meander from Dulwich.

I had a new 35mm camera to try out, so began to snap away almost instantly at autumn's first hints of decay. Unfortunately, having planned my route via roads, the South Circular is, by its own design, specific in its avoidance of anything interesting. It's an artery to the major organs of Streatham, Tooting Bec and Clapham Common, but manages to basically avoid all of these places unless desired. Endless blocks of flats sprouted as the sky did its best to rain before the road thankfully snaked around to reveal the greenery of Clapham Common.

After being distracted by the common's Victorian bandstand and several blue plaques – Edvard Grieg and Graham Greene being the most interesting – I found The Chase. This is Carter's road: a long display of huge Georgian properties eventually leading to Wandsworth Road. Yet something did not seem quite right. The road proudly displays several plaques of its own, specifically three to

celebrate a number of royal-themed street parties that have been held there in recent years. It's arguably now the antithesis of Carter's vision with its twee celebration of monarchy.

Wandering past Natsume Sōseski's and Dorothy Dene's blue plaques mere houses away (the latter reminding me of Carter's *Wise Children*), I found the house. Number 107 stood before me, looking clean, tidy and unoccupied. A quick google revealed that the house was last on the market for £1.5 million and, by all the evidence of the pictures online, was probably bought as an investment.

I thought back to my favourite picture of Carter, one of her sitting in her study with the view out of the windows revealing a pair of tower blocks, Amnesbury and Durrington on the Westbury Estate. The room in the picture is multicoloured, full of bric-a-brac, books, records; it's Carter's mind sprawling out from her skull.

The estate agent's pictures showed the room spotless, minimalist and empty. Show-home fodder. It was with a heavy heart that I accepted that a particular London, one whose culture arguably brought me down from the North, had long been priced out of existence. It's the story of London over the last thirty years told in a single room.

I wandered to the end of the road and looked at the tower blocks before finding a coffee and trying to read amongst the endless chatter of market concerns and 'new financial territories'. Clapham, with its rooks and Georgian decadence, had disappeared beyond Carter's world of myth, legend and indecency. There's a reason why, along with neighbouring Wandsworth, it's now nicknamed Nappy Valley.

I thought back to my favourite passage from the magnificent volume of short stories, *The Bloody Chamber*. 'She herself is a haunted house,' wrote Carter. 'She does not possess herself; her ancestors sometimes come and peer out of the windows of her eyes and that is very frightening.'

The ghosts in The Chase were, by contrast, sadly exorcised some time ago.

Published by Celluloid Wicker Man, 06/11/17

The Clapham Garages

It was during a walk last autumn in search of Angela Carter's old house when I first came across the garages. The walk had been a depressing task; a long, dull meander along the South Circular to Clapham.

After several miles of winding road, I found the area at the end unrecognisably affluent and cleaned up. I had naively expected it to reflect photos I had seen of Carter in the late 1980s, battered but lived in and filled with eccentric bric-a-brac. The Chase where Carter lived is now, by contrast, a prime property hotspot. The Clapham I'd come to find had long since passed, or so I thought. It was then that I walked down an alleyway that led to a set of garages behind Carter's road, and I was whisked sharply away to another realm.

Around halfway along The Chase there sits a wide entrance, designed for cars, which leads to the land behind. The concrete square is filled with old garages adorned with green and white rusted doors.

The walls all around are cracked and covered with dead leaves. Trees hang over the brickwork and sometimes intermingle with the streetlights. Walking through it quite by chance was like travelling back in time at least thirty years, similar in tone to the images I'd surrounded myself with before moving down to London a couple of years back.

The strange realms of *Callan*, *The Sweeney*, *Minder* and all those other London programmes had seemed to be filmed in an alien world full of open spaces, land left to its own devices and a surreal affordability. That London is as fantastical as *Forbidden Planet* in comparison to the city today. But these garages were absolutely part of that same world – somewhere the developers have forgotten – and, as I strolled around this mostly derelict space, I felt more than anything to finally be somewhere familiar.

I began to snap away with my camera, noticing all the unusual things left there. There were signs saying 'No ball games' but made of metal and with each letter three-dimensionally rendered rather than cheaply flat. There was explicit graffiti on almost every other door, though scratched in rather than spray-painted on as is the modern, Americanised way, and even the doors themselves seemed odd in their design, as if from a time now unusually passed.

The alleyway felt incredibly picturesque as the breeze rustled the leaves and rubbish on the ground. It felt not unlike some of the more emptied scenes from Michelangelo Antonioni's *Blowup* (1966), not least because, just over the way, hundreds of people were enjoying their Saturday with a variety of sports on the common, while others fought for highly sought after seats in expensive bistros and coffee shops. Clapham had been a noisy place to walk through but there was only the breeze in the garage square; the trees swaying, their leaves quietly hissing, and not a soul in sight.

I thought also of a number of paintings by George Shaw, and noticed later how my 35mm camera had produced images that had that same soft quality as Shaw's realistic work. In his painting *The Fall* (1999), a number of similar garages are captured with an eye that sees the same beauty in the decay, albeit Shaw's are a lot more dilapidated.

Another of his paintings, *The National Game* (2017), comes even closer to Clapham's garage realm, the way the concrete dips and creates little lagoons that reflect the trees back towards the sky. The painting also has that same mixture of doors and boards, hiding who knows what behind their secretive barriers; rusted Ford Cortinas used in dodgy deals, mouldy boxes of LPs, old DIY tools, children's clothes, a peach wedding dress from a happy day in a 1980s summer, dead rats and memories.

I can't be *too* romantic about this place, however. The houses in the road opposite cost well over £1 million, even though the area still has some of the direst of poverty further north towards the Thames. Carter's house was last on the market for a cool million and a half, and seems empty today. I've even found garages in other parts of the city whose rent costs more than my last flat in Liverpool did. Perhaps these little rusted boxes would be similarly expensive.

In other words, no land is safe, all space is profit, and all will be cleaned up and sanitised eventually, at least superficially. It's the same story for most of the city, especially in Zones 1 and 2. But this is the point. Such places, that have managed to survive the scrubbing, tell of a time when space was not a defined commodity; when there was still some sense of affordability and even an unfathomable beauty in the ordinary and forgotten brownfields of the capital. There's no slogan, no catchy marketing brand or price tag attached to this place. It just is.

In the London of today, it is an incredibly rare and lovely thing to find.

Published by Caught by the River, 30/05/18

Anita Brookner's Suburban Poise

We're all guilty of sometimes ignoring what is directly in front of us, especially in regard to where we live. Travelling sporadically (and with an admitted chaotic idiosyncrasy) around places in search of vague connections to culture means I'm probably worse than most for ignoring what is on my doorstep. The interesting things are always over *there* rather than *here*.

A quick hour's research and a wander outside my front door – leading to Herne Hill in south-east London, as it happens – revealed a wealth of interesting connections ignored for years. Since having moved further south in the city, I realise in hindsight how lucky I was to live there.

A few houses down from my old flat sits John Ruskin's grand mansion, which probably would have once looked out over greenery rather than estates. Down at the bottom of the hill sits the refurbished Half Moon pub, a place which attempted to gain a blue plaque a few years ago due to its connection with Dylan Thomas's drinking habits; the road opposite suspiciously called Milkwood Road. And further towards Dulwich Village sits Ardbeg Road, the surprisingly suburban beginnings of Ida Lupino, one of golden Hollywood's great leading stars and early female directors.

Of all the connections that came up, the one that resonated with me the most was the realisation of having, on an almost daily basis, walked past the house where Booker Prize-winning novelist Anita Brookner was born.

Dr Brookner was a precise and melancholy writer. Her literary success was as smooth and adept as her meticulous prose. From an early academic career, she became the first woman to hold the Slade Professorship of Fine Art at Cambridge University in 1967, after lecturing at Reading and the Courtauld Institute.

It was later that her fiction writing came to prominence, her first novel, *A Start in Life* (1981), aptly named to herald a new and pivotal shift in career. It was only a couple of years later that Brookner won the Booker Prize in 1984 for *Hotel Du Lac*, fending off stiff competition from J.G. Ballard's *Empire of the Sun* in particular. She went on to write over two dozen successful novels and received a CBE in 1990. She passed away relatively recently at eighty-seven, in 2016.

Brookner was born in Herne Hill, living in a family home at 55 Half Moon Lane. Her parents, Polish Jewish migrants, changed their name from Bruckner, and her father is suggested to have been a tobacconist. The uprooted family were not affluent and later moved to the smaller property at 25 Half Moon Lane, though Brookner would return to one of the bigger houses later in life.

Herne Hill typifies Brookner for a number of reasons. Her work is neat, suburban and yet also contains a calculated sense of social status and style; very much typical of the area. Often, Brookner is likened to the protagonists of her novels: equally calculated, prim and lonely. Yet most consider this image to be in part a concoction, a veil through which to dodge the increasing barbs that a phenomenal success such as hers brings. As Hilary Mantel suggested,

'Anita Brookner's critical fortunes show that it is possible to win a major prize, be widely read and still be undervalued.' Some things never change.

Visiting the house – though visit is hardly the word, with it being so close by – it felt a pitch-perfect expression of Brookner's creative world. The sun was ablaze on the day and the brief wander to the door that had meant so little on previous days was over in minutes.

The plants of the garden are kept appropriately neat, beaming in bright colours: the house is the absolute image of London suburbia. As the narrator of *Hotel Du Lac* tellingly suggests, 'My idea of absolute happiness is to sit in a hot garden all day, reading, or writing, utterly safe in the knowledge that the person I love will come home to me in the evening. Every evening.' It's incredibly easy to imagine the protagonist at home there.

I took my Polaroid photo, much to the bemusement of a gaggle of pensioners who loudly started talking among themselves about their own memories of Polaroid cameras while standing at the adjacent bus stop. The camera often elicits such responses: it's a nostalgia machine.

The house is certainly far more cheery than Brookner's general reputation, but this is in part the point. The reality of Brookner is generally as meticulously kept as the house's ornate garden. Of course, it's undeniable that some of that loneliness, channelled so effortlessly in her novels, does ring with a sense of truth outside of literary skill, instead born of experience. But it's not the full story.

Especially in childhood, this loneliness is insipid, dodged by later successes academically and creatively. I imagine a young Brookner, single-child lonely, in the house or the flat;

the dreary yet pleasant nature of suburbia confusingly seeping in. But then, walking back past 25 Half Moon Lane in particular, I realised that Brookner's old flat is now a popular and busy children's bookshop. What better monument to a figure so associated, rightly or wrongly, with isolation than a shop selling the best of antidotes to new, young readers, perhaps equally in need of worlds outside of the surrounding lonely, tree-lined streets?

Published by Caught by the River, 13/06/19

Muriel Spark's Peckham Collage

To ingratiate myself with London, I was keen to find some boundary markers in my local area south of the river to walk and explore. I'd only been to Peckham once before; to take pictures for an article about the locations of Michelangelo Antonioni's *Blowup* (1966) and to (fail to) view a flat on Spare Room, advertised by a performance arts specialist from Goldsmiths whose videos consisted of tearing her clothes off in lecture halls.

In spite of this, I was keen to explore the area again, though my location in West Dulwich made for a surprisingly long walk. I sought, therefore, to find some marker to define a map of the area in the hope of finding some happy accidents.

I noticed Muriel Spark's 1960 novel *The Ballad of Peckham Rye* while in a gallery shop on the Southbank, and was instantly taken by the overt sixties aura given off by its cover. Upon reading it, such an aura became more powerful, heightened by its array of literary imagery: secretaries, models of industrial business adapting to the new boom of American imported advertising techniques, and endless participation in a thriving and unpretentious pub culture.

It was all there alongside a heavily detailed mapping of the area. Or so I thought.

With research, it turned out that, like the London of *Blowup* which had last drawn me to the area, Spark had been working at her own London collage when portraying Peckham, mixing a huge array of local inspirations and amalgamating several places from nearby Camberwell Green. The real became mixed with the fictional.

However, there were still plenty of places to visit and they handily marked a relatively linear route through Peckham's more typical market roads right through to the Rye and eventually Honour Oak Park.

I started by Peckham Rye Overground and walked along the pavement, taking in the barrage of sensory experiences that the road provided. Every type of food seemed to be for sale, accompanied by a range of multicoloured designs, meat laid out like crazy paving and speakers blaring out so many different types of music as to almost feel like madness.

I'd started there because this was the quickest way down to the first set of Spark stops on the walk: a collection of increasingly repressive pubs and saloon bars.

Before hitting there, I walked past the road that led to the *Blowup* location, which gave a faint hint of nostalgia for the high summer meandering when I last saw it. The first scenes with David Hemmings's character, showing him leaving the workhouse where he took covert photos of the homeless, were filmed just round the corner, though the workhouse has long since gone and, if my geography is right, has been replaced by a rather nice digital workspace with a communal yard hidden behind (and, appropriately, a cinema on top).

I was there for Spark's locations, not Antonioni's, so I pushed on past the shops until the first pub appeared on my list. This was the Nag's Head and, though not in the novel under this name, it's almost definitely the pub that Spark refers to throughout out as the Morning Star.

However, it's not the same (and perhaps more famous) Nag's Head, known in Peckham as the drinking place of Del Boy and Rodney in *Only Fools and Horses* (that's actually in Greenwich and now known as the Pelton Arms).

On the opening page of the book, Spark lists a number of pubs as she recounts the initial mystery of the narrative: a young man, Humphrey Place, strangely spurning a girl on her wedding day due to the influence of a Scottish interloper, Dougal Douglas. She writes:

> He walked across to the White Horse and drank one bitter. Next he visited the Morning Star and the Heaton Arms. He finished up at the Harbinger.

The Heaton Arms was demolished and the Harbinger appears to be fictional, perhaps derived from a pub further north in Camberwell Green. Yet the White Horse mentioned is still there, and escaping the bustle of the high street on the right brings you directly to this incredibly English-looking pub. Seemingly picked up from a small country village and put down in the centre of Peckham, it stands out surreally, perhaps because it's directly opposite an impressively ambitious graffiti mural on a corner-shop wall.

Walking to the White Horse, an old artisan rug shop caught my attention. I realised that I was effectively walking the route that Spark's opening passages describe, heading down from these pubs at a natural pace, albeit without a drink and a spurned lover at the altar, towards the Rye. Spark gives further detail on the opening page:

> All the same, he appeared to consider the encounter so far satisfactory. He got back into the little Fiat and drove away along the Grove and up to the Common where he parked outside the Rye Hotel. Here, he lit a cigarette, got out, and entered the saloon bar.

The Rye Hotel, mentioned in the novel a few times, is still around and seemed a popular spot for the local ring-necked parakeets, as they squawked their way from the rooftops to the beautiful willow tree on the opposite side of the road. I didn't venture inside to see if the bar still retained its saloon, but this was the most obvious of Spark's locations based on the real Peckham.

In the spirit of the book, I walked on and stood in awe of the Rye itself: a huge and open green space taking up almost the whole view, sitting in stark contrast to the gritty urban character of the road a mere minute away. The characters in Spark's novel seem drawn there, almost always either passing through it or heading towards it, sometimes to settle fights but more often for unexplained reasons, as if it possesses some supernatural allure.

The day itself had a strange feel, initially overcast but with that type of whiteness in the clouds that hurts the eyes. The characters of *Ballad* had better weather for their meanders onto the common. 'They were moving up the Rye where the buses blazed in the sun,' wrote Spark. 'Their walk was nearly over.'

My walk was far from over and was only getting more surreal.

On the common, where supposedly 'the groom shot himself on the Rye', I was jumped upon by no less than three dogs, all salivating with a typical dumb friendliness. I thought that the strong smell of meat emanating from Rye Lane may have been potent enough to linger on my clothes, but then assured myself it was simply down to their inconsiderate owners.

The common was swamped by a circus currently in town, which seemed rather apt for Spark's novel; circuses seeming to recall post-war Britain in my mind's eye due to various films and television shows. Spark brings the circus of her novel further up the road, into the heartland of the terraces, the sawdust and hoops entertaining a false suburbia.

I was far from that part of Peckham, and soon right in the middle of the park, looking for Sexby Gardens, famed for its rose pergolas. This is where Dougal takes one of the factory girls for a walk. 'Let's go into the Old English Garden,' he suggests ominously.

I wanted to get a photo of the main archway through the garden, built into the park at some point between 1906 and 1915. However, a large pram sat in the way, so I made do with a few of the garden's many side-paths and arches leading to various ornamental objects.

Dougal's reasons for bringing the girl here are rather vague, as is the overall reasoning behind his manipulations of the characters of Peckham. He ironically extols that 'Peckham must have a moral character of its own.'

Apart from seeming an empty gesture, his walks add further ambiguity to his motivations. This was something that became clear when walking the mapped-out route of the book; that not only is *Ballad* a fiction set in Peckham, but it's a novel arguably set in a very fictional Peckham.

This discord between Spark's Peckham and the real one became most apparent at the end of this walk, where

I endeavoured to trudge up One Tree Hill, over the Peckham border into Honour Oak Park. According to Dougal, this place 'leads to One Tree Hill and two cemeteries, the Old and the New'. He then, with the polite consideration of a serial killer, asks his companion, 'Which would you prefer?' It's undoubtedly the most interesting spot on the walk.

Before ascending the hill, I walked up another road and found a beautiful contrast between a clearly ancient cottage and a brutalist block of flats; such is the character of the place. In fact, when later reading M. John Harrison's strange and disturbing novel *The Course of the Heart* (1992), it was this location that came to mind as the setting for the book's horrifying attempted ritual. I walked up the leafy hill path, finally to see the view out from One Tree Hill over the entire city.

The Honour Oak stood tall, replanted to commemorate Elizabeth I spending May Day there in 1602 with Sir Richard Bulkeley. The history of the area seeped through like the increasing rays of sunlight through the clouds and branches. You could almost hear John Dee rustling away in jealousy as he tried in vain to impress with alchemical conjuring tricks.

I stood on a Napoleonic beacon and looked out onto the view, reminded oddly of the opening of the short-lived music show *Naked City* which featured it in its ever-so-hip opening before treating viewers weekly to the excitable tones of Johnny Vaughan and Caitlin Moran.

Spark's fictional Peckham had been a haphazard, eccentric introduction to the place, highlighting a genuine otherworldliness to what is often portrayed as the simple embodiment of working-class London.

As Spark writes when finishing the odd story of Dougal Douglas and his manipulations of the area:

> The Rye for an instant looking like a cloud of green and gold, the people seeming to ride upon it, as if you might say there was another world than this.

Published by Celluloid Wicker Man, 19/09/16

Harold Pinter's *A Walk by Waiting*

'Dear Joe, I'd like to walk with you
From Clapton Pond to Stamford Hill
And on'
—Harold Pinter

Harold Pinter liked walking around London. It's often forgotten how vital traipsing the capital's streets was for him when considering how claustrophobic much of his theatre work is. Yet there is still a sense of place in his work, often highlighting many of his characters' obsessive qualities. They seem to never shut up about London.

It wasn't until learning about his friendship with his English tutor Joseph Brearley, and in particular reading the poem he wrote about this favourite teacher, that London's importance became more abundantly clear.

One of my own personal delights found in Pinter's work (for theatre and film) is just how London-centric it really is once picked up on. Whether it's Mick taunting Davies about the detailed routes he advises him on in Clive Donner's version of *The Caretaker* (1963), the grounded, isolating presence of the Hackney house in *The Homecoming* (1965), the upper-class enclave of his script adaptation for Joseph Losey's *The Servant* (1963), or the various London spaces that have popped up in television work such as *A Night Out* for *Armchair Theatre* (1960) and *The Collection* (1976) for Granada, London has always figured in his writing. Even that most oblique of his plays, *No Man's Land* (1975), has a kind of hidden London code spoken within it; various locales used as a double entendre.

After months of immersion in Pinter's work, and with a trip to London already planned, a Pinter-themed walk was inevitable. This wasn't, however, to be a simple meander regarding the odd theatre and film location.

The detail that Pinter put into his 1977 poem '*Joseph Brearley (1909–1977)*' – a poem dedicated to the inspirational English teacher who he went on countless walks with when at Hackney Downs Grammar School – meant a potential was there to walk its impressionistic routes, 'on, and on' as Pinter wrote.

Pinter mentioned the importance of these walks with both Brearley and his friends several times. In his talk at the David Cohen British Literature Prize in 1995, he discussed the importance of Brearley, who introduced him to writing by the likes of Shakespeare and John Webster:

> Joe Brearley and I became close friends. We embarked on a series of long walks, which continued for years, starting from Hackney Downs, up to Springfield Park, along the River Lea, back up Lea Bridge Road, past Clapton Pond, through Mare Street to Bethnal Green.

Pinter's description of the walk in his speech is far more detailed than its subsequent recreation in the poem. This is undoubtedly because its aim is to capture the fragmented nostalgia of the place, the feeling of discovery and perhaps a subtle release of melancholy at the man's death (the event that spurred him to write the poem). It was, therefore, a far more spontaneous form of map for a potential walk through Pinter's East London.

The walk began on a sunny February weekday, first getting the tube to Manor House station. The walk was not to begin specifically in the order of Pinter's poem or to be realised fully from walking the length between Finsbury Park and Hackney Downs; the two furthest points mentioned in regard to his walks with Brearley. This was purely due to time. Instead, Manor House was the beginning of the walk in order to explore the following lines:

Through Manor House to Finsbury Park,
And back...

Coming out of Manor House tube station, I walked down the beautiful pathway to the entrance of Finsbury Park. The park's design is one that feels similar to several Pinter settings, possessing a faded, genteel elegance of long pathways with arches of trees.

There was a community service group picking up litter, groups of lads dossing around enjoying the sun, and the jaunt felt instantly leisurely and relaxed. It soon became apparent that walking such areas did indeed sprout up almost constant conversation; there was a consistent conversational spark in and around the park that eventually led off into creative conversations about writing and other things with my walking partner, Harriet. Pinter and Brearley tapped into something important here: the raw material of flowing ideas through interaction with public spaces.

The poem refers to a reversal – 'and back' – so that was precisely what we did, heading back to the station to catch several tubes and an Overground train to Hackney Central. On the way back, I thought of Mick's elongated speech in *The Caretaker*, spinning Davies the tramp in a web of place names to taunt him and his inability to get down to Sidcup, where his important papers supposedly reside:

> You know, believe it or not, you've got a funny kind of resemblance to a bloke I once knew in Shoreditch. Actually he lived in Aldgate. I was staying with a cousin in Camden Town. This chap, he used to have a pitch in Finsbury Park, just by the bus depot. When I got to know him I found out he was brought up in Putney. That didn't make any difference to me.

The atmosphere changed when arriving into the bustle of central Hackney. Pinter's relationship with Hackney was complex. In an interview he gave for the ABC series *Tempo*, he was both critical and interested in the place and its influence on his work. When asked whether he liked growing up around there, he suggested that his experience was overall negative, further elaborating:

> No we didn't like it very much, we hated it. But I think we hated it in the sense that any young man growing up in any particular district hates it. And in this particular respect, Hackney was a kind of prison. Although we could get a bus and go out to Piccadilly in half an hour or so, we didn't have enough money to do it because the bus cost 10p or so in those days, and we were kind of cooped up and cramped in it...

Yet, when recalling his walks around the area as a whole, there's a great sense (and this was palpable even walking around it now) that there *was* a wealth of space to walk and talk in. It wasn't the worst London borough to have as a kind of prison.

We followed Amhurst Road, leaning right towards Hackney Downs. A high-rise shot up among the trees and the sun shone down on the relatively empty but pleasant lawns. A handful of joggers and cyclists were making their way around the paths, though no one was declaring lines of Webster into the wind.

> On the dead 653 trolleybus,
> To Clapton Pond,
> And walk across the shadows on to Hackney Downs

We strolled on, following the path parallel to Queensdown Road, and turned right onto Downs Road towards Clapton Pond. Downs Road was where the house for Caretaker Films stood, and where Clive Donner set up production and filmed the 1963 version of the play at number 31. Sadly the house was knocked down, though a handful of the same type of house still sit further down the road.

When discussing his time walking with Pinter and his Hackney Downs friendship group, the actor Henry Woolf also recognised in hindsight the importance of such a venture. Speaking during an *Arena* documentary interview for a film called *The Room*, he said that 'Wandering around Hackney and so forth… That traversing out of space in our heads… We didn't have any money to speak of so we spent an enormous amount of time walking and an enormous amount of time talking and reading.'

That idea, of 'traversing out of space in our head', of walking ideas into existence or substantiating already conceived ideas by walking some meat onto the bone, was clearly important to Pinter. As Woolf later went on to say, 'We bowled about and bought cups of tea and walked about and we didn't feel poor in spirit; we felt quite rich really.' This is a working-class experience of the city and the area; one that permeates a great deal of Pinter's work.

Clapton Pond glistened in the sunshine, its light creating shards of rainbow. We walked over its bridge, the vibrations of the busy traffic rubbing up against the oddly rural enclave. It's an intensely contradictory place.

Briefly moving away from Pinter's poem, we walked around the corner to Pinter's house in Thistlewaite Road, now adorned with a blue plaque to commemorate his time there. Pinter believed that the liveliness of the area had class links, suggesting that 'At the same time, we felt very much its qualities and liveliness and busyness. It was a very lively working-class district. It was living.' Whether that same busyness remains, in terms of class, is debatable. It was all a little too prim.

Continuing some way up the main road, we eventually found ourselves in Springfield Park. There was a specific reason for visiting, outside of Pinter's general writing and in spite of him mentioning the place earlier when detailing his walks with Brearley.

The poem also mentions a bandstand at Hackney Downs which is sadly no longer there. For the Super-8 film I was shooting at the time as a response to the poem, this seemed pretty essential, and so the bandstand in this park was to be used instead.

The views out over the valley were vast and dizzying. The bandstand was indeed a suitable substitute. We soon left Springfield Park, and meandered further, all the way along the main road towards Stamford Hill. This road has Clapton Terrace on it, the loop where Mick taunts Davies by driving him in a circle in the filmed version of *The Caretaker*. In terms of the poem, this was going back to the opening lines, which refer to the walk from Clapton Pond up to Stamford Hill.

Pinter said about Hackney that his engagement with the place was different to other areas he lived in later. 'The main thing about Hackney,' he admitted, 'was that it was *a place* as opposed to places you live in afterwards which are not places; you live in houses... You're not part of any district or place but in Hackney we were certainly part of the place.' After following his old haunts, it was clear that the area had a huge influence on his writing because it was, for him, a place rather than a space. Community was key.

Contrasting heavily with the claustrophobic settings of his many plays, the walk showed another side to this quintessential London writer; a side where ideas were walked into existence, peopled by park wanderers, lost souls and street-corner philosophers.

Published by Celluloid Wicker Man, 21/03/16

Doris Lessing's Dismay

An elderly lady was getting out of a black Hackney. There were reporters all around her, begging for interviews and photographs as she slowly manoeuvred herself out of the cab's heavy door, making sure that she paid the driver and didn't forget her shopping on the backseat.

'Are you photographing for a reason?' she asked briskly.

'We're photographing *you*. Have you not heard the news?' suggested an enthusiastic American.

'No?' she replied bluntly.

'You've just won the Nobel Prize for Literature.'

'Oh Christ,' she said.

This is roughly what happened on October the 11th 2007, when it was announced that Doris Lessing had won the Nobel Prize. Aside from being the oldest recipient of the award at the time, she was only the twelfth woman and the eleventh British writer to win the coveted prize. In other words, the news was monumental for British literature. And yet Lessing was nothing less than practical in her reaction.

She was returning from a hospital visit with her third son Peter, who cheerily remarked on hearing the news: 'Well, a certain professor must have died.' On the way back they had clearly picked up the week's food shop. The reporters trying to get quotes had to contend with Lessing carrying her week's vegetables. 'I'm sure you'd like some uplifting remarks,' she suggested. As many photographs of the moment show, she then proceeded to conduct her Nobel interviews sat on the tiled doorstep of her house in Hampstead.

Though not living in London until after the Second World War, Lessing and her house certainly embody a particular vision of London literature; that same type embodied by writers such as Anita Brookner, Judith Kerr and Angela Carter, where literature spawned from the grand houses of the capital. Though born in Iran and soon travelling and living in what is now Zimbabwe, Lessing eventually found herself as a telephone operator in Salisbury before finally moving to London in 1949. She divorced her second husband in the same year, London representing the new start of a marriage-free writer's life, concentrating on her work and her politics.

Search for images of Lessing online and the likelihood is that the photographs will be of her and her Hampstead house, either from the day of her Nobel win or from earlier interviews conducted there. Sometimes photographs have her situated at the window seat of the house, surrounded by pillows, cats and cacti. Others are taken in what looks to be an overgrown jungle of a garden at the back, the vines and nettles threatening to swallow the ornate garden furniture.

I often come back to the photographs taken on the day of the Nobel Prize, the furore over this decidedly modest, impatient woman, sat on her porch while holding either large bouquets of flowers or her head in her hands, dismayed by the chaos of it all. As she said to one interviewer, 'I'm trying to think of something suitable to say. What do you think I should say? Tell me what to say and I'll say it.'

Out of the four British Nobel laureates this century so far (V.S. Naipaul, Harold Pinter and Kazuo Ishiguro being the other three), Lessing's award feels the most everyday out of the quartet, simply because she was bizarrely the one who was door stepped by the paparazzi almost instantly upon its announcement, and even more strangely before the writer actually found out herself.

Certainly, if the award in my mind could be associated with a place, it could only be Lessing's front garden and its makeshift press conference with potted plants and a garden path of intricate black and white tiles, as well as a lavish green door.

After researching where the house actually was – a surprisingly difficult task, in that the house is not currently marked or celebrated as being that of a previous Nobel laureate – I journeyed to Hampstead looking for it. The area will never fail to surprise or feel unusual to my eyes, with its endless hills always far steeper than first imagined, and its erratic collection of upper-middle-class street furniture.

Getting off at the building site that was West Hampstead Thameslink station, I wandered through a cornucopia of Waitrose and pet salons before turning into the residential streets of Mill Lane.

Outside of the influence of new brands and businesses, the area's streets felt frozen in time; such is the protection of their original designs and atmosphere afforded by the area's wealth. Even the alleyways are strangely beautiful, almost exotic, like something out of a Frank Auerbach painting; their inner-city equivalents have largely vanished under glass and steel developments.

Turning off onto Gondar Gardens, and up a hill so steep as to threaten to tip over the cars parked along it, the house soon came into view. I wasn't sure what to expect, and was certainly greeted by nothing less than a (probably very expensive) typical North London house; no blue plaque or commemoration, just an ordinary building minding its own business.

Seeing so many commemorations of notable people all around London, part of me thought it was a shame not to mark Lessing's time in the house, especially with it being so overtly and humorously connected to that day when she seemingly stumbled onto what is still the most recognised literary prize in the world. But the ordinariness of the house is fitting and certainly in character for a writer who sat on the porch to give interviews to the world on the day when she was rightly recognised as one of the greats.

Published by Caught by the River, 19/08/19

Marcel Proust's Darkroom

Marcel Proust's bedroom must have been dark. Four volumes into his novel *In Search of Lost Time*, and it feels impossible to read the thousands of pages of his words without seeing them come into being in a barely lit Parisian chamber. Almost cocooned within this cork-lined literary nest, spreading memories like thin strands of cobweb until the early hours, I imagine Proust to have needed his room to be a shadowy blank canvas upon which his past played out.

There have been many depictions of Proust's bedrooms, often concocting a mixture of the various different houses in Paris where he lived and lay weary with illness, possessed by his need to write. On one winter's day while in Paris, I wanted to find some remnant of Proust's home, naïvely in the hope that it would still suggest something regarding its connection to the writer, at least in character.

Proust lived variously around Paris since childhood, first with his parents at 96 rue Fontaine in the 16th Arrondissement where he was born. His parents had moved there after their first house had been disturbed by the rumblings of the Paris Commune.

Though Proust lived in several other properties with his parents, alongside their famous trips away to various hotels and houses on the Normandy coast, the writer first lived alone after his parents had finally died. Entering his mid-thirties, he moved to 102 boulevard Haussmann in 1906. The writer soon took to his bed, a penchant for early nights being an admission that opens the novel – 'For a long time, I went to bed early' – and began work on the book that was to occupy the remainder of his time.

There's something about depictions of Proust's writing, or at least the process of his writing, that is refreshingly earnest compared to more romantic visions of being a writer, especially in pre-Second World War society. The process of writing becomes, for Proust, something that is isolating, another illness to add to his collection. It literally takes over his life as reams of paper pile up by the bedside. Find any depiction of him, paintings and drawings in particular, and they will undoubtedly sketch this lonely scene.

He epitomised the loneliness of writing.

Though recreations for such drawings will undoubtedly be taken from images from his last place of residence, 44 rue Hamlin and its bedroom which is famously recreated in the Musée Carnavalet as an exhibit, the loneliness was transposed from building to building. Rather than a desk, however, Proust was wedded to his bed. Recollection is best considered when comfortable.

It was Christmas Eve when I decided to go in search of 102 boulevard Haussmann. I was in Paris deliberately, equally alone and wandering in search of film locations and other sites for work. There was also an element of deliberate isolation; that after months of work, no energy was left for the sort of enforced social pleasantries demanded by Christmas. Paris, with its distinctly un-Christmas brutality, felt the right place to hang around.

Proust's house would be my first place to visit because it would, so I thought, set the tone for the trip overall. I hopped on the Métro to Opéra, hoping as well to venture to the nearby Hotel Scribe where the Lumière Brothers held their first film screenings and where Jean-Luc Godard filmed his science-fiction film *Alphaville* (1966). But it was in vain, as the hotel had changed in key with the luxury status of the area, it now being one of the wealthiest in the city.

I wandered on, closing in on the 8th Arrondissement, where, so I was constantly warned by garbled news websites, the *Gilets Jaunes* were causing chaos every Saturday. The area felt unusual at the time, simply because many buildings had their windows barricaded, their insides darkened with paranoid conspiracy. It only became apparent from walking further that every building attacked was a bank; windows smashed, faux-revolutionary graffiti sprayed upon stone walls and cheap wooden plywood acting as makeshift barriers against the cold.

Finally on boulevard Haussmann, suspiciously empty and with pavements blocked by building work, I began looking out for the building. I almost walked past the house in question, as 102 boulevard Haussmann is now a bank as well. Its windows were totally boarded up. Even its main door had been forcibly blocked.

A large plaque on the wall celebrated Proust's time there and had thankfully been left alone; the ire of the protestors aimed solely at what occupied the building. I snapped a Polaroid photo and sat on the hard wooden bench opposite, trying to imagine Proust's room now. It was still darkened, yes, but now by boards covering broken glass. I could picture him with ease, writing away as the world turned; barely looking up to see the turmoil unfolding away from the page.

Published by Caught by the River, 10/02/19

Georges Perec's Street-Watching

'Describe your street. Describe another. Compare.'

This was the mantra of French writer Georges Perec. Written in his essay 'L'infra Ordinaire' in 1973, Perec argued that the world around us, in particular the seemingly ignored domestic settings of urban modernity, provided almost infinite material for writing. Though initially examining fiction through a zoomed-in lens, in novels such as *Things: A Story of the Sixties* (1965), Perec quickly opened out onto the streets of Paris, the city's day-to-day life providing the ingredients for his more experimental writing.

Perec was also known for his linguistic experiments, breaking apart normal narrative structures with a range of self-imposed rules. Being part of the Oulipo movement of literature, one that turned writing into a complex, even mathematical procedure, Perec took on a variety of challenges, from famously writing a novel without the letter 'e' in *A Void* (1969) to using an early computer program to write *The Art and Craft of Approaching Your Head of Department to Submit a Request for a Raise* (1968). Most interestingly, especially in terms of place, was Perec's literary experiment *An Attempt to Exhaust a Place in Paris* (1975), a book whose experiment can actually be repeated off the page, and often is by young writers in Paris.

An Attempt follows a detailed place-diary written by Perec when sitting in the Café de la Mairie in place Saint-Sulpice. The small book is broken down into entries detailing the various aspects of the day on which he is writing, followed by what he can see from the window over a set period of time. It seems so normal that it's difficult at first to comprehend what writing down such things achieves, except a basic backdrop for, hopefully, something more interesting.

As the book progresses, however, details begin to repeat with an almost musical quality; the organic identity of a city living from day to day feels eerie to witness. Having read it multiple times, it feels like nothing less than being inside a living creature, its blood replaced by buses parking up impatiently, its architecture rendered as bones and joints, its wandering people as energy in search of a never-ending destination.

The city becomes cyclic, an ever-changing process. It's a surprisingly optimistic vision; that the dead cells are replaced and changed. The only static aspect is the writer himself, the witness.

One of my favourite photos of Perec shows him sat in the café whilst in the middle of writing and witnessing this scene. He is in the window of the Café de la Mairie, sat at a table with a packet of Gauloises, a notebook, a pencil, a packet of matches and an empty coffee cup. There's a curious mischief etched on his face. He was always a writer who balanced a playful sense of the absurd with an array of incredibly complex literary ideas.

'What we need to question,' Perec further listed in 'L'infra Ordinaire', 'is bricks, concrete, glass, our table manners, our utensils, our tools, the way we spend our time, our rhythms. To question that which seems to have ceased forever to astonish us.' Every action is some small mechanism or cog which in itself contains our own idiosyncrasies, the ordinary becoming almost fantastically strange when we realise how unconsciously absurd it all is.

Perec captures the feeling that sometimes occurs when we stare at words for long enough, where the meaning slips and the process of translating its shapes and squiggles becomes mysterious, almost unthinkable. The difference is, however, that the writer captures that same mystery with Paris; staring at it until it all seems unreal.

It was on a cold and lonely Boxing Day when I finally sought some human company in Paris, deciding to visit Perec's viewing spot at Café de la Mairie. I walked along through the frosty morning from Gare de Lyon, along the endless boulevard Saint-Germain before meandering into the labyrinthine streets and finding the square of Saint-Sulpice. Even on that day, there were people attempting to angle the perfect Instagram shot near the clichéd-looking Parisian buildings; people feigning to be in mid-walk as others photographed them. Windows were filled with expensive art, rare editions of books and small scraps of paper autographed by the likes of Paul Éluard and Guillaume Apollinaire. The area still drips with culture.

It was clear on entering the café that it was too busy to sit where Perec had, so I opted for an extra room the café had opened next door. Perec's words that open *An Attempt* run along the walls in a flowing typography; the café permanently marked by the writer's experiment. With some irony, it was clear that the anonymity of the café would no longer be possible from its window, with its coffee costing almost £7.50 and its endless array of moneyed Parisians photographing everything and debating in the main foyer, mostly about the *Gilets Jaunes* who had recently left their own mark on the area's buildings.

I sat alone looking out of the window. The buses still went by, people walked on, and the winter sunlight reflected off the walls. The creature continued living and the view from inside its urban corpus was as heady as it always was.

Published by Caught by the River, 23/07/19

Marguerite Duras's Winter in Trouville

In the summer of 1963, Marguerite Duras bought an apartment on the coast of Normandy. From then on, she would retreat to the safety of its pale light, travelling there often from her various homes in Paris and Neauphle-le-Château until the year of her death. Sometimes, she would venture to the room at more desolate times of the year, when the beaches were empty and storm clouds were heavy in the sky, especially when using the location for her filmmaking.

The apartment was housed in the grand building of the Hôtel des Roches Noires in Trouville-sur-Mer, and played a pivotal role in her work. When considering her unprecedented output, the first images that spring to mind are usually of Trouville; its vast skies, long beaches and cafés providing shelter from the elements.

Les Roches Noires, as it is now called, is an eerily quiet place in winter. Yet its architecture is filled with busier qualities, as if soaked in the voices of thousands of travellers from La Belle Époque; the era that its tall windows, ornate ceilings and extravagant stairways cannot help but suggest.

It was completed in 1866 by Alphonse-Nicolas Crépinet, an architect who, among other things, designed the tomb in Les Invalides for Joseph Bonaparte, brother to the First

Emperor. Constructed as close to the sea as possible, the building is remarkable in having survived the adjacent, relentless tides. On the right day, a view from its windows creates the illusion of being literally cast adrift.

Crépinet's building was a great success with the travelling rich of Paris, and became a symbol of the increasingly popular holidaying trends of the age. It was a veritable rival to the hotels in neighbouring Deauville, cashing in on the bourgeoisie's growing taste for coastal retreats and gambling. 'I will be staying at the hotel... where you will probably stay,' wrote Marcel Proust in a letter to

Reynaldo Hahn in 1894, 'because it is the best.' Proust would stay true to his word, holidaying often at Les Roches Noires and featuring it in his unfinished novel *Jean Santeuil*. Even Gustave Flaubert fell madly in love during a stay at the hotel, though he is commemorated for his connection to the area by a statue in Deauville instead.

My initial encounter with the building perfectly fitted those same romantic images. I first saw it in Claude Monet's 1870 painting, specifically a print that had faded into a foggy turquoise, hanging on the bathroom wall of a run-down Paris bar. Like so much that is shrouded by nostalgia, the lavish yet simple world depicted in the painting – the flow of dresses hidden from the sun by parasols, men gallantly doffing hats to passing women, and colours so soft as to be almost carried away on the breeze – masked the reality of Monet's life then. He was on the move due to the coming Franco-Prussian War and had nowhere to live, homing towards his native Le Havre up the coast and drawn by the possibility of new adventures further away in London.

Duras's relationship with the building feels similar to Monet's, albeit Monet could do little else except sit and paint it from the outside, being too expensive for the struggling artist at the time. Duras's similar sense of retreat is palpable in her writing from the moment she obtains a room there.

Her work, so often about loss considered in hindsight, increasingly resembled the view from the building's windows, heartache's horizon threatening to never cease until sea and sky became one. Whether in work about her colonial childhood in French Indochina such as *The Sea Wall* and *The Lover*, or more abstract work like *Emily*

L. or *Yann Andréa Steiner*, the voice within was always hollowed by loss, or at least in anticipation of it.

Loss permeates Duras's film work, too, with her voice and presence directly at its centre. She enters a more brutally confessional mode when behind a camera. Even when simply on script duty, such as in her most celebrated collaboration, Alain Resnais's *Hiroshima, Mon Amour*, Duras's work still contains stormy seas and subdued voices contemplating horizons, personal and actual.

Whether on film or in novels, the perspective gained from being in the building on Trouville's coast is often present, even in work made before she moved there. Emotional recollection seems unavoidably brought in on the tide.

When searching for images of the writer, one of the most prominent that appears is a photograph by Helène Bamberger taken in the foyer of the building in 1981. Ghostly with solitude, Duras is transfixed by the view out to sea. The building feels as if it has floated away from the land.

A huge part of her creative process is captured in this photograph. You can almost hear the ripples of her recollections. From seeing this photo, the building seemed key to understanding her complex body of work, not simply as setting but as stimulus.

Her work has a sea view, and I was determined to experience it.

The gates quietly opened for the car as we pulled up in front of the building, activated by a small device handed over by the agents in Deauville. Already, the fact that no one was around Les Roches Noires was apparent.

Being February, and with a number of storms due to hit the coastline that week, the Parisians (who undoubtedly own many of the lavish rooms in Les Roches Noires) were still in the capital, where they would likely remain until the weather warmed up. I had travelled there with my then partner, a shared gift for missing our anniversary a few weeks earlier due to the launch of a novel.

The building made me giddy with excitement as it was already clear which room was Duras's, deduced from a photo I had seen showing it to be a corner which partly faced the road as well as the sea. The fact that a Wi-Fi connection popped up on my phone simply labelled 'MARGUERITE' also helped.

The doorway within was curved and led to what was once the hotel's reception, the main room that Duras used for filming and for many of her author portraits. The sound of the sea haunted the corridors as if its rooms were filled with waves.

The alcoves that once housed the hotel's many keys were filled with old editions published by Gallimard, Folio and Le Livre de Poche. The picture of Duras taken in the foyer's main window was hanging on a wall; and then everything else was exactly as it always had been. The alluring sky-filled vista, the Art Deco chairs with their rounded arms and headrests, the delicate painting of nineteenth-century tourists along the border of the ceiling and, most hypnotic of all, the room's two opposing mirrors infinitely reflecting the space back upon itself.

The day was fading into evening, and after falling in love with our own small room – itself like a living painting – my partner and I sat together in the foyer and watched the sunset. In her underrated work *L'amour* (1971), Duras perfectly describes witnessing this same dusky view. 'In the distance,' she wrote, 'the sea is already oxidised by dark light, as is the sky.' Even *L'amour's* cover is adorned with a photo of this view, as if it completely summarises the text. The light was alchemical in its collapse and, seen through the thin panes of glass, invited our silence.

The vastness of the room (or perhaps the mirrored illusion of it) augmented our language, each statement hanging in the air for a few moments longer than usual, as if the very design of the building forced us to consider our words more carefully. Language requires greater care when in Les Roches Noires, its echoes heightening the speaker's self-awareness.

In her film *Agatha and the Limitless Readings* (1981), Duras breaks the cinematic form using this same patience naturally enforced by the building. She was rather proud of this, writing in an essay about her work that: 'All of the world's filmmakers are beneath what I write for the cinema.'

It was her filmmaking that first drew me to her rather than her literature, simply because it was more readily available. Her cinema was brazenly radical, unafraid of being texts as opposed to visual narratives, an unusual but essential extension of her writing. Her fellow *Nouveau Roman* writer Alain Robbe-Grillet felt the same about his cinema.

A scene in *Agatha* shot in the foyer highlights Duras's radical but stoic vision. Actress Bulle Ogier is walking slowly towards one of the room's mirrors. The camera is fixed and is there in the shot: we can see it clearly. There is no deception or clever angle to hide the bulky mechanism and its crew. Its presence is a quiet violence, becoming the watcher who Duras addresses in the voice-over. My life is real, she is saying, and so are my words, even when used as a voice-over for a film.

This is my winter.

That is my sea you can hear.

This is my heartbreak I am remembering.

I couldn't resist recreating this shot, falling into the infinity of the mirrors. I aimed my Polaroid camera dead centre and evaporated with the flash, providing the image with the sort of absence more typically expected from a film, albeit not one by Duras. It's easy to leave your body and its ongoing moment in Les Roches Noires.

That night, the inky darkness of the coast was all consuming. The sea continued to crash against the beach as my partner and I listened to the wind rattling the window frames. We soon faded into each other and disappeared as the storm met the shoreline.

'They are silent. They watch the progress of the outer dawn,' as Duras wrote in *L'amour*. That was our morning, too.

'You cannot drink here,' a man said abruptly in French the following morning. His voice was like gravel, rendering his words mere crumbling cadences before I slowly understood what he was saying. The rules restricting a variety of things in the historic foyer of Les Roches Noires had been neatly hidden in an ornate frame on the wall. Like the vital letter hidden in plain sight in Edgar Allan Poe's 'The Purloined Letter', it had been totally ignored. He was the caretaker of the building and, having already felt that it somewhat resembled the Overlook Hotel from Stanley Kubrick's *The Shining* – resulting in daydreams about what an adaptation of Stephen King's story would have looked like if directed by Duras – I thought it best to obey.

The foyer was alluring and inviting all the same. Its design makes it feel more than natural to sit there drinking and eating, watching the elements outside shift with the sands. The pleasure derives from knowingly sharing in pastimes enjoyed by travellers in eras gone by. It is a pleasure of continuity.

With drinking not being possible, my partner and I returned with just our books; mine a recently published collection of Duras's essays, *Me & Other Writing*, hers a novel by Françoise Sagan borrowed from the building's makeshift library. Reading there felt out of time, so to speak. We could have been sat within almost any period or, more unusually, no period at all.

'The sea seems to be sleeping,' suggests the narrator of *Agatha*. For all that could be gleaned from the view, only occasionally interspersed with a passing walker braving the storm, time felt frozen, asleep.

The place possesses a calming effect due to its illusions of temporal stasis. It was different to places specifically marketed as relaxing or inspiring. Images of wellness centres and ritualistic attempts at self-discovery were swept away by the salty air and quietude of the location; an ironic quietude considering the sound of the sea was always present, flooding the corridors.

Duras experienced this same tranquillity, perhaps explaining why she found such richly productive solace there. 'I do remember there was a kind of tranquillity stretching all over the sea and over us,' she writes in *Emily L.*, another of her underrated novels which examines loss on the coast, albeit one slightly further north nearer Le Havre. The sea retains strange qualities in her writing, often allowing for watery reflection.

After eating in Le Central, another of Duras's regular haunts near Trouville's casino where she drank copiously, we wandered through the shining wet streets before sheltering in a variety of cafés as a strong wind blew invisible blankets of sand through the air. A stencil of Duras was sprayed onto the wall of the public library, adorned with a quote suggesting an amorous affair between words and sentences: *'Faire d'un mot le bel amant d'un phrase.'*

Along the beach were a number of blue benches adorned with many names of figures associated with the area. I sat on the one bearing Duras's name and had my photo taken. Another rain shower threatened so the warmth of the room beckoned, boasting its endless panorama of the land around, viewed handily from the comfort of its bed.

Our trip was soon over, having shared Duras's view for as long as our small budget could last. We stood one last time in the foyer watching another afternoon drift into evening, the light stealing our breath. Colours smouldered so distinctively that, even in constant flux, they seemed almost solid. 'The air was blue,' Duras wrote in *L'amour*, 'you could hold it in your hand.'

When the azure caught fire and burned finally into charcoal, my partner took my hand and we wandered back to the room. Our eyes were still drenched in sky as we happily drifted together again as the tide murmured outside and the sea view faded to black.

Published by Port Magazine, 20/05/20

Thomas Bernhard's Favourite Hatred

'I prefer to be alone. That's my ideal condition,' the writer Thomas Bernhard once admitted. 'My house is really a great prison. I like bare walls. Bare and cold. That's best for my work.' He was discussing the complicated relationship he had with his country house in Obernathal, near Gmunden in Austria, a retreat away from the Austrian society he famously loathed.

Just like the narrators of his novels, such as those in *Correction* (1975) or *Extinction* (1986), Bernhard was an enjoyably contradictory persona, annihilating the things he seemed to enjoy as much as the things he hated. In spite of spending a great deal of his time in the house, the writer's relationship with the bustling capital of Vienna is arguably just as intriguing, complex and contradictory. Both of these extremes of place – the isolated rural and the bustling cosmopolitan – inhabit the same prose and the same mania.

Far from locking Bernhard in solitude, Vienna was another kind of prison: one built on a damning mixture of bourgeois sentiment, conservative Catholicism and the still persistent remnants of the country's association with National Socialism, especially in the upper echelons. But understanding Bernhard's work is equally about understanding Vienna, its coffee culture, its ghosts. Even if regularly isolating himself in his own 'memorial dungeon' in the country, Bernhard was a writer who reacted to the city as much as to the country.

Café Bräunerhof

Bernhard's array of novels glisten with vitriol. He created long, detailed attacks upon a variety of targets in the form of character monologues. Vienna is still famed for its literary café culture, and Bernhard was a large part of its image in the post-war years, but he undeniably railed against it at every turn.

A number of cafés in the city have a string of literary associations, but it was Café Bräunerhof that drew Bernhard. Search for images of Bernhard online and one of the first that appears, outside of those taken in his house, is one of him sat in the historic café, relaxing on the corner seat with a coffee and an array of newspapers. Yet what did he write about his favourite café? Something positive, perhaps? A segment from his novel *Wittgenstein's Nephew* (1982) illustrates Bernhard's biting contradictions perfectly:

> The literary coffeehouses have a foul atmosphere, irritating to the nerves and deadening to the mind. I have never learned anything new there but only been annoyed and irritated and pointlessly depressed... At the Bräunerhof, above which my friend had lived for years before we met, I am still put off by the foul aim and the poor lighting, which is kept down to a minimum – doubtless from perverse considerations of economy – and in which I have never been able

to read a single line without effort. I also disliked the seating, which is inevitably damaging to the spinal column, however briefly one sits there – to say nothing of the pungent smell that emanates from the kitchen and very soon gets into one's clothes.

As typical for Bernhard, it's difficult to tell whether he actually liked things or not. His manic rage dominates all.

The negatives induce a burning hatred; the positives elicit respect but nothing more. Nothing is safe from his critical eye, not even himself or the world of literature he inhabited. Yet neither is anything safe from his heart, his overriding joy at the strangest of pleasures. His writing is warmed by a friction between rage and joy. Bernhard is as unsparing in his adorations as his hatreds, which makes him refreshing, like strong coffee on an early spring morning. Nothing is done by half.

Visiting Café Bräunerhof, it was difficult to know what to expect. The Tripadvisor comments displayed as equally dismissive an attitude as Bernhard's narrator. If some were to be believed, the waiters – with their black suits, bow ties and silver platters – were Bernhard-esque characters themselves, cold-shouldering and ambivalent, almost insulting even. It would have been positively Bernhard-esque to be insulted by a waiter at the Café Bräunerhof. They were all, of course, wrong.

Café Bräunerhof is a time capsule like many Viennese cafes. There is no music – except live at weekends, when quartets gather to play a brief classical repertoire – no Wi-Fi, and very little light. The furniture is exactly as in the photographs of Bernhard sat there, and the newspaper holders are even the same battered type. In fact, nothing seems to have changed since his time there.

I sat down in a seat nearest to the door below a photograph of Magda Schneider (mother of Romy Schneider), the seat, in fact, where Bernhard is slouched in the photograph mentioned earlier. I ordered a coffee, soon arriving on a silver platter with the famously extravagant Viennese foam bubbling atop, and watched the other drinkers idling about.

A girl sat next to me reading a novel by Robert Musil, a pair of older men were debating in German about a story in one of the newspapers while sipping water mixed with spirits, and an American academic chastised her fellow drinker about how her research on Gustav Klimt had been appropriated without her consent for an exhibition booklet. It was, in other words, exactly like sitting in a novel by Thomas Bernhard.

'Yet for many years it was at the Bräunerhof that I felt at home,' Bernhard's narrator later admits in *Wittgenstein's Nephew*. It's a telling confession regarding his inspirations.

Grinzing

Bernhard was a writer full of surprises. He infamously stated in his will that his huge backlog of plays and novels was to not be published or performed in Austria after his death, since rescinded by his estate's executor in the 1990s. Equally surprising is to find that he was buried not somewhere near his retreat in Gmunden, but in Grinzing Cemetery just outside of central Vienna. After a morning spent in Bernhard's favourite café, it only felt right to make the pilgrimage to his place of resting. Taking the U-Bahn to the end of the line to Heiligenstadt, I went in search of the graveyard.

Grinzing is an unusual place, a mixture of imposing housing blocks and then an array of affluent streets and the suburbs as the incline of Lower Austria's dark forests begins. Walking out of the station and along, I was surprisingly greeted by the housing block used by Liliana Cavini in her controversial film *The Night Porter* (1974). The flats were the home of Dirk Bogarde's ex-concentration camp officer in the film. But soon these buildings faded into hills with much older, more lavish buildings.

People disappeared as if kept away by the steepness of the roads. I followed a bin lorry all the way up the final road to Grinzing Cemetery, itself camouflaged by a minor housing estate. Bernhard's grave, in spite of being there since 1989, was not on the map, unlike most of the other notable company he shared, including, appropriately, Gustav Mahler.

I walked and walked until finding what I knew to be his grave, drenched in ivy with intricate metalwork growing out of the greenery. There were only a handful of totems left by other devotees of his writing, nowhere near as many as some other writers' graves I had visited. Marguerite Duras, Marcel Proust, J.G. Ballard: even the darkest of writers had an array of pens, coins and debris left by their admirers.

Bernhard's prose defends his grave from such sentimental ephemera; his life was one long toying with death until his own eventual assisted suicide. Leaving objects of affection feels trite and almost contrary to what the writer would have wished. 'Everything is ridiculous when one thinks of death,' he once suggested when winning the Austrian national prize for literature in 1968; of all the times to choose to admit such a philosophy!

Instead of leaving a memento, I took a Polaroid photo of his grave, the ivy leaves shining in the sunlight. The view back towards Vienna was vast, and it felt just enough of a comfortable distance away for a writer who wrote such biting criticisms of the city.

I sat for a while in the surprising warmth of early spring, listening to the hooded crows argue, and content with their company alongside the dead writer. 'You are never truly together with one you love until the person in question is dead and actually inside you,' wrote Bernhard in his novel *Gargoyles* (1967). Never was a truer statement written.

Bernhard died the day before I was born, his manic character dissipating into the atmosphere. But it lives on, I hope, whether in those seeking the mathematical perfection of buildings in forests, in those desperately in search of the Gouldian transcendence of Bach, or in those trekking miles on lonely visits to the gravesides of writers long since crumbled into the ground.

Published by Caught by the River, 14/05/19

Viddy Well, Brother –
Stanley Kubrick's Thamesmead

Littered with some of the most startling images of British brutalist architecture ever captured, Stanley Kubrick's *A Clockwork Orange* (1971) is a social document as much as a dystopian science-fiction film. Based on Anthony Burgess's 1962 novel, the film follows a murderous gang of Droogs led by Alex (Malcolm McDowell) who indulge in violence and face the subsequent punishment and power of the state.

It seems a happy accident that Kubrick captured so much new architecture, with the director relying on an unusual level of location filming. In comparison to his previous film, *2001: A Space Odyssey* (1968), his budget had been slashed, Warner Brothers wanting him to prove that he could make a film on less money.

Relying on location filming was also fitting for Kubrick's creative aims for his Burgess adaptation: not to showcase a glossy, futuristic world similar to Arthur C. Clarke's, but one that was grounded in the present-day grimness of 1970s Britain. It was a threatening future lurking just around the corner.

Because of this, many of the locations chosen were everyday buildings, still new and experimental, whether it was Brunel University, the famous Chelsea Drugstore on the King's Road, or a Wandsworth Bridge underpass. As Kubrick suggested to Michel Ciment, he and his team researched the most modern buildings of the period through magazines.

'The locations were supposed to look a bit futuristic,' he suggested, 'and we did our preliminary location search by looking through back issues of several British architectural magazines, getting our leads for most of the locations that way.'

The film is evidently aware of the fashions in architecture of the period, and Kubrick picked the most overt examples, perhaps ironically, in that they are the examples that are essentially the most dated when observed today. It's a futuristic vision if the future is stuck in 1971.

The most startling architecture in the film is the estate where Alex lives with his parents, filmed in the brutalist project around Southmere in Thamesmead. Partly colouring the perception of the area's level of crime in subsequent years, Kubrick's use of the location presents the film's most astonishing visual space.

The whole area was rebuilt in the late 1960s, fashioned around a variety of angular buildings and slip roads, providing both expansive zones – including the marina lake seen in the film, supposedly designed to reduce crime via the calming presence of water – and cramped passages and alleyways. It was the supposed future of cities and only a few years old at the time of filming. Already, however, the failure of its design was apparent.

Crime became commonplace in the area, its network of passageways and tunnels perfect for a quick ambush or mugging. The crowded blocks led to social unrest. Drug problems plagued the estates and spread quickly. Rubbish piled up, with refuse areas idiotically placed under many of the housing areas, encouraging fly-tipping and vermin. Even merely walking through it must have been unnerving when lit only by its smattering of poorly placed street lights, rather like Alex's lonely walk back there; surrounded, of course, by piles of litter, perhaps inspired by the variety of bin strikes occurring in East London during filming.

Used in the famous scene of Alex's retaking command of the Droogs, the photography renders Thamesmead's buildings with an unusual feeling, simultaneously representing a morbid future and a failed present. Its realisation feels true to Burgess's original description of the scene.

'"As we walked along the flat block marina,"' he wrote, '"I was calm on the outside, but thinking all the time... Now it was lovely music that came to my aid. There was a window open with the stereo on, and I viddied right at once what to do."' It's impossible to reread this moment without seeing Thamesmead's tower blocks reflected in the rubbish-filled water, the strange steps leading down to the marina and the concrete designs jutting out with their unusual prisms and cubes.

On visiting the location, it became clear that much had changed and only very recently. The area has since accepted a development proposal in line with Crossrail, resulting in the total restructuring of the town. Alex's estate itself is now in the process of redevelopment and is being slowly demolished.

The main sequence of Kubrick's filming took place behind Binsey Walk in the estate, and a large gap now exists where the buildings once curved around the marina's water. All the entranceways were closed off, with only one opening left where the bins were once kept, now occupied by the homeless. Walking to the other side of the marina, a blue wooden panel blocked off access, but was eventually easy to bypass.

The contrast between Kubrick's images and the buildings as they are today is surreal. Whereas the Droogs walked upon pristine, cleaned concrete, the walkway is now overgrown. With the marina alongside covered in algae and wildlife now taking over, it felt more like J.G. Ballard's *The Drowned World* than Burgess's novel. The building seen in the background of the shot has already been totally demolished, so taking a photograph can only capture a fragment of how it looked to Kubrick's eye.

There's also clear resistance from the remaining residents to being moved from Thamesmead, even with the acknowledged social problems that evolved around the estate's design mere years after it was built. It seems highly ironic that, in one of the starkest depictions of dystopia in film, there appears to be more life in Alex's world than the real place today; the weeds growing confidently and the walkways cordoned off.

Kubrick's film presents spaces that reflect the cold brutality of binaries: good and evil, punishment and reform, present and future. The real Thamesmead is now crumbling into memory, but at least we have the images caught and documented in *A Clockwork Orange*; of days when Droogs fought on the gangway. It is, however, difficult to know which reality is really more dystopian.

Published by Little White Lies, 16/09/18

The Witches' School –
Dario Argento's Freiburg

It may be surprising to discover that one of the most
intimidating buildings found in 1970s horror cinema is a
German dance school. The building in question is a set
built for Dario Argento's chilling yet vibrant 1977 film
Suspiria, and is easily one of the director's most alluring
and hypnotic cinematic spaces.

With its lavish golden columns and bright pink walls,
it's astonishing how such dazzling, even camp, architecture
becomes so ominous a presence in the film. Even more
surprisingly, though the building was a set, it was inspired
by a real place rather than the dark corners of the director's
imagination. Argento took inspiration from a historic
building in the town of Freiburg where the film is set, and
so the academy in question has, in some sense, a ghostly
real-life twin that can be visited.

Suspiria follows American ballet dancer Suzy Bannion
(Jessica Harper), who is sent by her parents to a private
dance school, the Tanz Dance Academy in Germany. From
the moment she arrives at Munich Airport, strange events
begin to occur. Maggots drop from the ceilings, students are
found violently murdered, and the director of the academy
goes mysteriously unseen. On talking to the other girls, it's

clear to Suzy that something is awry at the school, and she follows her curiosity in search of links between the academy and the local folk legend that suggests it was founded by a malevolent Greek witch, Helena Markos.

With Argento being one of horror's great stylists, it's unsurprising to find his use of locations grand and Gothic. For much of the film, real locations ground the main school, as if its malignant presence blackens and infects everywhere around it. Be it Munich Airport where we first meet Suzy, or the foreboding Königsplatz where we see the blind pianist Daniel (Flavio Bucci) meet an untimely end, everywhere is tainted by the presence of this academy. The sense of dread is there in the locations from the off, but it's really part of an effective conjuring trick: creating a world around the school using real locations to hide the fact that the school itself is a set.

Argento achieves a strange authenticity in creating his dance academy thanks to the genuine building he borrowed from. Though not housed in the middle of a bleak forest as suggested in the film, Argento and his production designer Giuseppe Bassan were inspired by one of Freiburg's most famous buildings: the *Haus Zum Walfisch* or Whale House.

Sat in the centre of the university town, the house in its earliest form was built in the first quarter of the 1500s, and the restored building is in parts even more lavish and stylised than Argento's recreation. Though now housing part of a museum and a bank, the building is most famous for being the brief residence of noted scholar Desiderius Erasmus. The plaque seen on the outside of the real building celebrating this link is mischievously recreated by Argento for his set, knowing the irony of having an occult conspiracy housed in the refuge of one of Christianity's most noted humanists.

On my visit, it was difficult to walk around Freiburg without the film's famous soundtrack by the band Goblin playing over and over in my mind. Though far from the atmosphere of the film, with the surrounding Black Forest being more picturesque than unnerving, it was impossible to shake the music and its eerie melodies. Wandering quickly through the Old Town quarter and its narrow cobbled streets, the dramatic pink of the Whale House soon came into view.

The main entrance recreated by Argento is tucked away in Franziskanerstraße and was suitably quiet. The bikes of students were chained up along the front, while someone from the bank sat with a sandwich by the steps. Seeing the building in real life shows how brilliant Argento's facsimile really is, though it was telling from wandering around the back and seeing an even more extravagant entrance that the director took what he needed from the building and nothing more.

With the visit over, I sat in a café just around the corner, comparing the Polaroid photo I took to pictures I had of the film set on my phone, still quietly debating whether something else had been captured in recreating the building. Argento's whole cinematic project plays with the balance between garish, kitsch style and an unsettling sense of the real.

In his earlier giallo films, this is a clearer relationship, as he was always using real locations for largely earthly narratives of murder. But there's something strange about the inspiration in choosing this building and design, something that makes *Suspiria* far more effective; as if he unconsciously tapped into the potential of the genuinely otherworldly – perhaps even the occult – and unknowingly recreated and preserved it for future purposes as yet unknown.

Published by Little White Lies, 20/04/19

Jacques Tati's Tativille

Jacques Tati understood space as much as comedy. Not content with perfecting poetic laughs and visual witticisms, the director arguably also defined on screen the evolution of post-war European architecture, examining its innovations and problems as much as any individual architect or theorist.

Tati was subtly critical of some of Modernism's designs and buildings, finding humour in how people either accepted or struggled against the changes required to adapt to such calculated spaces. For Tati, these buildings sought to tidy up humanity, streamlining lives and denying wandering.

The relationship between old and new worlds is perfectly contrasted in 1958's *Mon Oncle*, which, unlike Tati's other films, goes to great pains to accentuate this collision rather than simply focus on the modern replacements. *Mon Oncle* is less about a linear narrative and more about a journey into the small everyday details of an increasingly mediated world.

It follows Tati's comic persona, Monsieur Hulot, as he navigates the changing town around him. He lives in a chaotic brick building, rides his bike around the town, and visits his nephew (Alain Bécourt) who lives in the automated world of the Arpel family; a world whose design is slowly spreading throughout the town.

Hulot's exploits come from trying to adjust to this world, and often failing. He causes dismay at the factory owned by his brother-in-law (Jean-Pierre Zola). He accidentally partakes in the practical jokes of local boys, and struggles with the changes as the cobbled roads are smothered with tarmac for cars. Most of all, Hulot shows how this new age of architecture plays into the façade of keeping up appearances.

Even though the buildings of his films are mostly designed and built especially to highlight the fallacies in the architecture, some of his locations are real. In *Mon Oncle*, Tati relies on the illusions of buildings, whether it be the wonderful ramshackle house we see him walking through via windows on each level, or the strict lines of the Villa Arpel and its absurd water fountain shaped like a fish. Tellingly, only one is celebrated by architects today.

However, it was the real-life Parisian suburb of Joinville where Tati took inspiration for the old world feel of *Mon Oncle*, and indeed, it makes up for a large chunk of the location filming when the film is not using fake buildings. Monsieur Hulot's house, for example, was still constructed and filmed in the suburb even if ultimately an illusion.

Joinville is notable for its cinematic history. It housed a successful film studio, where a number of French and American films were produced from 1910 all the way to 1987, when it eventually closed. Alongside this film heritage, Joinville eventually housed 'Tativille' for the director's next film, *Playtime* (1967); a huge metropolis of skyscrapers and blocks created solely by design and illusion, which took longer to construct than the actual filming itself.

The town is, however, most present in *Mon Oncle*, and indeed opens the film, the rustic old French streets deliberately shown in stark contrast to the building sites of the new suburbs. As Tati famously once said, 'Geometric lines do not produce likeable people.' It was the real Joinville where he found a warm, genuine humanity.

Though much of the film was shot at La Victorine studios in Nice, the film's title – scrawled in chalk on an old brick wall – was shot in Joinville. After the credits have appeared on building-site signs, we cut to a pack of dogs led by the sausage dog that lives in Villa Arpel. He runs with the loose pack, from the older roads and scrublands to the straight streets of concrete, enjoying the derelict space in between the area's many archaic lampposts. Tellingly, the pack of dogs was largely unplanned and built into the film, Tati becoming so attached to them during recording that he later found them homes once the filming had concluded.

Travelling to the suburb on a lonely winter's day, I went in search of this very particular wall from the film's opening title. It stands at the intersection of a quiet street not far from Joinville-le-Pont train station. Walking from there, the street stretched out, travelling alongside the water of the Marne. The new buildings along the high street almost knowingly mimic *Playtime*'s designs. The area cannot shake Tati's vision. I later visited the road that is named after him, Allée Jacques Tati, as well as the statue that now commemorates him further up the street.

The old brick wall has survived the development that Tati satirised, but only just. The wall stands between rue de Paris and rue de la Procession, and it's not difficult to imagine Monsieur Hulot suddenly zooming around the corner on his VéloSoleX. The building which once stood next to the wall, however, has been demolished and replaced with a plain new build.

Tativille's straight lines were always going to win out in the end, though it's pleasing to find a few of the old walls still standing in quiet rebellion, just as Monsieur Hulot would have wanted.

Published by Little White Lies, 05/08/19

François Truffaut's
Nouvelle Vague Illusions

If asked to think of a single image that defines French New Wave cinema, it's likely that the commonest answer would be that of three lovers running across a bridge. The runners are two men and a woman, though the woman is dressed in baggy men's clothing. They hop and skip in a carefree fashion down some steps towards a narrow walkway above a cacophony of railway lines, before sprinting to the opposite end. It's really that simple.

The scene is from François Truffaut's third feature film, *Jules et Jim* (1962), and showcases everything that made the *Nouvelle Vague* a breath of fresh air: youthful vibrancy, energetic camerawork and emotional detail all rendered in an endlessly cool visual style. Another dominant aspect of the *Nouvelle Vague*, borrowed partly from the *Cinéma Vérité* movement, is the use of real locations over sets; *Jules et Jim* being typical in its extensive use of a variety of locales.

The drama itself contains one of cinema's most famous *ménage-a-trois*. We follow the pair of friends of the film's title: Jules (Oskar Werner), a shy Austrian writer and Jim (Henri Serre), an excitable Frenchman. They bond over the arts and both fall madly in love with an ancient statue when on holiday. Meeting Catherine (Jeanne Moreau), who bears a remarkable resemblance to the statue, their relationship variously changes in accordance with Catherine's volatile behaviour and the world around them.

After the war, which separated the friends, they meet once again in Jules and Catherine's house in the Black Forest, the pair having had a daughter. Soon things begin to unravel as Catherine not only switches regularly between which of the friends she wants to be with, but with other men in the area, too. In typical Truffaut style, the film spells amorous tragedy.

Truffaut's film travels extensively, from Parisian streets to Alpine lodges. But its most effective and enduring moments occur in the French capital, so it seemed right to scout out one of the city's locations, the bridge being the most evocative image from the film. Of course, the film's narrative is really haunted by bridges, and not simply by the one in question.

Under a bridge joined to quai de Montebello, Catherine jumps into the Seine in her first attempt at suicide (though this may simply be a demonstration of her power over the two men). The relationship at the heart of the film also concludes on a bridge, which finalises the ultimate tragedy of the lives on show, the relationship literally driving off a broken bridge.

However, the scene of the trio running over the walkway is far more optimistic than the film's other bridges, even if it's still tinted with foreshadows of the melancholy to come. The scenario acts to convey two aspects, the first being Catherine's unpredictable nature. The trio walk down the steps to the bridge, on which she decides to race them all the way to the other side. She bolts off ahead before the final count, leaving the two men lagging behind.

Truffaut surrounds the runners with shots of the bridge, its metalwork designed to keep crossers from any possibility of getting down onto the busy train lines snaking out of Gare de Lyon. The bridge scene in some ways encapsulates the destiny of the trio, with no choice available other than to continue on in a straight line, right to the end.

The other use of the bridge is to show the first burgeoning of the *ménage-a-trois*. At the end of their run, Catherine asks Jim to help her move her cases the following day, rather than Jules. The latter shrugs off the implication of some affection between his friend and the woman he is slowly falling for by distracting himself with a witty jibe about teaching Shakespeare. But the first signs of the affair are there, and undoubtedly the three runners are effectively changed from when they first walked carefree down the steps, descending another set at the bridge's west end as potentially different people.

The original passerelle de Valmy has changed dramatically but, with there still being a footbridge in the same place, I wandered through a wintry Paris in search of it. The steps which the trio walk down start between avenue Winston Churchill and rue Marius Delcher, and descend towards the multitude of train tracks.

However, one set of steps has since been removed, with the new bridge sitting higher to accommodate the increase in trains, wires and tall railway equipment. The metal fencing that enclosed the characters has been removed and replaced with a much lower fence, allowing for a particularly brutal industrial view out over business parks, factories and other grey buildings huddled around the railway.

After taking the Polaroid photo, I began to walk to the other side of the bridge before accepting that it would be more in keeping with the spirit of the film to run. In spite of some engineers walking behind me, and perhaps causing them to think I had committed some crime, I sprinted through the winter air to the end, regretting the naïve decision only a few seconds after starting; feeling admiration for the trio of the film who kept up the pace right until the end.

I caught my breath by the other steps, noticing a grim, defunct escalator on one side and the steps which the characters walked down on the other, still surprisingly close in design to how they are seen in the film. It was, however, apparent that the Paris Truffaut captured was long gone, hidden beneath grey warehouses, cars and concrete. It was certainly no longer a bridge for lovers to run across, star-crossed or otherwise.

Published by Little White Lies, 10/03/19

Agnès Varda's Avoidance

Cléo from 5 to 7 (1962) is a wandering Parisian odyssey. With only her second feature, Agnès Varda showed her understanding of the city to be more astute than most of her equally cosmopolitan contemporaries, filming a journey through some of the capital's most picturesque and unique urban landscapes. Shooting in the streets and buildings of the Left Bank, Varda achieved a refreshing level of authenticity to her urban portrait. With such authenticity comes a multitude of possible pleasures for the film location enthusiast, with almost every frame of the film presenting a potential visit.

Varda's melancholy film follows a day, or more precisely two hours, in the life of Cléo (Corinne Marchand), a famous singer plagued by paranoia over an impending biopsy result. Her worry drives her to wander and explore Paris, sometimes forgetting her problems via friends and chance encounters, sometimes overcome with anxiety over what a potential illness could mean for her life and career.

Cléo is forced to live with chance rather than the accustomed control she is clearly used to exerting. Varda's film is essentially an anxiety map of its lead character stumbling through a day without full agency, in which the long way round is taken to get a simple answer.

As much as being a narrative, *Cléo from 5 to 7* is a cartographic document. The strength of the film comes from the veracity with which Varda captures the journey at the film's core. Paris is not fragmented but recreated as earnestly as possible, showcasing genuine haunts and realms from the period's art scene in a way only someone totally immersed in it could have known.

Being shot in this way, and with the screen filled constantly with images of Parisian walkways, buildings and streets, a full walk of the film is entirely possible, so long as its occasional taxi journey and bus ride is taken into account. Whether we would see the same city as Cléo does with her morbid gaze, however, is another question.

With so many potential locations to choose to visit, it was difficult to find one that summarised the whole film: how can a film explicitly about journeying be contained within one image? The closest answer I found was the scene in the film's finale, in which the thoughts haunting the character come to a strange, corporeal anticlimax. Cléo, along with a local soldier (Antoine Bourseiller) she has picked up as a wandering companion, finally go to the hospital to get her results.

They meet the doctor (Robert Postec) driving along the road just in time, casually giving the diagnosis out of the window of his car before departing and leaving the pair staring in amazement. But what are they watching as the shot moves off with the camera: their fears drifting away, the waste of time of the last two hours, the hope of a city seen anew?

The shot in question, in which Varda quite literally drives the camera away from the pair, is filmed on one of the cobbled roads outside of the cours Saint-Louis, the road leading to the famous L'hôpital Universitaire Pitié-Salpêtrière. Though originally starting out as a factory for gunpowder, it became a hospice for poor women, and also a prison for prostitutes. The building is equally famed for its Catholic chapel, the St Louis Chapel of Salpêtrière, commissioned by Louis XIV and designed by the same architect as Les Invalides.

Now one of Paris's most successful teaching hospitals, Cléo was in fine company in being one of its attendees. Michael Foucault and Lady Diana died there, while the hospital is generally known for its famous patients, including Alain Delon and Gérard Depardieu.

The location is interesting in the film as it really is its endpoint. Even if the film went on wandering, which would be an equally Varda-esque thing to do, this would still be the turning point, the peak. The meander we have seen throughout the whole film has been an avoidance of this place and what it represents for the character.

When Varda carries that camera away in the doctor's car, it's a telling gesture; a nod to the paranoia of the film but also an acknowledgement of its serendipity, the joy of a journey unplanned. As Lauren Elkin observes in her beautiful assessment of the film in her book *Flâneuse* (2016), 'The car pulls away and the camera with it: Cléo's shock rendered in movement, a quick back zoom travelling. Travelling shots for a travelling director.'

The film was shot during the spring equinox of 1961 and it was certainly a nicer day than my wintry visit. Walking along boulevard de l'Hôpital and trying to avoid the street-sweeping cars which drive at unusually fast speeds along the pavements, I eventually came to the gates of the hospital. The railway line from Gare d'Austerlitz runs on a raised track along the road, under which a small shanty town of tents huddled underneath, sheltering from the rain. A friendly security guard greeted me as I wandered in and started to work out which of the two roads Cléo and her soldier wander back on.

In 1961, Cléo could not have been in a better place to receive her medical news, of hope for healing. 'This neighbourhood,' she says, 'is full of hospitals. As if one were better cared for in the 13th and 14th Arrondissements.' The statement has a stark irony today considering the other vagrant wanderers taking shelter just over the road, left to walk with no end in sight.

Published by Little White Lies, 04/07/19

Film & Television

Mapping *Cléo from 5 to 7*

Cléo from 5 to 7 (1962) was only Agnès Varda's second feature film, an astonishing fact to consider. In its eighty minutes or so of running time, the director demonstrates a high level of visual and formal innovation, notably in the realm of cinematic mapping.

The film is framed around a woman walking, following in the footsteps of the mournful title character as she travels across Paris, all captured with intense geographical detail. The film is not only an enjoyably unique exploration of coming to terms with illness and mortality, but a snapshot of Paris in 1962, and even its cinematic culture.

What really allows Varda's film to stand out from its peers is how its perambulatory eye fills the screen with specific places; so much documentary detail, in fact, that a book-length essay would be worthier to cover the sheer number of interesting references to buildings, clothes, cars, objects, people, antiques and other paraphernalia that appears on screen. Even the tiniest of things seem to relate to the character's worries and concerns.

Varda's film is filled with superstition, its opening sequence of a tarot card reading draining the colour from the character's life and everything she sees. Cléo's own mortality hangs heavy over her journey, and the film explores Paris through this unusually dark emphasis.

Ultimately, Cléo finds that fear itself is largely self-perpetuating, but it was traversing the most everyday of scenarios that buffers the news of her final diagnosis. She is in search of headspace as much as physical space. But what did she see on her journey? Recounting it creates as strange an effect as filming it.

Her day:

Cléo leaves her fortune teller and walks down the street to a café, where she meets her assistant (Dominique Davray). This assistant consoles her while she spills her coffee. They overhear a couple arguing before venturing to a hat shop. 'Everything suits me,' Cléo insists, and she buys an expensive winter hat in spite of it being summer. Time is potentially extended for her by the purchase; maybe she *will* see the next winter, after all. They take a taxi to Cléo's flat and are harassed on the way by men. They laugh it off, but Cléo's darkness returns on seeing some unusual carved ornaments in a window.

Art students block the street while the taxi's radio witters of whiskey shampoo, the Algerian War, Kennedy and 'Free the Bretons'. A poster of Luis Buñuel's *Un Chien Andalou* is on a wall outside the flat. Inside, Cleo plays with a variety of kittens while enjoying her extravagant bed, a piano and other furniture. Her lover (José Luis de Vilallonga) pops round briefly before a pair of musicians – one of whom is the film's composer, Michel Legrand – visit to show her some new material. A sad song makes her weep and she leaves the flat in a black dress to wander again.

Cléo walks down the street and disturbs some pigeons. A man is performing, swallowing frogs. She flees in disgust as the eyes of men continually watch her. She heads to Le

Dôme on boulevard du Montparnasse and plays her last single on the jukebox. There are paintings on Le Dôme's walls which she looks at while she drinks cognac. The street beckons again.

Another performer disgusts her with a needle poked into his arm. She finds solace in a sculptor's studio, where her friend (Dorothée Blanck) is modelling for a class. They leave together in a car and travel to her friend's partner's cinema to drop off some reels. They watch a short film, with cameos from Anna Karina, Jean-Luc Godard, Eddie Constantine, Jean-Claude Brialy and Sami Frey. The film is, in fact, by Varda, a short ode to silent comedy called *Les fiancés du pont Mac Donald ou (Méfiez-vous des lunettes noires)*.

The women leave and walk to Le Dôme again, but there has been an accident and they decide to take another taxi. Cléo gives her friend the new hat before she leaves and is dropped off in the park. She strikes up a conversation with a soldier on leave from Algeria (Antoine Bourseiller), distracting from her worries again. They catch a bus together to the hospital, so much detail and conversation in between, arriving to find she will need two months of treatment but should be fine. Her worry drove her frantic steps, but she knows herself better now.

Why list these events? This maelstrom of information can only provide a glimpse at the endless detail of Varda's masterpiece. Critiquing the film in a traditional way (this means this; that means that) doesn't quite work. Its structure is too wandering, too drifting, like a Situationist artwork, but one that remembers to have a heart.

From recounting the bare bones of what is seen on Cléo's journey around Paris on that sad day, Varda's insatiable curiosity is obvious, and that is the real key. She understands that the ordinary has its own draws and wonders, even allowing a cursed woman to briefly forget her upcoming ordeal with illness. She didn't need any mindfulness or self-help; simply the ordinary street life of Paris. Such curiosity in the everyday, in things, thoughts and wanders, is really the raison d'être of Varda's filmmaking as a whole, and it was Cléo who first walked it into being.

Published by Little White Lies, 30/05/18

An Inventory of
Chantal Akerman's Flat

Fifty years ago this September, Chantal Akerman made her first film. It was a short, comical fragment about distraction and suicide called *Saute Ma Ville* (1968). Following Akerman herself running up to her flat, the film then shows her gradually making a mess of the kitchen where she has locked herself, taping the gaps in the door and windows ready for a slow death by gas. The screen is filled with a random assortment of objects, all abstractly dealt with by the manic character that may or may not just be Akerman messing around. Here is a list of things we see:

A small bouquet of flowers which are dragged up a flight of stairs and into the flat. They may have been bought in a shop or perhaps stolen from outside a stand, rather like the camera that was used to shoot this film. Or maybe they were a gift from someone sentimental.

A button for the lift reading 'lift' which is manically pushed though the lift is not actually taken. The lift is raced by Akerman, running up the stairs, though she loses as the lift is a lift and, being a lift, is actually faster than Akerman running up the stairs.

A poster on a door with an angry-looking Smurf on it standing under the caption 'Go home!' The Smurf is actually

Judge Smurf, a minor character from the cartoon series that barely appeared at all and which, when searching online, can only be found in the form of a physical toy rather than an image. Judge Smurf may be fond of hard boarders and possibly hold resentment, even xenophobia, towards those who live outside of the Smurf community (hence 'Go home!', as well as the fact that Father Abrahams, the Dutch songwriter who brought musical fame to the Smurfs with a variety of novelty hits, was a supporter of Hendrik Koekoek's populist Farmer's Party and recorded a hit single with the politician blaming Arabs for the 1973 oil crisis).

Two smaller pictures to the right of the Judge Smurf poster. One is of a photograph of Akerman herself with the words 'C'est Moi!' scribbled underneath, just in case the character forgot she was playing Akerman, or a performer playing someone else but who was really Akerman performing all the same. The other photograph is what looks at first to be a hand hanging down over a black background. It feels deathly and is probably not Akerman's hand, though nothing is impossible. Closer inspection reveals it, in fact, to be the face of a man looking away in disgust, probably at being misidentified as a hand that may or may not have been Chantal Akerman's.

A roll of dark sticky tape which is probably more accurately duct tape, due to its colour. It is, however, too thick to be duct tape, so, judging from its size alone, it must be Sellotape. The tape is hanging from a door handle in between being used to fill the gaps so that gas doesn't escape. It's also used later, to seal the window.

A bottle of wine which is already open. The wine is red and potent enough to make Akerman choke a bit and stare into the camera when drinking it. This is because the wine is red, and only those of a totally psychotic disposition can drink long since left-open red wine and not in some way grimace through to the fourth wall of their lives in despair as its solidified fragments trickle down the throat.

A black mac coat with white buttons and a white shawl. This is stored in a kitchen cupboard, which is far more logical a place to keep such things than first considerations suggest; of all of the rooms in the household, only a bathroom is liable to get you wetter than a kitchen. Akerman knows this, explaining why she dons it and a white headscarf when she mops the floor, which is covered in kitchen paraphernalia.

A box of Brio dishwashing powder. Brio the company now tend to make dishwashers rather than dishwashing powder. Akerman did not own a dishwasher in 1968, like many people, and her primary concern, judging by *Saute Ma Ville*, was to get the dishes washed as quickly and painlessly as possible before killing herself.

A pair of black shoes and some boot polish, which is then used to polish Akerman's legs until her white socks and skin are darkened. Polishing shoes before death is a wise choice, as the worst thing that could happen when someone finds your body would obviously be for them to exclaim, 'Look at the state of those shoes, I'd have died of shame anyway if I'd worn them in such a state.' However, polishing legs with shoe polish is not very sensible.

A copy of *Le Soir*, the daily Belgian newspaper with liberal leanings. *Le Soir* had a notably excellent crossword section in the 1960s (probably), but was also threatened with bombs for continuing to publish the cartoons of Charlie Hebdo in later years that showed the Prophet

Mohammad. It has not blown up yet (unlike Akerman's flat, which is about to).

A burnt bouquet of flowers. This may be the same bouquet as seen earlier in the film (along with a box of confectionaries). Both may have been a gift from some relationship and the reason why Akerman is contemplating suicide (the relationship, not the flowers themselves, which, while rather pathetic, are also charming in their own weak way). This is normal, as relationships often tread the fine line between flowers and suicide. These flowers are burned on the stove before the gas is left to run, perhaps in an effort to die via carbon monoxide like Sylvia Plath. However, a voice in the film cries 'Bang, bang!' and it is suggested that Akerman's character, who may or may not be Chantal Akerman, has died, not through death by carbon monoxide poisoning, but by an explosion caused by the gas coming into contact with the match. She is dead either way.

Published by Celluloid Wicker Man, 30/04/18

The Quiet City of *News from Home*

Chantal Akerman's *News from Home* (1976–77) is a visual diary reflecting a very personal episode of her history. A feature-length film of sorts, it seems born out of cathartic necessity rather than simply creative ambition.

Akerman had been working throughout the 1970s, and *News from Home* was made after her critical appreciation had grown in stature, largely thanks to the impossible-to-ignore vigour of her four-hour 1975 feature *Jeanne Dielman, 23 Quai du Commerce, 1080 Bruxelles*, as well as her coldly erotic *Je Tu Il Elle* (1976). *News from Home* feels like a project from someone earnestly haunted by certain memories, perhaps even guilt, at the sacrifices necessary to achieve her overall creative goal, choosing to look back for a moment and create something smaller in scale in comparison to films she could have probably made at that point.

News from Home is first and foremost a visual document of 1970s New York. The film has no strict narrative, but instead spends time capturing a sense of place; one surprisingly sparse for a city that supposedly doesn't sleep. Akerman frames New York with a beautiful, moody atmosphere, brought over from the earlier *Hotel Monterey* (1972), creating an Edward Hopper-esque aesthetic of low-lights for low streets.

The Hopper comparison is one often discussed, but Akerman's film genuinely manifests his ideals without the intention of mere mimicry; the two artists sharing a general interest in the interpretation of space and light. These are the shadowy dawns and dusks that drape a spectral sheath over the everyday rumblings of American city life.

'Maybe I am not very human,' Hopper once suggested, 'what I wanted to do was to paint sunlight on the side of a house.' Akerman channels this idea, and also answers the question that Hopper rhetorically poses: what does such urban light really look like?

Akerman moved to New York in the early 1970s to become a filmmaker, though not before working numerous low-paid jobs, infamously but appropriately selling tickets at a porn theatre to buy her celluloid stock (which likely allowed her to watch the city safely during all those mysterious hours usually unseen by the majority of the public).

Akerman's film is a manifestation of the very human desire to want to document the sun on the side of the house, the *Nighthawks*-esque hotel, the empty streets, and the early-morning train station. But she also quietly suggests that it's only humanistic to do so if shot through with personal reflection. She's not a disinterested observer hovering above it all but an active participant.

New from Home is connected to Akerman's personal life through the presence of a voice-over reading out letters sent to the young director by her mother when she first moved away. In other words, she was living in this city to make her work, and, to do so, she was forced to have a more sparing relationship with her parents.

Capturing light is something to do when parents are far away. It's still humanistic, but Akerman is clearly addressing some self-accusation, some guilt lingering from her earlier days of creative struggle. It's a natural phenomenon, but one that sits in contrast to the growing distance clearly present in the letters themselves.

The viewer never hears what Akerman sends back, tellingly, but it's obvious that her replies became less frequent, less personal. She chose to hide the life she was leading in order to stay true to her own creativity. The mother's voice becomes cloying and increasingly desperate to know what her daughter is doing to sustain herself. Akerman doesn't even tell her she is moving apartments until long after the event, in spite of receiving a steady flow of money, support, and even occasionally clothing.

Akerman has to walk the streets to create her work (both in the sense that she worked her jobs in the city, and in the physical sense of actually shooting the film herself). By doing this, she needed to throw off the loving shackles of her home life. Yet it also seems like a pertinent sacrifice in hindsight; if she hadn't succumbed to this, painting her city with the same moody pallets and philosophy as Hopper, then perhaps Akerman would not have become the creative success that allowed her to eventually return home (a theme she would explore in *Les Rendez-Vous d'Anna* (1978), which hints at an appropriately negative outcome).

News from Home is one of the most affecting critiques of the creative process and the personal sacrifices often required to fulfil them. Akerman's film suggests that this results in a loss of humanity, but not in a negative or permanent way.

The city is consolation in itself for the sacrifice.

Her distance and selfish determination to create would flower into a startling artistic talent, but the journey was always circular rather than simply linear: the city, another, and then another.

No mother stood a chance.

Published by Celluloid Wicker Man, 16/06/14

All the Lonely People:
Les Rendez-vous d'Anna

Chantal Akerman's early features have one aspect in common: all are suffused with loneliness. In her first fiction feature, *Je Tu Il Elle* (1974), a character wanders between lovers old and new but is always confused as to what she really wants, eventually content with isolation. In *Jeanne Dielman, 23 Commerce Quay, 1080 Brussels* (1975), we follow a woman trapped in the monotony of a mysteriously empty life with her son. Even in her documentaries, Akerman possessed a vagabond approach haunted by solitude.

The peak for Akerman's loneliness is arguably in her film *Les Rendez-vous d'Anna* (1978). More so than her previous films, Akerman affirmed the melancholy of constant travel through her most ambitious set of visual scenarios.

Les Rendez-vous d'Anna follows film director Anna (Aurore Clément) as she travels around Europe attending screenings of her films. On her way, she meets a man in Germany, Heinrich (Helmut Griem), who she initially takes back to her hotel to sleep with before being unable to go through with it. She instead opts to meet his family the next day and hear the story of his sad life.

She then travels again, meeting a friend of her mother and, eventually, her mother herself (Lea Massari), in whom she confides her first experience of intimacy with another woman. Finally, travelling back to her home city, she goes to a hotel with an ex-lover (Jean-Pierre Cassel) before ultimately ending up alone in her flat, listening to answerphone messages.

Journey

Akerman herself was a traveller, venturing around the world with only a vague sense of belonging. Anna is clearly a shadow version of Akerman, a distanced film director who is unsure as to what she really wants from life. In many ways, she becomes the marionette of her film producers, wandering in a daze through a variety of European cities, not quite sure why she is really there.

Her life is a zoetrope of lifeless train stations, banal hotel rooms and late-night cafés. She fails at intimacy in almost every instance and, played over the backdrop of a reduced editing style, the film captures the engulfing stasis of loneliness in all its silent grace, even when constantly on the move across landscapes.

The opening shot is almost a mission statement for this loneliness. A fixed image of a German train station shows a coldly symmetrical composition of stairs leading down from the platform. We hear a train arriving, though the camera refuses any break in the stasis. Huddles of people busily rush down the stairs, shuffling on to the next short moment of their lives.

One woman, our protagonist, detaches herself from this crowd, perhaps unwillingly and with little choice. She heads to a phone box but the camera still refuses to move: Akerman even denies her the company of the viewers themselves as she makes her call. She finally wanders back down the stairs, which are deserted; her work (or perhaps her love life, it's uncertain in this instance) has separated her from everyone.

The film's travelling is similar in tone to this scene, with a rigid inability to find any destination. Though she converses with fellow travellers on trains, Anna rarely takes anything in. So many of the conversations that float her way are one-sided, allowing others to express and detail the problems they cannot otherwise share. She becomes a key to unlock the frustrations of those around her on these tedious journeys, though she never ultimately resolves her own turmoil.

The journeying means she's never really there, never fixed, always clock-watching for the time of the next train or meeting. Anna is a phantasm of the city, never able to establish anything as the momentum of her work drags her on, casting everyone around her to the wayside of the train lines.

Motherhood

A strange emotional haze is present throughout large parts of the film. The feeling finds a symbolic visual in Anna's first hotel visit. The room she is staying in has large windows, covered with a thin, white curtain obscuring the view. Anna pulls it back and the camera follows her, creating a hypnotic image of a determined attempt to regain clarity. But behind the obscured image was only further evidence of how alone she is; how empty she feels on this meaningless meander back home. The emptiness gains greater specificity as the conversations between her and a variety of people amplify her solitude.

When she visits Heinrich's family, the conversation revolves around his own failed marriage, but the presence of both his mother and daughter frames Anna's life in interesting ways. We barely see them converse, and Akerman skips the potential scene of them all eating together. Instead, we hear of the dinner in hindsight, where Anna is then asked for her opinion of the two women. It highlights Anna's dual role as daughter and as a childless woman. The whole scenario cannot help but feel constructed to highlight her isolation and the parallel world she potentially could have inhabited as a mother herself.

In journeying back to her own mother, the distance becomes clear: this is a rare occurrence for Anna, as if facing her mother highlights her own childlessness. The wandering journey of the film seems a failed search for the children she never had, confirmed finally by her empty, decidedly single flat in Paris at the film's conclusion.

It also partly links to the muted sexuality of the character. She is unable to fully commit to any one liaison or even bother to conclude them. In a later scene when her ex-lover begins to explain his own isolation, he professes his ideal world is one where he is a woman who has one child, dedicating his life to it. It's as if every aspect of reality unconsciously derides Anna's position.

It speaks of a quiet, constant and very real social pressure.

Sexuality

Sex is icy in Akerman's film, though this is part of a continued trend from her earlier cinema. In *Je Tu Il Elle*, the daringly extended lesbian sex scene is really one of the coldest in

1970s cinema (contrary to its constant GIF-ified presence on websites like Tumblr and Twitter). The characters are so unsure about what they want that they resort to literally throwing their bodies clumsily towards one another in the hope of rekindling the romance that was once there. It's almost a confused violence rather than passion.

Akerman employs the same effect in *Les Rendez-vous d'Anna*, with the failed sex scene with Heinrich, the man similarly throwing his body at Anna, trying to evoke some reaction in return. But she remains passive, lifeless. Later on, revisiting her ex-lover, the sexual tension of the scene similarly fizzles to nothing, with both characters instead enraptured by the vast city that lies outside of the window before the man becomes ill.

The only sexual satisfaction Anna has is in the past tense, recounting to her mother the moment she fell into bed with a woman in Italy, itself seemingly only by chance. The moment of this admission is unusual in that both Anna and her mother are themselves in bed, frozen and unsure how to react. It feels as if Anna is trying to explain to herself what happened and why she still phones the woman, though she never gets an answer, of course.

She professes love but it sounds hollow, with the overwhelming context of the film colouring it as yet another lost moment in a series of empty steps to nowhere. Sex is a strange performance, in which it is no longer possible to indulge with total abandon when the knowledge of people's ultimate transience is a persistent spectre. There's nothing left but the self when cut loose from the emotional responsibility towards others, even when merely expressed through physical lust.

Ghostly Repetition

Akerman has a final, tragic trajectory for Anna. It's not simply that the apartment she eventually finds herself in is cold, empty and with the lights off, but it's the answer machine that ghosts the lost moments of previous days when Anna was travelling.

A number of voices speak from the past. One is possibly the Italian woman she has been trying and failing to call at various points on her journey. Some are friends expressing a desire to meet, perhaps for more reasons than simply amiable company. But the most blunt is from her producer, suggesting that another such tour is about to come up, meaning yet more travelling. This time it will be through various cities in Switzerland. It's a quietly brutal realisation of stolen agency: that Anna's life is circular and out of her hands.

Considering the freedom Akerman expressed in her documentary film *News from Home*, this film feels like a crash down to earth: growing older and realising that the things that matter have long been trampled to pulp under a desire for artistic expression and success.

Anna's journey has this circular shape because that is what constitutes loneliness; its never-ending monotony, its lack of physical fixation. When Akerman addressed some of these issues in *Jeanne Dielman*, she did so by extending the length of shots, repeating household rituals and movements as Delphine Seyrig tried to normalise her own behaviour and isolation, albeit a static one. In *Les Rendez-vous d'Anna*, Akerman has evolved and is looking at a different type of isolation.

Rather than being one whose illusion would collapse if the confines of the four walls of domesticity were broken, this loneliness of total freedom dogs a woman across a whole continent just as persistently, toying with the constant dissatisfaction that a hollow life ultimately nourishes. It makes for what is surely one of Akerman's strongest films, but also one of her most honest; in which she faces head-on the drifting reality of a creative life.

Loneliness never felt so inevitable.

Published by Celluloid Wicker Man, 14/10/19

The Temporal Disjoints
of Marguerite Duras

Marguerite Duras never gave cinema an easy time. Adapting her own stories into feature films, the writer, rather than compromise the unusual qualities of her books, instead experimented and destabilised the narrative aspects of film to suit her needs.

Like her contemporary Alain Robbe-Grillet, Duras made many attempts to transplant the elements of voice from her literary work into film, usually involving one specific technique: the detaching of the voice from the body of the performers. Much has been written of the disembodied voice, especially in audio-visual theory that focuses heavily on the surreal presence of voice-over dialogue in popular cinema (with particular interest in film noir), but Duras's striving to make the form fit her own narrative style often meant that her work defied some of the more conventional practices.

When first watching her brilliant 1975 feature *India Song*, a sense of the uncanny was present from the very start. It was only some way into the film that it became clear why this was; that the voices we hear the characters communicate with are in the soundtrack, rather than diegetically there. We do not see them speak. The place of the film's setting suddenly becomes out of joint, out of time.

The narrative is opaque and, rather like Robbe-Grillet's *Last Year in Marienbad*, it follows a group of interconnected characters wandering through a large mansion, dreaming each other into existence. Actors such as Delphine Seyrig and Michel Lonsdale look on at each other, acting the meaning of their dialogue but never opening their mouths to speak it. There could be several reasons for this, but the decision is part of Duras's overall experimentation with the voice-to-narrative relationship. The overriding feeling in *India Song*, even with the luscious costumes and splendour, is that the film's visual is dramatically within the past tense; that we are watching ghosts looking back, the glamorous dead reliving their favourite local haunt.

Duras's smaller-scale films use similar techniques, in particular disrupting the sense of place by knocking its sounds and dialogue out of sync. In many of her shorter films, the voice is again disembodied but has no specific ownership or source, creating the feeling that the film is haunted by unseen spectres.

In her 1981 film *Agatha and the Limitless Readings*, a similar scenario to *India Song* is played out in the desolate seaside resort of Trouville. The rupture is even more exaggerated, perhaps to highlight the film's role as an essay, with cameras being seen in mirrors and with actors (including Bulle Olgier) improvising their way physically around the large rooms and wintry beachscapes.

The fact that the narrative is addressing childhood memories, including an incestuous relationship, perhaps begins to explain why this distancing technique is opted for by Duras. The traumas – sexual, colonial, and emotional – are almost too dramatic to face head-on and would be rendered melodramatic by their simplistic recreation. Duras slips the characters into the past, the present always off screen but echoing through the soundtrack.

The same seaside resort can be found in a number of her films, though not always using the same technique. The ensemble drama *Woman of the Ganges* (1974) uses the same set-up but keeps the dialogue and the visual attached, creating a lesser effect and film. The disjoint is, however, retained for the short film *L'homme Atlantique* (1981), made at the same time as *Agatha*.

The main character's voice is lost entirely and given over to Duras's instead. The disjoint frames the film further as an essay; her writing style often finding drama in essayistic styles. The same rings true for her films.

In *Agatha* in particular, the questioning highlights the very process of filmmaking, almost as if Duras is satirising cinema or at the least questioning its legitimacy for dealing with personal, dramatic issues (the same contradictions that Michael Haneke has been dealing with for most of his career). The fact that this technique is adhered to, in spite of using some of the most famous French performers (who possess some incredibly distinctive voices), shows how important this questioning is for Duras. Even France's most celebrated stars are denied the connection of their voices to their lips when Duras is behind the camera.

Perhaps most interestingly, the form breaks down in a film where the voice is retained. In *La Camion* (1977), the structure, while having the voice disembodied throughout several shots of a lorry on a journey, is grounded by Duras herself reading and discussing the script with Gérard Depardieu. Even if the disjoint is, on a visual level, lesser in this case because the sound can always be reframed back to the setting of the drawing room where the reading takes place, the film is the most temporally fluctuating of Duras's features. The lorry's journey feels to be through time as much as space.

The disjoint instead comes from inverting the filmic process, amalgamating a practical element of the film's production (the script reading) into the very narrative itself. More than simply allowing a camera to be shown in the reflection of a mirror, Duras breaks apart the whole of the cinematic process, à la Jean-Luc Godard, allowing access to the emotional resonances of the work but through an open break that evidences an unusual level of trust in the viewer.

Published by Celluloid Wicker Man, 26/02/18

Jean-Luc Godard's Libidinal Circuits

Jean-Luc Godard often explored the relationship between politics and the spaces it influences. The more recognisable turn of modern urban spaces happened to coincide with his own sharp turn towards political questioning, especially in films such as *Tout va bien* (1972), *La Chinoise* (1967), and *Week-end* (1967), looking in particular at a factory, an inner-city flat, and a busy roadway. These spaces provided more than a backdrop for Godard's political arguments: they visually manifested them.

The best example of this relationship between space and politics is, however, in another film he made in 1967: *Two or Three Things I Know About Her*. The film, a kind of dark visual cousin to Jacques Tati's *Playtime* (1967), was spawned from the magazine *Le Nouvel Observateur*, which published an article, followed by a series of responsive letters (always a dangerous indulgence), regarding the subject of casual prostitution increasingly practised by middle-class women.

The rise in such a phenomenon was linked to various social changes. After all, this was only a year before the riots of May '68; the permissive society had been in full swing in the west for several years; and the general social unrest in many nations led to a time of stark change.

Godard ties the ideas down to two specific factors, instead of simply the bubbling-up of the 1960s habit of sloganeering for revolution:

The social pressure exerted upon society, especially woman, by materialism.

The effect that the power of such materialism has on the living spaces of the urban and suburban areas, around Paris especially.

The two aspects are linked explicitly in the film, mixing Godard's burgeoning essayistic style with a fictional dramatisation following suburban housewife Juliette Janson (Marina Vlady). After dropping off her child at a day-care centre, she is shown to embark on her usual day of casual prostitution.

Essentially, Godard is one of the first filmmakers to tie post-war materialism and sexuality together, arguing that the sexual revolution would ultimately mean commodification rather than the easy freedoms it promised. The fact that he does so with a keen eye on the psychogeographical aspects of Parisian development during the era only shows his further skill in addressing multiple ideas, at least at that point in his career. It was a creative skill he would arguably lose as he became more and more militant.

The film opens with a statement connecting the concept of 'Her' (*Elle*) to the spatial area of 'The Paris Region' (*La région Parisienne*), and this is the film's chief gambit: the blurring of the female body with the living spaces of Paris.

For Godard, both are for sale.

It's worth noting that the film was made in the same year that Guy Debord, the shambolic Situationist who connected commercialism with urban change well before Godard, published his most definitive work, *The Society of the Spectacle*. Surprisingly, with the rest of the film's numerous literary references, Godard failed to reference Debord, as the two were on the exact same lines on this matter of place and commodification changing social mores.

This being said, Debord rejected Godard's work on the grounds that its own (then admittedly waning) obsession with popular culture undermined his general radical position, still speaking to the commercial masses; such is the po-faced seriousness of most hard-leaning political artists. Professing an inverse ratio between accessibility and authenticity is a common trait of such radical artists and their petty infighting, even today.

Hindsight shows Debord to be overly judgemental in the case of Godard's 1960s output; he would soon be making just the kind of impenetrable political treatises that Debord saw as the future, and Godard would spend the next decade paying for it in creative purgatory as he went further down the cinematic and political cul-de-sac.

Their ambivalent relationship aside, Debord suggested the same effects of the changes in the living spaces within post-war cities that Godard encounters in *Two or Three*. In *The Society of the Spectacle*, Debord suggests why this is, writing that:

> Urbanism is the mode of appropriation of the natural and human environment by capitalism, which, true to its logical development toward absolute domination, can (and now must) refashion the totality of space into its own peculiar decor.

The natural fallout of this is not only visual (the film basking in the developments of many typical high-rise blocks and motorways) but also social. *Two or Three* looks to this fallout, where the race towards consumerism (itself a circular journey that can never be completed with its desire for infinite growth) is only achievable for household women such as Juliette if they also sell their bodies; the social and physical body being 'refashioned' into the 'peculiar décor' of urbanism.

This relationship, however, must have some greater enabler than simply the desire for the latest gadgets, fashions and household goods, which is basically how Godard naïvely frames it.

To somewhat counter this simplistic aspect of the film, Godard makes the link between the design of these spaces, built out of (and for) materialistic consumption, and the potential for the women to, in a sense, throw off the moral mores of middle-class life through the very architecture they live around. It's a not dissimilar escape explored by Luis Buñuel in *Belle de Jour* (1967) around the same time, with Catherine Deneuve released from her class responsibilities by casual prostitution. It's a fetish many European directors, chiefly male, indulged in throughout the 1960s.

Many shots show Juliette outside one of the high-rise blocks, suggesting that a 'landscape is like a face'. This builds a link between the space where she lives and the space of her body; the link which pushes her to seeing prostitution in the spare hours of her day as being perfectly sensible.

The film has some bizarre moments because of this link, especially when considering the paranoia over the way women are forced to operate in these spaces. Godard throws suspicion of prostitution upon *every* woman in the film. Even when they don't for one moment suggest the possibility of selling of their bodies for sex, there's an underlying suspicion that any woman living comfortably in this area is doing so only by means of prostitution. It's a misguided, misogynistic absurdity. Understanding women has hardly ever been one of the director's strengths.

The point, however, is that he's not extending such potential simply out of paranoia, but out of a growing disgust at the system that is effectively forcing at least *some* women into such situations. Godard lays the blame at the feet of the developer, the politician, and the prefect of management at the company Spatial Planning, Paul Delouvrier, who oversaw many of the real developments used in the film.

Going on the programme *Zoom* (1966), Godard went head-to-head on the subject with government official Jean Saint-Geours, the results of which were telling. In the debate, Godard links prostitution to outside factors, suggesting the simplistic Marxist-tinged view that any person working for solely commercial purposes (such as advertising) is working in a form of prostitution anyway, and that both mental and physical forms of selling oneself are an outcome of the consumerist environment.

'To me,' he argued, 'it's not an individual phenomena but a collective one.' We are all technically hookers of some form in Godard's eyes, which perhaps shows the unabashed ridiculousness of such May-'68-ish thinking.

Jacques Tati was far more effective in critiquing the same modern developments of Paris in the phenomenal *Playtime* (1967). The buildings of that film, the famed

'Tati-ville' set, mocked post-war architecture with absolute precision. They also, unsurprisingly, did not simplistically turn their female occupants into sex-workers, and Tati did not require a lecturing Marxist treatise on political autonomy to sell *Playtime* as a work of art, either.

In Godard's defence, Saint-Geours fared no better on *Zoom*, describing the difference between casual and committed prostitution with all the subtlety of a pimp. 'One is a case of over-adaptation to our consumer society,' he argued, 'the occasional prostitute who quickly realises that a comfortable life requires money... The other is a typical case of a maladjusted woman gradually destroying herself.' This crass overview is typical of the period in its blanket assertions: women doing this are either greedy or lowlifes. He does, however, make the assertion that 'nothing encourages these phenomena more than large cities'. On that point, he and Godard were in agreement.

The final scene of the film, a moment in which consumer product packaging fills the screen, is an unusually poignant one. The shot shows a strange alignment of various boxes of household products on the grass outside an apartment block, rather like a model plan for the development. If attention has been paid to Godard's imagery throughout the film, the likeness between these boxes and their adjacent housing development will be obvious.

Godard is making one final stark statement: that, like those small boxes which hold the product, the buildings hold their own contents for sale – the occupants, the people, the women – in the same commodified way. Their ability to sustain themselves in the area is a fallacy: to live in these boxes is to be turned into a product, a product which must be sold if you desire to live in the boxes in the first place.

C'est la vie.

Published by Celluloid Wicker Man, 25/01/16

Fernweh and *The Green Ray*

I recently finished a draft of a novel which follows a lone woman cast adrift by the news of her father's suicide. Her grief manifests in a strange obsession with the town of Strasbourg, where she decides on a whim to stay over the winter. In one part of the novel, my character looks into the concept of fernweh, though her research of the concept was as much for my benefit as hers.

The concept, roughly speaking, is the feeling of those who feel the need to travel with no attachment to home, even though home is where everyone at some point ends up. It's neither an opposite of *unheimlich* nor simply another way of addressing wanderlust, its twee and optimistic cousin. Instead, it's somewhere in between, and not always a positive psychological perspective to share.

In my book, this feeling is negative, and I believe that the momentary characterising of the term as such came for me when watching Éric Rohmer's film *The Green Ray* (1986) during the writing.

Rohmer's film follows a young, nervous woman called Delphine (Marie Rivière) who has been left hanging in more ways than one. It's summer, and all her plans to travel are in tatters. Her relationship has recently collapsed, and her best friend has dropped her from their planned trip to Greece as she has a new boyfriend. The film follows Delphine on her three attempts to get away from Paris to various holiday destinations before reluctantly admitting defeat and returning earlier than planned each time.

She is first stuck awkwardly with a group of couples near the sea, and is unable to fit in. Then she visits the Alps, but is put off by tourists. Her final trip to a beach resort finds her frustrated at the role she is forced into as a lone woman on holiday. Even Paris is unable to satiate her changing emotions, the need to get away growing again each time.

The film then jumps track to her final failed holiday. During her departure back to Paris, she meets a man she instantly connects with. She decides to travel with him and finally sees 'the green ray': a rare optical phenomenon that sometimes occurs before the sun rises or sets, a green spot or flash briefly shining. The ray has esoteric qualities, with Delphine having earlier overheard a conversation about Jules Verne's writing on the subject.

In the film's final moments, she cries at the sight of this light and a whole host of emotions and realisations overwhelm the character. It's one of Rohmer's strongest, most beautiful conclusions.

However, the mentality that led to her seeing green ray itself is more interesting than the finale. Delphine spends most of her time feeling on edge, suffering from anxiety attacks brought on by the horrifying mechanics of flirting when newly single. Single life seems pointless when fresh out of a long and serious relationship. The breaking of long-term relationships renders the theatre of single life absurd (and vice versa).

On paper, Delphine could be said to have wanderlust in very general terms, but it's too optimistic a concept to do justice to her worries and melancholy. Fernweh is a far better diagnosis of Delphine's state of mind.

She's detached enough from her home in Paris to drift. Anything is better than wasting the warm months in the city where she lives, and her break-up has coloured and changed Paris for her anyway. This drifting only returns her home out of unhappiness rather than homesickness. Unlike the travel-blogging appropriation of wanderlust, with its Instagram-friendly editing of filtered vistas, such actions fail to satisfy (and never really can satisfy) the sadness inside Delphine as she carries it with her.

It's only by chance that she meets someone, finally: a man who does not turn them into farcical performers in some elaborate game leading to empty sex. Chance hangs heavy over the film, embedded in the narrative via the overhearing of Verne's folkloric interpretation of the ray.

The evolution from fernweh to wanderlust is the film's last shift, but Delphine is still forced to look within herself in that final moment of happiness and chance. Perhaps the tears are flowing at the realisation of further drifting to come.

In that moment, however, she rekindles briefly a youthful daring, even if, by doing so, she's also looking back upon all the mistakes and loneliness that led there. Finally finding true escape is overwhelming, even when it only flashes for a second as the sun sets.

Published by Celluloid Wicker Man, 21/05/18

Cartography in *Le Pont du Nord*

In 1946, Jorge Luis Borges published his story 'On Exactitude in Science'. The piece is a fragment of a fictional 1658 volume written by the equally fictitious Suárez Miranda. Its story addresses the role of cartography, relying upon the ironic endeavour of a group of cartographers attempting to make a 1:1 scale map, the map referring back to the original with such precision that it sits like a second skin over the very place it was designed to map.

It's a typically Borgesian impossibility. Yet it was when reading this short that I started to think about cinematic mapping, about the time-image and cinema as a temporal medium as a whole. In other words, how certain possibilities deemed impossible in the plastic art of mapmaking found a familiar guise in cinema. With this, the first film that instantly sprung to mind was Jacques Rivette's strange but hypnotic *Le Pont du Nord* (1981).

Rivette's film follows two women (played by mother/daughter pair Bulle and Pascale Ogier) as they attempt to solve a mystery that takes them all over Paris. The city is in flux; being gradually redeveloped with buildings crumbling or demolished, land left to grow over and even central Paris feeling unstable. The city becomes a game, quite literally, with the narrative structured around the Game of the Goose.

A map of the city appears throughout, modified to account for this game's restrictions, further enhanced by mysterious packages sent by the ominous Max (Jean-François Stévenin). Tying the film into Borges is a relatively reasonable proposition, considering that the paths lead to some centre, resembling a labyrinth.

The film takes on more of Borges's ideas from 'On Exactitude' in that the mapping of the city, 1:1, feels tangibly possible in the film, the process of filming at times measuring the city through time and physical space.

Rivette is one of the directors who embodies best Gilles Deleuze's concept of the time-image and its basis in cinema. Time is no longer subordinate to movement in the images that are captured, according to Deleuze; time itself becomes directly present rather than merely represented. Limiting cuts and edits refuse to ease its passing. The viewer should *feel* time in its rawest form.

When Rivette films Pascale Ogier riding her moped repeatedly around a roundabout adorned with lions (Le Triomphe de la République in particular) the space is mapped by the literal time it takes for her to explore it. It's not the entirety of Paris, but it's certainly a temporal cousin to Borges's ambitious mapmakers; if the unnamed cartographers were filmmakers instead, they would likely resemble Jacques Rivette.

Rivette maps streets in real-time, or as close to real-time as is possible before cutting between segments. It's not an exact fit (he still cuts, even within scenes), but the drive is there, as is the potential to extend it. He tellingly had already tried a more extreme version of this in *Out 1* (1971), resulting in a film that was over twelve hours long. The most open-minded of producers, even in 1971, probably had to have words with the director.

We forget sometimes when looking at maps that they are a measure of time as much as they are of space, even if not accurate but merely an insinuation, an estimate. This is a palpable element in Rivette's film.

When the characters examine their maps, especially when comparing a variety of maps they have come across – using one to decode the meaning of the other – I thought of what Borges said in his short story. 'In time,' he wrote, 'those Unconscionable Maps no longer satisfied, and the Cartographers Guilds struck a Map of the Empire whose size was that of the Empire, and which coincided point for point with it.'

I can't quite make the link to what this says about Rivette's film, when really the maps and their meaning are deliberately unfathomable. But I feel for sure that the link is there somehow; an attempt to find a new understanding to an evolving reality: the reality of Paris.

In other words, the two characters were themselves in a map of sorts, created by their own movements; where certain roads and places were mapped in the scale of 1:1, drawn with the cartographic randomness that can only be achieved via physically drifting through streets and through time with a film camera.

Or it could simply be a meaningless game.

Life, like cinema, can be like that.

Published by Celluloid Wicker Man, 12/03/18

The Wastelands of *Série Noire*

A man dances in a wasteland. It's a damp, empty landscape consisting solely of grey, sticky mud and the odd rock. A burst tyre lies next to a large pool of water where the man has parked his cheap car. Paris tower blocks rise depressingly in the distance: this is the very edge of the city, forgotten vistas where no one bothers to visit.

And yet the man dances. At first he seems nervous, looking around with the wide eyes of an animal expecting to be attacked. He runs back to his car, diving for cover, before slowly stepping back out into the mud, about to reach for something: a gun of his own?

He pulls out a personal transistor from his tattered Burberry mackintosh and hits the play button. He begins to bop to the rhythm of the music that crackles out, putting the radio on the car bonnet as he begins an invisible waltz to Duke Ellington through the rubbish with a woman who isn't there.

This is the opening of Alain Corneau's *Série Noire* (1979), an adaptation of Jim Thompson's *A Hell of a Woman* (1954). Unlike Thompson's novel, the film opens with a sequence that suggests nothing but the sadness and desperation of its lead character, and with what feels like a deeply Gallic irony. Corneau was assisted in the adaptation by author Georges Perec, and I believe this to be one of the reasons for this opening; where a place is chosen to express the loneliness and attitude of the main character, soon to be shown as unstable, violent and hopeless, rather than something more dramatically typical.

The film follows Franck Poupart (Patrick Dewaere), a desperate door-to-door salesman, as he hatches a plan with underage prostitute Mona (Marie Trintignant) to steal money she has earned from her pimping aunt (Jeanne Herviale). The plan becomes complicated by both Frank's suspicious boss (Bertrand Blier) and the fact that the young girl is playing games of her own.

This opening scene is, however, a concoction of Corneau's and Perec's alone rather than Thompson's. The writer opens his novel with a scene adapted further into the film when Frank finally meets Mona; something that makes sense in an American cultural context (character and narrative being the dominant Hollywood lynchpins, at least until it sold out to pure spectacle). What is it, then, about this wasteland scene that Perec and Corneau thought made it ripe material for opening with, rather than sticking with the novel's jump-starting of the relationship between the two leads?

This landscape, filmed in the Parisian suburb of Créteil when it was still being turned from a functioning quarry into a drab post-modernist dystopia, is returned to regularly, always in Frank's car. It's a landscape of murky morals, and is clearly important to the film.

The first problem that concerned Perec and Corneau was how to transfer the character of a typically American novel to France without too much rupture. Perec himself was enlisted to work specifically on this problem, as detailed in a behind-the-scenes news report that interviewed both writer and director.

Perec seems an unusual choice, especially as his role specifically relates to dialogue; his novels are more often than not devoid of it. But Perec needed money quickly, and turned to cinema for a more regular income than publishing his long and complicated novels. Still, Perec's linguistic skill with dirty and brutal *argot* drags the film fully into a Gallic mode, and he more than justified his presence.

There's something very Perec-esque about this opening, as well; its seeming pointlessness to the narrative showcasing a detailed quirk of the main character that helps to understand his mentality but little else. In typical Perec fashion, place comes to be much more than a setting, a heightened reflection of a character.

Everything that occurs in the film can be considered as a knock-on effect of this character's instability. Therefore, a scene showing the range of his delusions and fantasies arguably foreshadows the whole of the film's grimy, desperate narrative. How low do you have to be to dance alone in a Parisian suburb's quarry?

Perec suggested in the interview to coincide with the film's production that there was a certain 'zooming-in' narrative effect that, though increasingly present in novels then (especially his own work), was actually something owed to cinematic narratives more than literature; the audience subjected to a closer and closer inspection of a world in miniature.

It mirrors Perec's own narrative tricks, especially in *Life A User's Manual* (1978), which gradually builds interconnecting stories of a housing block by getting closer and closer to the lives of the individuals who live there (and in a level of intense detail). Film arguably does this, too, albeit in a far more accessible and less experimental way, as description of the surroundings and action is not needed. The right *mise-en-scène* can detail what would take pages of prose in a novel. Perec was envious of cinema's ability to do this.

I like to imagine the opening of *Série Noire* occurring on the page in the style of Perec's prose. He could have produced a wonderful novelisation of the film, the sort of back-and-forth strangeness of adapting a film adaptation of an already existing novel no doubt a perfect puzzle for the writer. The amount of detail could have been potentially spectacular: the information of the area in which it is taking place, what is happening there (including an itinerary of the horrific building plans), what was there before, the make and design of the man's car and where he bought it, the history of the music that plays on the little stereo (a very grainy Ellington recording by any standard), and a detailed description of the dance that the man performs.

Broken down into its component parts, the viewer not only gets a sense of how isolated the character is, but a huge array of secondary information that has certain accumulative effects as the film progresses. The rest of Corneau's film is more typical of that period's noirs; what I sometimes call icy-noir. It was a genre perfected by Jean-Pierre Melville, especially in *Un Flic* (1972), but also found as a general aesthetic in quieter, non-crime films including Chantal Akerman's *Les Rendez-vous d'Anna* (1978).

Icy-noir is filled with wintry films, often shot with what looks like a filter of light blue over the camera lens. *Série Noire* has this look as well, but adds extra layers through Perec and his influence of place and detail; where a man dancing in a forgotten muddy patch of land outside of Paris gains a great deal of meaning, and becomes the most beautifully unnecessary opening scene in French cinema.

Published by Celluloid Wicker Man, 12/02/18

Snails and Death in
Diary of a Chambermaid

When I think of the films of Luis Buñuel, the first image from his oeuvre that comes to mind is that of the corpse of a murdered child. Her legs are strewn among the branches in a deep, dark wood. Snails are slowly making their way across her skin.

The image in question is from Buñuel's 1964 film *Diary of a Chambermaid*; a relatively straight film for the director and lacking the overt surrealism that he was known for.

Based on the admittedly trite novel by anarchist libertine Octave Mirbeau, the narrative follows maid Céléstine (Jeanne Moreau), who takes up residence in the country house of an eccentric, troubled family.

She indulges the various male employers' needs and fetishes, which range from simple flirtation to a leather boot fixation. An abrasive gardener with fascist leanings, Joseph (Georges Géret), is most enamoured with her, however, though this doesn't stop him violently murdering and raping a little girl called Claire (Dominique Sauvage) on the estate. Determined to prove his guilt, Céléstine tries to plant evidence and have him charged. But the man's political leanings, in an age of rising fascism, guarantee his freedom. The film ends in Joseph's new café in Cherbourg as a fascist parade proudly marches by.

The film is essentially about the violence and fetishism that goes hand-in-hand with organised hatred. There are so many subdivisions within the film through its variety of characters, however, that to generalise about its intention can undermine its detail. The main theme is, of course, fascism: its sleazy rise, the hatred and hypocrisy that propel it, and the silence that contributes to its growth.

It may be for this reason that I find the image in question so poignant, so disturbing and yet so in touch with the land, too. For the director, there really was blood in the soil.

The central murder at the heart of the film is never seen, but instead is abstractly portrayed. Joseph is taking his cart through the woods when he comes across Claire. She was merely wandering through the trees, collecting snails and eating blackberries. He offers her a lift, but she refuses and goes back into the forest. He carries on his way, but thoughts clearly begin to circle within him. He checks the surroundings to make sure no one is around before leaving the cart and running into the forest after her.

Buñuel cuts to an obvious piece of symbolism, first a hog running in the forest and then a baby rabbit, before cutting again. This time the image is stark and not strictly chronologically measured, as clearly some minutes have passed between cuts. It now shows the girl's legs intermingled with the bark and bracken, black blood covering her skin.

Most essential is the way Buñuel films this image. Snails are making their way slowly across her legs, escaping from the basket she had put them in. There's so much potential reading into it, some of which is horrific (the slimy trail being left on her legs, etc.), that it's surprising to find it doesn't last longer than it does. Such is the nature of the scene, however, it's likely that its short length was in avoidance of potential censorship.

There is an intriguing relationship to place in this image, a disturbing naturalism in the relationship between violence and the rural location. The snails crawl over the dead girl's legs like they were just another branch or log, and the legs are filmed as if now part of the forest; mere foliage or debris. She becomes one with the soil through the violence committed against her. For all its blood-and-soil wailing, this is the hypocrisy of fascism: the only blood in the soil will ultimately be that of the innocent.

Buñuel had a noted love of insects and invertebrates since before his filmmaking began. His image of ants rummaging around in a hand in *Un Chien Andalou* (1929) is one of his most famous. Ants are in this film, too, crawling over a glass shed which is quickly smashed by an incoming piece of rubbish from the film's aggravated neighbour. But the snails are the most horrifyingly memorable.

Buñuel once admitted that he had 'always found insects exciting'. He never specified precisely *what* was exciting about them, however. The strangeness of insects and animals generally in *Diary of a Chambermaid* evidently creates a potent symbolism – especially in an earlier scene, where a butterfly is literally obliterated by a rifle shot – but I return again and again to the snails making their way over the dead girl's legs.

The image reflects the quiet perversity on display throughout the whole film, the brushing aside of every moral fibre by unrepentant ideological violence. But there's also a sense that the land will grow over everything eventually, even the frustrations of those isolated in country houses; those who ultimately enable such fascism to fester through mere boredom or disinterest. As Céléstine suggests, 'It's strange, how the country always seems sad. I guess people don't have much fun here.'

Published by Celluloid Wicker Man, 04/06/18

The Nowhere Road in *The Discreet Charm of the Bourgeoisie*

The Discreet Charm of the Bourgeoisie (1972) is a perfect example of a narrative film dissolving into a surreal dreamscape. From its title alone, Luis Buñuel's obvious target is middle-class idolatry, but, for a film full of incredibly stark images, there's one visual motif which stands out from the other surrealist political attacks.

Discreet is punctuated, whether in dreams or reality (or perhaps both), by a recurring visual of the film's six main characters walking endlessly along a country road. It's in this simple scenario where *Discreet*'s most subtle political comments form.

The walking often marks the end of a scene, or, occasionally, a dream sequence. The three men and three women walk in a rush along a road rather than on a pavement. There's no traffic and the surroundings are overtly rural; it could easily be the same road where the pair of unfortunate cyclists from Robert Fuest's horror film *And Soon the Darkness* (1970) meet their fate. Both films make the most of the eeriness of such a space; eerie not least in that its nervousness is a daytime phenomenon, rather than a more typical night setting.

There is, however, more to this visual than its simplistic description here suggests. The pace of the walkers suggests a potential destination, their determinedness becoming more apparent as the film progresses. Are they late? Running away from something perhaps? Either way, the group fails to progress. In fact, it appears that they revert to similar points earlier in the road, implying an ominous and endless treadmill purgatory.

The editing also gives an oneiric character to these moments, with each cut moving the arrangement of the six people into different places. In one cut, the couples of the group walk together, but in a second cut, they are dispersed. Perhaps the image feels more surreal than it actually is because of its unexplained placement in the film. Taken alone, it's nothing more than a simple, unexplained image.

The scenario is never mentioned or acknowledged by any of the characters. Even in the overt dream sequences, the most bizarre moments are concluded with a character waking up, highlighting that all before it was a dream. These segments have no such clarity, instead popping up as if taken from an entirely different narrative altogether. Added to this are the clothes of the group, which are clearly more fitting for the various social occasions the film is built around. They are dinner-party smart but appear to have taken a wrong turn and ended up in the countryside.

Buñuel initially wanted the characters of the segment to grow wearier as the film progressed; later dropping the idea in fear that it would be too obviously symbolic. The scenario does still retain its sense of symbolism (it is, after all, disconnected from any semblance of the main narrative, so has no other real function), but what symbolism can this be?

Throughout the film, Buñuel connects the bourgeoisie to urban or suburban dwellings. They blend in with their lavish backdrops, opulent houses and offices; a social camouflage hiding their immoral indulgences such as drug smuggling and casual affairs. In the flat landscape of the countryside, the characters have nowhere to hide. They stick out a mile. Therefore, they are forced to do the only thing possible for an animal caught in the open: get moving.

The landscape highlights their dreariness, effectively removing the *Wizard of Oz* curtain of their power. Their dangerousness is their ordinariness; their true colours more obvious when in contrast to a backdrop in which they cannot disappear under tables or into bedrooms.

And so they walk. Buñuel forces them into a situation in which they can do nothing but stand out for all to see. The act of walking, one which they are rarely ever shown to do for more than a few feet in the rest of the film, is a torment, a humiliation. They have no destination in spite of attempts at showing the confidence that suggests a potential end to their walk. They *appear* to know where they are going. But how many fallible managers or bosses have we all recognised with that same Wile E. Coyote-faith in running off the cliff? Probably too many to recall.

On and on they walk until the very last shot of the film. Buñuel may have shot them, literally, with a sub-machine gun minutes before (and in the safety of their own house *and* before eating as well) but this final, unending punishment of walking is the director's last attack upon the group.

It's ultimately reminiscent of a quote from Rebecca Solnit, whose words, despite discussing the positive release that walking provides, also express the reverse, which Buñuel seizes upon and sentences his bourgeoisie to. 'Many people nowadays live in a series of interiors disconnected from each other,' she wrote. 'On foot everything stays connected, for while walking, one occupies the spaces between those interiors in the same way one occupies those interiors. One lives in the whole world rather than in interiors built up against it.'

It's the hellish level playing field that they have always dreaded, blisters and all.

And so they walk for eternity.

Published by Celluloid Wicker Man, 22/02/16

The Emotional Landscape of *Scenes from a Marriage*

Scenes from a Marriage was Ingmar Bergman's first successful attempt to work in the medium of serialised television. The six-episode series following the highs and lows of a marriage signalled many changes the director would make during the 1970s.

Though a later cut of the series' six episodes was edited into a whole film for American audiences, several unfortunate changes to the drama were made in order to accommodate its new, shorter running length. This is not a list of the many changes and the negative impact of losing many of those elements has, but is instead an exploration of one particular aspect lost in the edit; one that I believe is vital in structuring the emotional relationship of Bergman's drama.

Scenes follows the turmoil of a marriage in gradual disarray. A full decade's worth of vignettes are shown of the matrimonial pairing of Marianne (Liv Ullmann) and Johan (Erland Josephson) as they continue to meet on and off for various reasons after an affair leads to a messy separation. While much of the drama remains largely intact in the film edit, it loses a key motif: a structural, landscape-infused pillar found in each episode's end credits.

At first, losing the credits of a television show may not seem too important to the overall drama. Yet, it's what Bergman actually did with them that undermines the film edition, to the point where it resembles little more than a curio by comparison.

At the end of each episode, the credits do not appear in full but are read by Bergman himself. He lists the performers and the technical staff, the name of the episode, the production and its filming location on the island of Fårö. Already, this can be seen as an unusual practice, especially because Bergman fails to announce his own involvement.

More important, however, are the images which accompany this reading. Bergman doesn't have himself filmed for his credit reading, nor is it something theatrical akin to Orson Welles's occasional reading of the main players (particularly in what remains of *The Magnificent Ambersons*). Instead, all six episodes of the series end with specific footage of the landscape of Fårö, with Bergman inviting the viewers to reflect upon such images.

Like in so many of his films, the landscape of his island home plays an important role. All of this is lost in the film version, often moving between claustrophobic spaces, where great emotional trauma and turmoil chaotically flows and with little context as to the gaps in time between the chapters. These little landscape postcards seem a vital cleanser, in particular in the darker episodes.

In the first episode, titled 'Innocence and Panic', the viewer is shown Marianne and Johan being interviewed by a lifestyle magazine on their tenth wedding anniversary. The journalist wants to know what makes a successful marriage, and her questions dislodge some of the problems that are clearly embedded in the relationship. They later witness their friends' bickering, which turns poisonous, showing the married couple what a supposed bad relationship looks like. It appears to be a different world to theirs, but really it's just a foreshadow of what is to come.

To end this episode, Bergman opts for a zoom shot of the Fårö landscape at sunset. This is one of three landscape shots that involve some sort of slow zoom out, and it seems an important editing tool. Here, and in the next episode, the landscape allows the perspective of the initial focus of the shot to slowly come into view. The first two episodes of the drama itself do the same thing for the pair's relationship (with a more chaotic effect). This also features in the last episode, after everything has happened and the decade that has taken up the series is itself put into focus.

The first landscape shot shows a sunset; the landscape approaching dusk. There's a fog enveloping the ground. The reflection of the sunlight in the water could easily be read as highlighting the reflection that the pair have been witness to in the failings of their friends' marriage (that of Katrina and Peter, played by Bibi Andersson and Jan Malmsjö).

It's a gentle moment, but one that suggests the sun is setting upon the marriage as a smooth-running arrangement (and one which further builds as the landscape shots are clearly in some sort of chronological order).

The second landscape is the same as the first but further inland. The episode, 'The Art of Sweeping Things Under the Rug', sees Marianne question herself as she succumbs to the domineering presence of parents. The credits begin with a close-up of a frost-covered stone which zooms out to reveal a wall in the landscape that was hidden from the first set of credits. The wall separates the two characters: one increasingly fragile, the other confident enough to flirt with a co-worker at the university.

Similar visual themes build as the marriage disintegrates. In the next episode, 'Paula', Johan's affair is revealed (along with the fact that he is leaving his wife and children to go and live with his mistress). The landscape shown is clearly at night but now moved to a beach where a lonely, rusted boat sits upon the shore while a pathetic lighthouse fails to give proper light to signal danger. These two objects paired together effectively reflect the state of Marianne in particular, who had no warning as to the intentions of her husband when he walked into their holiday cottage that night. Marianne saw no warning light and crashed violently against the shoreline, left to rust and decay alone.

Other themes seem even more literal though less effective. For example, in the episode 'The Vale of Tears', the credits reflect the title by being a very simple close-up of rain falling upon water, while the following episode's climactic violent encounter emphasises a dead tree after the pair have eventually agreed to sign the divorce papers. Again, both shots are static and reflect the lack of emotional progress apparent when the two characters are in each other's company.

The final episode shows the ironic pairing of the two characters long after they have both remarried. In 'In the Middle of the Night in a Dark House Somewhere in the World', they decide to spend a night together for what would have been their twentieth anniversary, ending up at a friend's lodge. Marianne has a nightmare and wakes up, with Johan comforting her.

In some ways, it seems that the last five episodes could have been playing over in their dreams, or have even been recollected. The landscape in the final episode shows an ambiguous timeframe (it could be dawn or dusk), and in this sense it reflects the unavoidable ambiguity of their relationship's future: is it really over, or is it always to be as habitual as a sunrise or sunset?

Bergman provides the viewer with one more landscape shot, showing two separate houses reflected in the water. The sun hovers between the two with a gentle gleam. A huge lake ripples out; landscape meeting water meeting sky. The sun could be rising or it could be setting, but either way, the characters are left with only the landscape for comfort: strong with indifference and brutally reflective.

Published by Celluloid Wicker Man, 03/06/15

Walking Despair in *La Notte*

By the early 1960s, the glamorous hedonism of Europe had reached a new peak. The scars of the Second World War had given way to new youthful vigour, at least for those who could afford it. The hollowness of this new hedonism became a theme in cinema of the period, but nowhere more so than in Italy.

In films such as Federico Fellini's *La Dolce Vita* (1960) and *8½* (1963), the lives of the rich and fashionable were gradually picked apart, showing the emotional void beneath the sharp suits and little black dresses. Style had eroded emotional substance.

Yet it was another Italian director, Michelangelo Antonioni, who more critically dramatised this distinctly urban pessimism, notably over the course of a trio of films known as the 'Alienation trilogy'. Bookended by *L'Avventura* (1960) and *L'Eclisse* (1962), it is in Antonioni's 1961 film, *La Notte*, where his critique of the rich jet-setters hits hardest.

La Notte is set over roughly a single day. We follow Giovanni (Marcello Mastroianni) and his wife Lidia (Jeanne Moreau) as they are subsumed by their shared silence over mutual infidelities. Giovanni is an author with a novel just released and a launch to attend. First, however, the couple must visit their sick friend Tommaso (Bernhard Wicki) in hospital – the visit upsetting the pair in different ways.

During the book launch, Lidia wanders further into town to where the couple first lived when married, wondering whether she should have chosen the dying man as her husband rather than Giovanni.

She watches life go by, far from the social milieu she now inhabits, before she is picked up by Giovanni. They visit a lavish club before attending an equally expensive party, where they both flirt and almost cheat on each other; Giovanni with Valentina (Monica Vitti), Lidia with Roberto (Giorgio Negro). Having failed to find any meaning in fidelity or infidelity, they walk one final time together as the night meets the morning.

Although it's named after the night, a large portion of Antonioni's film unfolds in the daytime. It's a wandering film for the most part, the characters only washing up on the shore of the party out of boredom later on.

The opening titles are distinctly urban and sketch the cityscape of Milan perfectly. Contrasts fill the screen, between the rubble of new developments and the sleek new lines of post-war architecture, all scored by inhuman electronic hums; as if the city is evolving into an alien landscape. The sky is haunted by helicopters, disturbing weary hospital patients, not dissimilar to Fellini's helicopter-filled opening in *La Dolce Vita*.

As in his swinging London film *Blowup* (1966), Antonioni fills the city with diggers in the process of streamlining spaces into appropriate habitation for these cold, lost people. At one point, Lidia leans against one of the unforgiving walls as her emotions get the better of her. The concrete support fails to help her stem the tears; it's as uncaring as the people around her.

So she walks.

Lidia wanders the streets with no particular purpose, except perhaps to escape her reality for a time before the coming night; a night where she knows she must wear a mask to hide her unhappiness. Communication in these streets, as in so many of Antonioni's films, never reaches its intended destination but simply echoes and reverberates between the walls of buildings before dying away.

Such walking shots feel closer to the Italian Neorealist films of the 1940s than the hip, avant-garde films of the 1960s. Then again, so does the architecture that Antonioni momentarily zones in on as it is destroyed; all piles of bricks, the corpses of more human buildings. Lidia looks to a world that once was, its remains stacked between the new blocks as it crumbles to nothing before her eyes.

Later, at the party, one character says: 'Don't look at me like that: I know I'm showing signs of ageing.' Bodies are like buildings in Antonioni's world; old things quickly become ruins awaiting demolition.

When the night does finally arrive, it comes in the form of a party. Similar to Fellini's skill in portraying the milieu of the era, Antonioni's parties always feel authentically extravagant. The characters talk endlessly about culture as a means of avoidance, taking every opportunity to turn away from their emotional reality. These are people who write articles about Theodor Adorno and invite Umberto Eco to their gatherings (resulting here in a genuine cameo from the writer); anything to avoid the absence in their hearts, the void of meaning in their lives.

Why face your collapsing marriage when you can talk to Umberto Eco over a glass of red?

The night fizzes with potential, especially for romance (or at least sex), and affairs spark before coming to nothing. Even this latent eroticism is only momentary. Rain arrives and seems to wash inhibition away for a time. Water patters onto the patio and into an inviting swimming pool. It fills the silence, just for a moment.

It's no wonder that Lidia walked earlier. What else was there left to do? When the party is finally over and the night is fading, Lidia and Giovanni wander again. In the end, the only landscape left for them is a fake one: a golf course adjacent to the house. With all its faux pleasantries and quaint challenges, it's a landscape that reflects their denial over the truth of their lives: that their friend in hospital is dead and their relationship is drained of any further meaning.

There is nowhere left for them to walk.

Published by the British Film Institute, 21/01/21

Sex and Landscape in *Zabriskie Point* and *The Last Movie*

Late last year, I watched two films back-to-back that effectively explored one very unusual theme: sex and the landscape. Viewing Michelangelo Antonioni's *Zabriskie Point* (1970) followed by Dennis Hopper's directorial debut *The Last Movie* (1971) highlighted a number of unavoidable connections between the films.

Both films were products of the American counterculture coming up against the concrete wall of early 1970s Nixonisms; both feature the disintegration of a moral core via various endeavours (in *Zabriskie* it's architecture, development and student politics; in *The Last Movie* it's cinema itself); and both films deal explicitly with the relationship between sex and landscape.

Zabriskie follows the meandering journey of Mark (Mark Frechette), who is mistakenly identified as the killer of a policeman at a race riot on a student campus. Stealing a plane, he flies out to the desert, his life becoming intertwined with the daughter of a rich property developer, Daria (Daria Halprin).

Some way into the counterculture adventure, the two find themselves in the sandy desert of Death Valley. The pair are deliberately characterised as curious and childish, playing at first in the landscape with youthful abandon. A sex scene occurs as a climax to this abandon, protracted by slow-motion photography as Mark and Daria roll around the dunes.

Antonioni covers their skin with this sand. As the cuts reveal the lovers to be less and less clothed, they gain a new sandy couture. In some shots, it's only the movement of their bodies that reveals the pair to actually be in the shot; their sexual union morphing them deeper into the topography, to the point of camouflage.

As the scenario progresses, Antonioni opts for an even more unusual effect. He fills the landscape with other couples of varying partnerships and orientations to accompany the original pair, their sexuality activating an erotic spirit latent in the earth.

This was the scenario that landed Antonioni in trouble with the authorities at the time, with performative outrage at supposed genuine orgies being filmed in a public National Park masking a real desire to ban the film: a protest, really, against its overt anti-American streak.

Yet the scene in question is one of the film's most important, as Antonioni is clear in showing what the linking of these two characters physically does to the film: it augments the very perception of the landscape from which the film takes its name, rendering it sentient and writhing.

The fact that the two leads sparked up a genuine romance during the filming, albeit a romance that did not last, is hardly surprising. The power of their attraction is shown to conjure a landscape brimming with its own sexuality. They simultaneously characterise it and become a part of it.

Dennis Hopper's *The Last Movie*, on the other hand, shows a similar and brief scenario but only in order to contrast it later on with a typically American commercialisation of sex and the body. Perhaps the sense of connection between the two films is further compounded by the fact that Hopper married Daria Halprin in real life a year after *The Last Movie* was released, the real and the fictional intriguingly weaving together.

The film follows Hopper as Kansas, a staffer on a Western shooting in Peru. He loses his love of filmmaking due to an accident during production, and opts to stay on in the town and live there. He partners up with Rose (Toni Basil), a local prostitute who plied her trade to the crew during the shoot. Things become chaotic as the local villagers become obsessed with recreating some of the scenes from the film that Kansas was working on earlier, misunderstanding that it was wholly fictional. Kansas soon lashes out at all around him and is eventually lost in the ritual of the fake/real film.

When Kansas and Rose's relationship is shown to be at its peak, Hopper opts for a sex scene for the two characters at a local waterfall. Their bodies are shown to fit snugly into the mould of each other, as well as the rocky outcrop of the waterfall.

Kansas wants this simplistic life away from the brutal monetary world of cinema, losing himself briefly in the moment, before Rose ultimately forces them both to return to the town and its array of bars and bordellos.

In sharp contrast to this sex scene, Kansas's psyche is ravaged by the town. He's shown to gradually mistreat Rose, seeing her as a commodity far and away from their moment by the waterfall.

The couple later pay (along with some fellow American visitors) to watch two women have sex in a backroom. The moment is a deliberate contrast to the earlier scene by the waterfall, when the pair of characters almost dissolved into the landscape through the pleasure of each other's bodies. The sex show is so contrived that even the characters wince at its fakery. Most importantly, however, is the fact that it takes place between four walls.

Antonioni predicted (arguably with some naïvety) where such a negation of sex and landscape would lead: the explosion of a kind of proto-revolutionary embodiment. *Zabriskie* is most famous for its final sequence of various commercial products (as well as Daria's father's home) blowing up in slow motion; almost orgasmic in its editing, intensity and repetition. It shares a similar thematic journey to *The Last Movie*'s eventual moral collapse, though has an optimism that seems more apt for 1970 than 1971, with Nixon's re-election looming.

Hopper's film, on the other hand, knows that the moment of dissolved identity between body and landscape is fleeting; a growing impossibility in an increasingly violent world. Mediation of the body (especially of women's bodies), and the threat to the landscape more generally by developers, is unavoidable. Both are coming from the same powerful place.

The two films capture a moment where the landscape, far from being the bastion of healing, sexless chastity that it's regularly portrayed as today, comes to life as the most beautiful of erotic expressions, even if ultimately the lovers of both films inevitably return to the suppressive conformity of a bed and a ceiling above them.

Published by Celluloid Wicker Man, 09/01/17

The Breeze in the Trees of *Blowup*

If asked to choose a particular sound that defined London in cinema, I wouldn't choose the bustling noise of traffic or an iconic piece of soundtrack music. It would, in fact, be the very simple but endlessly mysterious sound of wind rustling through the trees in Michelangelo Antonioni's *Blowup* (1966).

Having visited all the locations from the film last summer for the British Film Institute, it was a surprise to find, when visiting Maryon Park in Charlton where many of the film's famous sequences were shot, that Antonioni and his sound recordist Robin Gregory had merely emphasised something that was already there rather than creating an impressionistic illusion.

This was doubly surprisingly considering how much Antonioni augmented the visuals of his locations, famously painting the grass in the park and the tarmac on the road so that it looked exactly as he wanted. This emphasis on the breeze, and its grounding in a very particular everyday reality, is where much of the power of these sequences in the film is arguably derived.

In narrative terms, the park sits at the heart of the film, though ironically it is geographically at the very edge of the rest of the real locations. Thomas (David Hemmings), a photographer, pays a fleeting visit to the park after perusing in a nearby antiques shop. He slowly echoes the footsteps of a pair of lovers whom he photographs, only to be confronted by the woman, Jane (Vanessa Redgrave), who mysteriously doesn't want the photos developed.

The film revolves around the back-and-forth journey of these photos before Thomas realises, after developing the reel and gradually blowing up the photos, that he has accidentally captured a murder. He then visits the park several times, first finding the body of the murdered man and then finding it has disappeared, before finally disappearing himself after watching a group of mimes play tennis in the park's public court.

Maryon Park is, in other words, at the centre of the narrative vortex of the film, with each visit spitting Thomas back out as irreparably changed, even if he fails to realise such a change to have occurred.

For all these moments in the park, the sound of the wind rustling through the trees is heightened, being almost the only sound to occur there apart from the occasional snap of Thomas's camera and the final game of mime tennis (which in itself is a puzzling moment, in that an imaginary game eventually produces real sounds).

Antonioni had relied on this rustling effect before, in particular in the Rome-set entry for his Alienation trilogy, L'Eclisse (1960), but it feels more apt for London, not least because the city has more trees than Italy's capital.

The soundscape hints towards an otherness in the space, one that's far and away from the hectic noise of Yardbirds gigs, fashion shoots, chaotic threesomes and drives around Notting Hill. For a film with a notably famous soundtrack, one by Herbie Hancock, its virtual absence throughout in all but the opening and the very final moment (along with the odd instance of being listened to by characters on record players or vaguely faded into the background) raises questions about what the sound of the breeze through the trees is doing to the film as a whole.

In Julio Cortázar's original 1963 short story, the nature of the wind gets a mention, and though originally set in Paris, it's worth quoting as it at least highlights its deliberate inclusion. 'It's rare that there is wind in Paris,' wrote the author, 'and even less seldom a wind like this that swirled around corners and rose up to whip at the old wooden Venetian blinds behind which astonished ladies commented variously on how unreliable the weather had been these last few years.'

It seems that Antonioni ran with this aspect. Thomas initially sees it as representing some sort of peace and contentment away from his hectic photography studio rather than anything particularly meaningful. When he mentions the photos he has taken in the park to his manager Ron (Peter Bowles) (importantly, before he has developed the reel and seen what is on it), he mentions this calmness as a defining factor. He's at that point unaware of the change that has taken place since his visit. The continual transition of Thomas's own realisation – of both the inane qualities of his life and what he has really seen in the park – becomes overt and eventually unavoidable.

Even after developing the photos, the act of doing so seems to allow the park's sounds to bleed into his studio. The change they enact on Thomas's perception of the world cannot be undone; the breeze drifts through his studio as the realisation sets in.

The sound of wind rustling the trees of Maryon Park becomes a sonic leitmotif for this transition of character; a realisation that something was missed the first time around. The link between this idea and the character comes from an engagement with the outside world, where the park and Thomas develop a symbiotic relationship far beyond what he initially perceived would be the outcome from his casual wander to snap a few casual rolls of film.

The final irony of this is that such a realisation ultimately destabilises the character to the point where he disappears. When the end titles of the film appear, Thomas fades from the park, the awareness of the mime of his current existence beyond salvaging. Antonioni shows the logic of this moment as, instead of the breeze in the trees dominating the soundtrack, the Hancock score plays instead, drowning out the sound just as the realisation of his non-existence effectively drowned out Thomas; so much so that he fades from the grass and into the breeze.

Published by Celluloid Wicker Man, 03/04/17

Air-Con Spaces in Alan J. Pakula's Paranoia Trilogy

A man is following someone up an escalator. The space around them gleams with inhuman malevolence, as if it was designed as an arena for violent conspiracy. Soon one of the men will be dead, yet this is hardly surprising as the building they are in is as cold and uncaring as the powers that built it.

This scene is from the second film in Alan J. Pakula's powerful Paranoia trilogy, *The Parallax View* (1974); a film that builds suspense through deliberately playing upon the banal malice of such spaces. Alongside *Klute* (1971) and *All the President's Men* (1976), Pakula's films defined an ongoing architectural trend: the adoption of what could be called air-con spaces.

These empty corporate zones, with greater and greater acceleration, have become shorthand for political underhandedness, unnerving surveillance and a very secretive violence. Whether they be empty inner-city hotels, conference spaces filled with lonely escalators, vacant offices or shopping malls after hours, these very American realms were the sites of conspiracy and corruption that slipped in and out of the genuine political reality of the early 1970s.

All three of Pakula's trilogy utilise the increased tension of the country in this era. There is menace in the ordinary here, something malignant brewing since the Cold War escalations post-Second World War, exasperated further by the assassinations that scarred American politics in the 1960s. These are the traumas driving Pakula's films, the trilogy a cathartic release of paranoia over the political machinations deployed by a variety of US governments and organisations in the period.

Following on from his 1969 feature debut *The Sterile Cuckoo*, Pakula began to express such concerns in *Klute*, an inner-city fable concerning a private detective (Donald Sutherland) and his search for a missing executive who is connected to call-girl Bree Daniels (Jane Fonda). Though the air-con spaces of this film are limited, they are essential to the contrasts within the drama.

The executive who ordered the investigation, Cable (Charles Cioffi), conducts a campaign of terror against the call-girl in order to hide his role in a disappearance. Essentially, this is shown to be overseen from his high-level boardroom; low-light, misty views, absent morals.

The building for those scenes was in fact 26 Church Street in Lower Manhattan, and Pakula shot the location during the construction of a much larger set of air-con spaces adjacent to it, seen outside the executive's windows. Learning that those cranes seen behind Cable are building the World Trade Centre only adds to the unnerving poignancy of Pakula's film.

In one particularly effective moment, Cable is seen in the space listening to a revealing tape. The scene alerts the viewer to the truth behind Bree's worry over being secretly observed. It's far from delusional but part of the increasingly common reality of the Watergate era which the trilogy defines itself through. The camera slowly tracks through the shady boardroom until Cable stands up, the camera implying his looking down, before cutting to Bree's much lower and more typical apartment.

This is the contrast, the change occurring in the era; where the suspicious individuals who inhabit these spaces have both a technological and symbolic ability to observe all below them, whether the rest of the public likes it or not.

Pakula achieves the ultimate in air-con spaces in *The Parallax View* as the film's culminating act of violence (one which defines the whole narrative) takes place in a conference centre. A journalist, Frady (Warren Beatty), is uncertain as to the straightforward portrayal of a political candidate's assassination at the Seattle Space Needle. He follows a trail of dubious characters, leading ultimately to the so-called Parallax Organisation and a further plot.

Another assassination is due to take place in the conference centre where the dress rehearsal is underway for a senator's political rally. The centre is a vast and intimidating space where suited men lurk in the shadows, staring from behind curtains or from high up in the roof-rafters. Even the outside of the building has a horrific, reflective quality seemingly designed for purposes outside of anything even remotely human.

Pakula deliberately frames the beginning of this final scene with emphasis on these dead exteriors. It's actually a composite of two real buildings, the Central Civil West Courthouse and the Los Angeles Convention Centre. Pakula was clearly spoilt for choice in this era for potential locations.

Inside the space, the musical score dies down, instead making the most of the strange ambience of such places, usually consisting of the hum of lights, the swirl of fans and the breeze of the air-con, as well as the quintessential vacuum cleaner somewhere further into the labyrinth. This quietude is only interrupted by the practising of a marching band preparing for the evening's rally in the main hall. Yet, behind the twee fanfare, men are gathering in the corners, haunting the corridors with an air of officialdom.

They are organised: the space is theirs.

When Pakula puts characters into these spaces, something unusual happens. While Frady and the man he is following are standing on the escalator, their presence is unsettling, even abnormal. These spaces may possess the usual shorthand for human interaction but having their facilities used by only a small number of people highlights the absurdity of their scale.

The rows and rows of empty tables prepared for the rally show the true hollowness of the event, the senator's voice occulted to a tape machine that repeats even after the assassin's bullets have ripped through his diaphragm. It's this scale that ultimately is the undoing of Frady, locked into a framing of political assassination and forced to scurry in the rafters of the huge complex until he leaves the space in the only way left open to him: a body bag.

The two films lead naturally to *All the President's Men,* the final reality of the trilogy coming full circle with its dramatic rendering of the genuine conspiracy of Richard Nixon's Watergate scandal. Interestingly, however, something has changed.

The counterattack against the unseen powers, threatening those who possess the information needed to bring the truth out into the open, is also fought from an air-con space. The office of the *Washington Post* reporters Carl Bernstein (Dustin Hoffman) and Bob Woodward (Robert Redford) is just as much an air-con space as the others, but it's fitting that the war of information has now moved entirely into these realms.

The film even opens with a perfect embodiment of the air-con space: the break-in at Democratic Headquarters, showing the moment when the trail of conspiracy first becomes evident. The office feels an eerie place as the five Watergate burglars make their way through the carpeted corridors, furnished with bland fittings and objects.

The blandness of such spaces is essential; bland seems harmless but is often anything but. The ubiquitous surveillance potential channelled in these films comes from both fiction and reality, however. It need not be said that *All the President's Men* builds on the reality of this period of politics but, equally, the era of Watergate invades the previous two films as well as others.

In the same year that *The Parallax View* was released, Francis Ford Coppola defined this feeling of being permanently observed in *The Conversation* (1974), a film full of long glass windows hiding telescopes and audio-surveillance equipment. The architecture of this period seems purpose-built for surveillance; impossible places that expose the presence of any person unsure in the ways of covert activities.

Even Scorpio (Andy Robinson), the manic killer from Don Siegel's *Dirty Harry* (1971), finds purchase in the potential anonymity and surveillance of these buildings, making his first killing from one of their rooftops. These buildings often favour psychopaths and madmen, official or otherwise.

Modernity is now defined by these air-con spaces. The events that happen within them become increasingly surreal, though lessened with the general bizarre bent of today's politics. These are spaces where Christopher Walken can literally fly through the air, as in Spike Jonze's video for Fatboy Slim's 'Weapon of Choice' (2001); the lobby of the L.A. Hotel hauntingly emptied, allowing such a strange scenario to seem perfectly natural.

Such spaces have become the norm, even in Europe, where the designs have been somewhat imported from America. Yet, with our political age and direction seemingly dictated by the choices and actions taken within these spaces, others have followed on from Pakula's first steps to explore the dangers they house.

J.G. Ballard examined the same potential perfectly in his last period of writing after the millennium. Though his earlier fiction was concerned with similar architecture degrading the morality of its occupants à la *Crash* (1973) and *High-Rise* (1975), his later novels bask in the violent potential of the newly gleaming corporate realms.

This comes to a violent head in his novel *Super-Cannes* (2000), where the conference centre aesthetic has created such boredom for its middle-class occupants that they revert to extreme, racial violence as a release. In novels such as *Cocaine Nights* (1996) and *Kingdom Come* (2006), air-con spaces again become surreal backdrops for middle-class terrorism and the potential consumer fascism of shopping malls. Even BFI Southbank itself becomes an air-con space for Ballard in *Millennium People* (2003); NFT 2 now a place of unfolding psychological terrorism with its thin carpets and uncomfortable sofas.

Ballard was building on Pakula's vision, where architectural inanity was a ploy. As London is increasingly turned into one large air-con space consisting of empty luxury flats, Westfields and conference centres, Pakula's trilogy becomes more and more of a stark warning of the impending danger within the corporatisation of space.

This could be seen decades ago in Mike Leigh's *Naked* (1993), as Johnny (David Thewlis) talks his way into an empty corporate high-rise and ventures through its corridors with the night-watchman, Brian (Peter Wight). Johnny seems even more manic in this space than in most of the film, reverting to full conspiracy and paranoia as he predicts the end of the world at the oncoming millennium. His delusions almost ring true, but not because of any compelling argument: it's simply because he's putting forward such a prediction in the empty air-con space of an office block. The apocalyptic and the banal sit remarkably comfortably together.

Whether following the assassination of a politician, the surveillance of a call-girl or a politically unscrupulous break-in, paranoia exudes from these spaces, making these films both unnerving and thrilling. With such ideas breaking loose from the cinematic world, however, dominating cities and suburbia across the West and elsewhere, Pakula's air-con spaces define our current climate, our collective digital scream as municipalities of glass and steel increasingly dominate our everyday spaces, forever surveyed.

We are undoubtedly living in their mould; now simply ghosts glimpsed on closed-circuit TV, watched by persons unknown.

Published by Sight & Sound Magazine, 06/10/17

The Violent Countryside
of *Straw Dogs*

By the 1970s, the malevolence of the English landscape was unavoidable. The presentation of rural realms had gradually evolved on screen, becoming places of unforgiving ghosts (as in Lawrence Gordon Clark's *A Warning to the Curious* (1972)), of devils (as in Piers Haggard's *The Blood on Satan's Claw* (1971)), and of human violence (as in Michael Reeves's *Witchfinder General* (1968)).

Though some English landscapes on screen preserved some sense of romantic detachment, in the likes of John Schlesinger's *Far from the Madding Crowd* (1966) and Joseph Losey's *The Go-Between* (1971), the landscape's tainted reality had finally clawed its way back through several centuries' worth of Romantic Pastoralism.

Modern-day green and pleasant lands were suddenly haunted by unnerving violence and trauma, the transition arguably defined most disturbingly and effectively by American Sam Peckinpah's first non-Western feature film, *Straw Dogs* (1971). Along with Ken Russell's *The Devils* and Stanley Kubrick's *A Clockwork Orange*, it was a film that gave the British Board of Film Classification a number of sleepless nights in 1971.

Straw Dogs is based on Gordon M. Williams' novel *The Siege of Trencher's Farm* (1969), and it follows newly married couple David and Amy Sumner (Dustin Hoffman and Susan George) as they return to live in the latter's small home village in a remote part of Cornwall. They are faced with a cold welcome by the locals who are unhappy, and perhaps envious, that Amy has married an outsider (an academic figure, no less).

Some of the local men, including Amy's old flame, Charlie (Del Henney), are hired to fix and renovate the farm that the couple have moved into. But the pressure builds as David is lured away by the men under the pretence of helping them in an early morning hunt, only to then lose him deliberately. Charlie doubles back and forces himself on Amy, with a second man then forcing him to collude in her second rape. Amy keeps both attacks secret.

The tension rises further after Amy's breakdown at a local gathering, forcing the attackers to leave. The pair later help a man, Niles (David Warner), who is run over. Unbeknownst to them, Niles earlier accidentally killed the daughter of the local drunk, Tom Hedden (Peter Vaughan); another uncomfortable factor with the character's special needs being the supposed cause of the manslaughter. The film concludes with an incredibly violent siege on the Sumners' house led by Hedden, resulting in some of the most violent and brutal deaths in popular 1970s cinema.

Straw Dogs garnered a variety of controversies, chiefly for the ambiguities surrounding the assault of Amy. The narrative not only implies that it was a natural outcome of her earlier teasing of the men, but frames her as somewhat enjoying the first attack by her former lover. It's only when the second man attacks that she is shown to unambiguously struggle. There's little doubt that the film's notoriety today derives from this deeply uncomfortable presentation of assault, yet there's much else in the film that essentially aligns with more esoteric films from this period; most notably its relationship to landscape and its strain of locality functioning as a toxicity that remains deep in its isolated soil.

The majority of the film's drama stems from the notion of outsiders and insiders; that people have more right to live in (and live *with* people from) an area when they are born there. It's telling that Peckinpah was chastised by the original people of the area used for the filming of such a characterisation. The residents of the village of St Buryan were incredibly angry at the film's portrayal of their community, especially because many occupants had taken part as extras, unaware of its content or context.

The 'local shop for local people', as famously expressed by the couple in *The League of Gentlemen*'s Royston Vasey, has a doubly horrific effect during the patriarchal 1970s; that local men have the automatic rights to local women's bodies, with or without consent. The attachment to the landscape bizarrely grants such access.

Women's bodies in *Straw Dogs* sit in line with actual facets of the landscape. They may as well be those of livestock (a visual appropriately realised a year later in Michael Ritchie's *Prime Cut* (1972)). As with many dramas set in rural communities in this period, isolation is essential to the social make-up and breakdown of morality. The skewed localism of the soil, without the intervention of social or moral progress of the wider community, sours further when left to stew.

In this sense, the film shares a great deal in common with Reeves's *Witchfinder General*; another Western posing as an

English equivalent of sorts. Again, isolated rural plains give rise to a continued violence against women and, more generally, between male rivals.

Apart from both films being shot by director of photography John Coquillon, whose eye imbues the landscapes with inescapable vastness, both films also highlight the lapse in morality sometimes brushed aside more easily in Spaghetti Westerns in particular. Whereas the epic nature of American landscapes (and its faux Italian/ Spanish equivalent) seems to attenuate the moral implications of such violence, the English landscape is too canonised as peaceful to create the same atmosphere. In many ways, it heightens this tense effect through contrast and irony (now marked doubly so, considering the Sumners' house is itself a pricy, self-catering holiday cottage).

Peckinpah ultimately distorts the cause of such events for his own dramatic ends; his film is only an accidental rather than knowing critique of England's fetishist relationship to certain types of landscape. Yet the Cornish vistas he filmed cannot hide the conscious nastiness of such localised violence even if, in narrative terms, the soil's almost sentient qualities seem to contrast with such horror.

The landscape is the root of the bloodlust.

Published by the British Film Institute, 02/06/17

Horror's Pleasure of Distance

One of my favourite moments from Alfred Hitchcock's *Psycho* (1960) is not a typical choice considering the film's many infamous scenes. Rather than showers, murders and other more memorable images, I particularly love a relatively bland scene later on in the film. It has narrative development in its eerie punch line, but has little else on screen in terms of Hitchcock more generally: it's utterly perfunctory in comparison to most other things in the film.

The scene captures something I've found in a range of horror that is difficult to describe: a pleasurable sense of distance from a place of horror that has been already mentioned. Whether this is distance in terms of the characters and the space they inhabit at that moment, or in the viewer's sharing in that warmth away from a place where horror is seeping out into everyday life, this distance is something I cherish when I come across it.

The scene in *Psycho* is late into the story, when the narrative is following Lila Crane (Vera Miles) and Sam Loomis (John Gavin) as they search for the missing Marion (Janet Leigh). Marion was on the run after stealing money but made the unwise move of spending a night in the Bates Motel, where she was murdered by Norman Bates (Anthony Perkins).

In the scene, Lila and Sam are in the house of Sheriff Chambers (John McIntire) after paying an unsuccessful visit to the Bates Motel, where Norman was suspiciously unhelpful. The pivotal moment is that, having seen the figure of Norman's mother in the window of the house overlooking the hotel (and Norman having spoken as if his mother was alive), the sheriff drops the scare that Norman's mother, someone we have heard speaking throughout the film, has been dead for some time. 'Well, if the woman up there is Mrs Bates… who's that woman buried out in Greenlawn Cemetery?' he asks.

At that moment, I am *glad* to be in the sheriff's house; more than glad, in fact. It's a kind of morbid cosiness. The viewer has some pathos as to what is going on, though not the full picture of Norman's illness just yet. Either way, there's a distance between the two spaces.

The Gothic horror inhabiting the motel and mansion is very deliberately mentioned while in this small-town, homely room with a figure of authority present as well. The moment is eerie but it's a pleasurable distance, a sense of far-away malevolence. It heightens the feeling of leaving such safety, heightening the tension of returning to face the gruesome reality of the Bates Motel and its macabre history.

I often think of the ghost stories of M.R. James working in a similar way. While talking on a podcast a few years back, one of the points I raised in regard to why James's readings of his ghost stories at Christmas likely worked so well was because of this similar contrast.

This contrast, in his strongest stories for me, often involved a wintry, desolate landscape in which spectres and unnameable revenants were approaching, seeking violent retribution upon the curious. From a warm Cambridge fireside at King's College to an empty Norfolk beach in winter, the sense of distance is the same.

I'm grateful to the various narrators of James's stories, always really James to my ears, that they conjure these images when we are at a pleasing enough distance to enjoy them. They are gifted a quality that implies the reader/listener is some way away from where such horrors occurred or, worse, are occurring in that very moment. 'A Warning to the Curious' does this especially well, though equally, the feeling is similar when watching any number of the BBC's adaptations of his work.

I think, too, of the moment in Jonathan Miller's *Whistle and I'll Come to You* (1968) where the image of the protagonist, Parkins (Michael Hordern), lying in bed is overlaid with images of the beach where he found the whistle. It's not a pleasant realisation for the character as the landscape and its menaces are seeping into his hotel room. For the viewer, we are given a brief moment of distance and feel the cosiness of that creaking hotel; glad not to be out there in the cold Norfolk night.

Perhaps the most alarming and effective example I've encountered of this feeling is in H.P. Lovecraft, and, more specifically, in the story 'The Case of Charles Dexter Ward'. In Lovecraft, this distance is part of the general mechanism of his work as the creatures at the centre of his stories are often beyond full description and comprehension; if the reader is to remain sane, that is.

Lovecraft relies on testimony from characters within his stories as to the horrors going on elsewhere rather than dramatic renditions of them. There are often cries in the distance. In 'The Case of Charles Dexter Ward', I've never felt such an acute sense of pleasurable distance, though it was, on first reading, unnerving enough to almost slide from pleasure into genuine anxiety.

In one segment, characters in a cottage recount what is unfolding on a coastline near the farm, where the intrigue of the story swirls like sulphurous vapours. Some sailors and military are sent to investigate (and end up fending off) *something*. The reader is not taken along with the sailors on their errand and does not witness what happens to them. It's the absolute opposite to what would happen in a Hollywood thriller equivalent, no doubt basking in an endless and disappointing CGI rendition of Lovecraftian creatures.

Instead, Lovecraft provides evidence of people either returned from whatever it was that happened, or people in a nearby cottage who heard and glimpsed fragments of what was going on. There are several different distances are here.

Lovecraft writes that 'It was just before dawn that a single, haggard messenger carried a conviction which his mere words could never have conveyed: for though he was a seaman well known to many of them, there was something obscurely lost or gained in his soul, which set him for evermore apart.' He then describes the scenario that left him this way through 'muffled' sounds, before screams from the actual farm itself are heard and followed swiftly by silence.

All of this is told second-hand, implied, judged or related. It's never in the moment, just like the insinuations about Norman Bates's mother gaining greater effect when placed away from the horror quickly becoming apparent at the

Bates Motel, or how much more pleasing it is to learn of cursed Saxon crowns when sat by a Cambridge fireside.

'A wailing distinctly different from the scream now burst out...' wrote Lovecraft in his unnerving short story. My first, and still consistent, reaction to this is simple: what a pleasure it is that such an affair is related from *afar*.

Published by Celluloid Wicker Man, 09/07/18

The Urban Wyrd

One of the key criticisms of theories surrounding folk horror is its emphasis upon the rural landscape. How can a genre really encompass rural horror films such as *Witchfinder General* (1968) and *The Wicker Man* (1973) while also discussing more obviously urban-set horrors such as *Quatermass and the Pit* (1967)?

While key works of folk horror cinema seem to broadly focus on rural landscapes in which to set and conjure their horror, by setting up such a rigid parameter for defining films in the genre, it does neglect some of the most popular and effective examples. This brief assessment aims to balance the rural emphasis often found in discussions of the genre with some of the more urban examples, labelling them 'urban wyrd', and showing the links to their rural cousins, as well as several important differences.

When putting together a presentation about folk horror for a conference in Belfast last year, some of the preparation for it was to try and anticipate criticisms and potential questions that would be asked afterwards. The question that I most feared at the time was a relatively straightforward one, and went something along the lines of 'What about *Quatermass and the Pit*?'

A question about Nigel Kneale's drama would have produced an unforgivably long silence on my part at the time, as there was simply no answer. My ideas surrounding folk horror were uniquely based on the idea that the rural landscape isolates individuals and communities, and their narratives functioned in various directions from this initial premise.

In any of its variations, whether the 1958 BBC television version or Hammer's big-screen adaptation by Roy Ward Baker, Kneale's story simply didn't fit with the strictness of any reasoning put forward at the time about folk horror. We have come a long way since then, with the genre now an effective little cottage industry for academic writing.

The 1967 Hammer version of *Quatermass* did not have any rural-derived skewed belief systems in parallel with, say, that of Summerisle or medieval England. If anything, such beliefs function in the drama instead as a race memory lying dormant in all of humanity, the demonic alien insects uncovered during the development of a London tube station having influenced humanity's more violent and tribal impulses.

In total opposition to other films discussed, it did not have a rural setting, and was firmly placed in a built-up part of London, albeit a mostly studio-based recreation (with only a few genuine shots around central London and Chiswick in the film version, while Cheapside is briefly seen in the television version). While the story definitely had a manifestation of some form due to an ancient, hidden power (another common trait of folk horror films), the relationship between its summoning and the previous levels of drama were complex and not simply ritualistic. In other words, *Quatermass and the Pit* was an enjoyable but frustrating spanner in the works.

Or was it?

For some time now, my idea of the chain of folk horror, an idea where landscapes lead to the isolation of communities, paving the way for skewed morality and eventually summoning and violence, have been critiqued, dismissed and used in a variety of ways (perhaps arguably too much). Yet, this example was demanding a reappraisal of several of its tenets well before the cottage industry of folk horror took off.

In many ways, the way to rethink it was to effectively work backwards, if only because Kneale's play does at least have the typical folk horror outcome, where the Martian alien, responsible for the majority of our religion, folklore and fascism, manifests over London to enact a human cull for the survival of the species. This was the desired outcome, but what was the dramatic pathway that led to it?

The summoning of this creature was inherent within us as a race memory, but also embedded within human curiosity itself. Perhaps curiosity can be fed further into the idea of skewed belief systems in that, like a lot of horror, a complete lack of awareness towards potentially dangerous or unnerving elements is itself a form of skewed belief system. It certainly doesn't relate to the reality of being confronted with danger in more typical genres. M.R. James especially made great use of this human fallacy in a number of his stories: a warning to the curious indeed.

In order for the chain to work in more traditional folk horror, the landscape *must* lead to isolation, on screen or off. The initial problem with applying the chain to *Quatermass* was that the sort of isolation required for folk horror seemed theoretically impossible for a film set in central London. After re-watching the film and the television version, as well reading several works on Kneale himself, it seems that the answer is relatively straightforward.

The urban geography of *Quatermass* is very distinct and specific. In one of Kim Newman's various analyses of the film (mentioned in detail within his British Film Institute book on the film), he suggests that *Quatermass and the Pit* is more claustrophobic than the other *Quatermass* films. Indeed, *Quatermass and the Pit* is one of the most isolated and claustrophobic portrayals of London ever put onto film.

London in the film is just as isolating as Summerisle; an effect achieved by a closed-in set that renders a busy street in London as somewhere oppressive and self-contained. It may as well be surrounded by water or miles of empty farmland. The idea of urban geography creating of sense of isolated claustrophobia is very much a trait within several films on the outer periphery of folk horror, especially those obstinate 'Why are they folk horror?' films. The most obvious example is *Quatermass* because it often crops up within the most basic of folk horror discussions. Others, however, are perhaps just as deserving as being part of the discussion.

The most interesting film that springs to mind is *Death Line* (aka *Raw Meat*) (1973). An underrated shocker by Gary Sherman, the film follows the abduction of several people on the London Underground (again linking thematically with the film version of *Quatermass*). These abductions are carried out by a rapidly diminishing group of underground, subhuman cannibals; workers from the building of the tube who were left down there and forgotten about.

While no supernatural elements occur, the violent cannibalism and horror still seems very folkloric; as if the narrative could be something a youngster would be told in order to stop them misbehaving on the tube. Survival also seems essential to the urban variation of the chain. Disturbingly, there is little difference between the inhabitants of Summerisle burning a man to help their crops grow and a regressed human kidnapping people to eat from Russell Square. Both scenarios seem utterly necessary to the individuals involved for their survival, once the morality has been skewed enough by social isolation.

There could be a backlog of films to discuss once this idea is opened out. However, several films that could fit into this idea are most definitely not folk horror. Alfred Hitchcock's adaptation of Patrick Hamilton's *Rope* (1948) is a great example of urban wyrd, yet is most definitely not folk horror. The characters are entirely isolated within their city apartment, their morality utterly skewed (by their university education, of all things), their actions derived from some sadistic Übermensch ritual with the outcome being their own supposed confirmation of superiority over their social peers. Even Hitchcock's *Frenzy* (1972) seems built on these elements, though it's merely a digression (along with Michael Powell's *Peeping Tom* (1960), Douglas Hickox's *Theatre of Blood* (1973) and a variety of others).

The point in question is that these other films are not folk horror. Yet the urban wyrd can draw a parallel line with the genre that can help explore and discuss the more anomalous, difficult films that often crop up.

By aligning *Quatermass and the Pit* and others within the urban wyrd, strands within folk horror become far more tangible, as well as overarching themes of British counterculture horror as a whole. The city is undeniably as weird as the fens and the fields that dominate the genre.

After all, folklore haunts urbanity's streets with equal aplomb.

Published by Celluloid Wicker Man, 13/04/15

The Outsider in *Quatermass II*

The characters in Nigel Kneale's work rarely like an outsider. The drama of his plays is often built around small groups of people at odds with some unwelcome stranger. The oppositional group will be diametrically opposed in spirit, character and morality for a variety of reasons; sometimes for more pulp purposes, such as aliens in a space invasion scenario, but also more earthly images of townspeople entering closed rural communities.

The electronics research group in *The Stone Tape* (1972), for example, envisage an unseen enemy in the form of their Japanese competitors, while a town vet in his episode of the series *Against the Crowd*, 'Murrain' (1975), is treated with disdain for disbelieving local superstitions about a supposed witch putting a curse upon a farmer's cattle. Not only do these beliefs build tension in Kneale's dramas, they show strong links to the landscape in which the stories are set.

The best example of Kneale's narrative device, however, can be found in the various adaptations of *Quatermass II*, made by the BBC in 1955 and later into a film by Hammer Studios in 1957.

Kneale's tendency for such a device can be explained by a number of elements, but the most obvious and predominant one is the political climate in which he was writing. His general themes stem from the emphasised island mentality brought about due to the Second World War; a time when the outsider was necessary to demonise, if only for more general propaganda (think of Alberto Cavalcanti's *Went the Day Well?* from 1942).

This type of thinking is at its strongest in times of conflict and the immediate years post-conflict. It's arguably an extension of 'narrow nationalism', as Anthony Giddens once suggested in a column for the *Guardian*. Add to this the paranoia over the increasingly volatile state of the Cold War, and the Knealian formula becomes an expression of the mentality for the United Kingdom of the 1950s.

Kneale himself said as much in the introduction to the script published in 1979. 'It was 1955,' he recalled, 'an uncomfortable time. There was much public concern about a new brand of bureaucracy, which manifested itself in the form of secret establishments: giant radars reputed to endanger human life and concealed huge plastic pods; germ warfare establishments behind barbed wire; atom-proof shelters for chosen administrators.'

Quatermass II fits this model well, as it showcases a range of different effects of the supposed outsider which predominantly augment the state of the English landscape. It must also be remembered that Quatermass as a character (at least in the television adaptation) is himself an outsider after the scientific and moral failures of his own experiments in the previous instalment, *The Quatermass Experiment* (1953). Perhaps the lack of support for the character from various officials throughout the narrative is due to this position, but it does seem rather ironic. As Kneale wrote, 'Quatermass himself would be the lone figure, doggedly worrying his way through officialdom's barriers and pat explanations to get to the horrifying truth.'

Quatermass II is concerned with the fate of Winnerden Flats, a rural community that has been demolished and modernised to make way for a suspicious food production plant which turns out to be harbouring a special environment for an alien creature. This location presents a number of problems for Kneale in regard to the outsider and the landscape.

In spite of much intrigue occurring in government, and at Quatermass's own rocket research laboratory, the real drama occurs when Kneale moves the narrative to the desolate plains of the rural community, as it gives him the opportunity to use the concept of the outsider as a boost of tension (even when the outsider is not really the drama's main protagonist: the real outsider is, of course, an aggressive alien).

In typical Kneale-esque fashion, the fear of outsiders from the city is proven to be fallible; they have the means to uncover the uncomfortable truth about the project that the locals have been blindly working on. In a twist of sardonic wit from Kneale, the close-knit rural community of the village are themselves harbouring an outsider, only one from space, a creature that intends to colonise the planet once it has grown.

In his viewing notes for the play, Andrew Pixley highlighted the mindset that Kneale felt was becoming the norm in society because of this blind and unquestioning nature. 'At the time,' Pixley believes, 'Kneale was very concerned that people took too much on trust from the authorities. Grasping the sense of paranoia about new, potentially dangerous scientific establishments, he wrote of what could happen if an apparently beneficial advancement or research site was in fact in the hands of the enemies.' The main aspect to point out from Kneale's perspective is that outsiders change (or at least want to change) the environment to suit their own needs for the worst. Yet, ironically, only another outsider in this drama is in the position to point this out.

The outsider, in both the context of people from the city and the creature from out of space, has destroyed the local environment and placed guards around its newly occupied area. It's not hard to draw comparisons with both the evolution of the Bloc States and the increasing global paranoia over nuclear war; the people outside your community have the power to not only adapt your environment for their own needs, but the ability to completely destroy it if they wish. It's the ultimate expression of national state paranoia.

Kneale would move in the complete opposite direction for his next instalment of *Quatermass*. In *Quatermass and the Pit*, Kneale would conclude that evil was already here before humanity rather than from somewhere outside, going so far as to suggest we were all aliens, all outsiders. This change may have been due to the world evolving around him, but there is little doubt that Kneale channelled a great, national paranoia into his work, especially because the very essence of the land was so increasingly scarred by the same wire fences and inhuman architecture that we still arguably take for granted today.

Published by Celluloid Wicker Man, 26/01/15

Fox Hunting in Wyrd British Cinema

Few events symbolise the brutality of the countryside as effectively as fox hunting. It highlights the class divisions still present in this country far more powerfully than most other country pursuits. Aside from the obvious power on display by those who still, quite illegally, partake in it, even before its ban in 2004, it had become a symbol of the ultimate violence of the land-owning classes.

Thankfully, the arts have always seen fox hunting for what it is – outside of the clearly inane arguments for it being either pest control or the upkeep of tradition – and no medium has highlighted its violence more brilliantly than cinema.

Films of the wyrd landscape tradition especially have tapped into the nasty hypocrisies and power displayed by fox hunting, and have provided damning critiques for a number of years now.

Thoughts of this idea first began to reverberate when watching Michael Powell and Emeric Pressburger's underrated film *Gone to Earth* (1950). Adapted from the novel by Mary Webb, the film follows the doomed romance between a gypsy (Jennifer Jones) and a fox-hunting squire (David Farrar), all taking place in a lavish rural landscape.

Fox hunting takes centre stage in the drama. Even the title refers to the call given when a fox has disappeared on the hunt. But Powell & Pressburger understood the symbolic potential in the act, especially as a tool to comment on rural class divides and misogyny.

The gypsy, who has a pet fox which is later killed (as is she) by a pack of hounds, plays the role of a fox; with the overtly masculine squire resorting to similar violence and coercion in order to obtain her, even after she has married the local vicar. As is often the case in such films, the landowners treat everything on their land as theirs to do with as they please, even if those things are actually living creatures.

This same theme was heightened several years later in Terence Fisher's adaptation of *The Hound of the Baskervilles* (1959) for Hammer Studios. There is, of course, a natural horror to the act of fox hunting that lends itself well to the genre, though Fisher does something more than just use it as a backdrop.

The film's opening is centred on a group of young men fresh from the hunt and dangerously high on the kill. Fisher shows the natural escalation of the characters, where they see the local servant girl (Judi Moyens) as just another creature to be taken. She is chased across the moor; no doubt in the same way they chased the fox earlier, though a more sexual charge is present.

There's a clear link in both of these films between the act of taking an animal for granted – killing it needlessly for some bestial pleasure – and the taking of a woman's body, both for sexual and violent pleasure. The line between the two is deliberately blurred.

Horror would find other interesting uses for the hunt. In Roger Corman's Edgar Allan Poe adaptation, *The Tomb of Ligeia* (1964), hunting frames the whole of the film's opening. After the initial prelude, the first post-credit sequence is a detailed portrayal of a fox hunt. This is partly to show the difference in attitude of the lead character as he uses the hunt as a ruse to meet a woman (again linking the hunt with sex). But the whole sequence then has later consequences, framing the individuals as deserving the horror to come (especially as it's animal-based vengeance, albeit in the form of a demonic cat rather than a fox).

There are few scenarios better to act as shorthand for grotesque upper-class English characters than to have one waving the corpse of a fox about, such as Derek Francis's Lord Trevanion does in Corman's film. There are undoubtedly many examples of this, arguably too many to list.

Disney used the nastiness of such violence to build a message of caring into their underrated 1981 animation, *The Fox and the Hound*. But the final example I want to draw attention to is not a film but a music video, because it addresses a further issue easily equated with the clear unfairness of the fox-hunting set-up.

For Dizzee Rascal's 2007 single 'Sirens', foxhunting is used as an effective framing of inner city racial inequality and the inherent violence of it. What is so effective about the video, apart from its stunning 35mm aesthetic, is that it manages to displace the act of fox hunting into an overtly urban environment and still make it seem plausible, the gentry effectively exerting their violence everywhere. It's a superb example of the urban wyrd.

The most powerful shot of the video contains a mounted hunter in a small urban flat, attempting to chase the rapper, though the final sequences of men and women dousing their faces with blood (hinted at potentially being that of a working-class Black man) is one of the most powerful and stark images to be found in twenty-first-century music videos.

What is clear from this, and all the previous uses, is that fox hunting, while commenting on a number of inequalities, is ultimately a symbol of power, unfairness, and the belief that financial status gives a free pass to just about any action. With the still prevalent occurrence of hunting with dogs on private land, even after the ban, it has never had a more depressingly potent effect on screen.

Published by Celluloid Wicker Man, 07/10/17

The Landscape in
British Pursuit Films

In the British tradition of the chase-and-pursuit drama, there are several reoccurring themes. The idea of a lone individual being chased through different landscapes by a group was popularised in Britain by media in the Second World War, though it was around long before then. The basic set-up in the loose genre has an individual wanted for some crime or misdemeanour (sometimes falsely). They are pursued by various parties; from the law, who believe they are guilty, to the genuine guilty party that wants an innocent individual silenced.

The most interesting aspect of this sub-genre in its British guise, however, is the varied relationship between the individual (after they have escaped a more urban environment) and the rural landscape used for concealment.

Often such landscapes appear late in the narrative and long after the initial crime has been committed. Most importantly, the main character on the run will have used up all their available means in urban areas, often realising that, through the betrayal of suspecting locals to the relevant authorities, built-up places are not safe if they wish to remain free, or even alive.

It's at this point that characters so often find themselves in hills, pastures and mountains; a last desperate attempt to avoid their pursuers by using dangerous elements of a particular landscape to aid them in their bid for freedom.

One of the earliest examples of this drama in film is Anthony Asquith's *A Cottage on Dartmoor* (1929), but already the genre does something unexpected. The narrative happens in flashback and follows a hapless barber who, in a fit of jealous rage, attacks the lover of a woman he has fallen for, only to be sent to prison. The film concerns his escape from Dartmoor Prison into the valleys of the bleak landscape as he enters the lonely cottage of a couple.

Apart from the fact that the character on the run is actually guilty of his crime, *A Cottage on Dartmoor* shows an opposite of the norms for landscapes in the form later on. The landscape is actually the undoing of Joe (Uno Henning), but through his own choice. The couple have forgiven him for what he did and try to help him to escape, but ultimately fail.

Knowing that any attempt to get back to the cottage will result in the police killing him, he deliberately chooses death, broken-hearted and defeated upon the lonely moors. For an example of how this would work in a more typical scenario, think of Pip in Charles Dickens's *Great Expectations* successfully aiding and abetting escaped prisoner Abel Magwitch on the moody Essex marshes.

In later films (albeit adapted from earlier novels), the landscape would become a refuge for the weary fugitive, often enabling their escape as well as providing vital information. The enemy often seems to reside in rural landscapes, too, as if they find the terrain to their advantage as well.

In 1915, John Buchan wrote the spy thriller *The 39 Steps*. This was later popularised and amended with modern themes by Alfred Hitchcock in 1935, producing perhaps the most typical and entertaining of chase-and-pursuit dramas.

Richard Hannay (Robert Donat) has been falsely accused of murder after accidently becoming involved in a ring of spies. The hapless but resourceful Hannay is pursued through towns, cities and railways by both the police (who want him in connection to the murder), and the gang of spies (who want him because he has too much information to be allowed to live). Eventually, after being caught several times, he escapes into the Highlands of Scotland, where a supposed friendly agent lives.

Hitchcock creates a stunning backdrop out of the Highlands, using a mixture of atmospheric studio recordings and some rare early location filming. It would be a trait he would continue to utilise, most famously in *North by Northwest* (1959), albeit in vivid Technicolor. Such was the strength of Hitchcock's filming in those segments in the Highlands that they also came to define the varied later screen adaptations of Buchan's story, in particular Ralph Thomas's version in 1955 starring Kenneth More.

More important is the narrative use of this landscape. In spite of it being essential for Hannay to traverse, it feels like a natural conclusion to the mystery of the spies, at least for the main character. The locale is also where he finally convinces someone that he is telling the truth, albeit in the warm confines of a remote Highland hotel.

The film is famous for its silhouettes of figures on the skyline, and these moments show when the landscape briefly betrays the character. Once back into the rock and gneiss, however, Hannay is untraceable and only returns to the clutches of his enemies when he enters the home of the main villain, whom he mistakes for an ally.

Mixing both the guiltiness of Asquith's film with the hidden landscapes of Hitchcock's, Charles Crichton's *Hunted* (1952, sometimes known as *The Stranger in Between*) tells a very mixed, vaguely similar tale of pursuit, where the danger of the urban environment becomes part of the narrative. Dirk Bogarde plays Chris, a jealous husband who has just murdered the man who was seeing his wife behind his back (echoing *A Cottage on Dartmoor*). Upon committing the murder in a deserted warehouse, he discovers that a boy has seen him, and abducts him for fear of being given away.

Quickly, it becomes clear that the boy, Robbie (Jon Whiteley), was also running away from an adoptive, abusive household, so was only too glad to be taken. Though Chris tries various urban areas for solace, his luck runs out and he instead jumps a train that takes them to the hilly areas of the north, and eventually to Scotland (again).

It becomes a challenge to traverse the area itself (after all, Robbie is very young), but, in a different way to *The 39 Steps*, the landscape *does* offer refuge from their pursuers. Even when they eventually escape to a sparsely inhabited fishing town in order to steal a boat, the rural location provides enough safety for the pair to almost get away with it. As it turns out, it's only Robbie's oncoming illness that actually scuppers Chris's bid for freedom.

The final film to mention (but by no means the last of this kind) is *Rogue Male* (1977) by Clive Donner. The film was made for television and adapted from the 1939 novel by Geoffrey Household, which is as much a key text in the movement as Buchan's novel.

Following the narrative of Sir Robert Hunter (Peter O'Toole), *Rogue Male* documents Hunter's failed attempt at killing Hitler (played by *Grange Hill* regular Michael Sheard), and then his subsequent escape back to England from Austria after being initially caught, tortured and chased by the Gestapo.

Originally adapted for cinema (albeit to much lesser effect) by Fritz Lang under the title of *Man Hunt* (1941), *Rogue Male* subverts several of the landscape norms established more widely in the genre.

The main character's problems first occur within the rural landscape as opposed to an urban one, contrary to his plans. When Hunter eventually does seek somewhere to hide, he chooses the hills of Dorset, where, unlike the other films' characters, he sets up camp, literally digging himself an underground site to live in with his adoptive cat Asmodeus.

The landscape is subverted again when he's eventually caught by the Gestapo, the place threatening to become a tomb. Luckily, Hunter is more resourceful than his Nazi counterpart and eventually comes through thanks to a makeshift weapon, though he is clearly grateful to the landscape for help in his initial subterfuge and success in escaping.

While this is only a general overview, from these films alone it can be seen that the relationship between landscape and the genre is more complex than a mere backdrop. The rural locations are not simply an excuse to break up the urban monotony, but essential to their structure.

Circumstance changes the way these narratives portray such landscapes and hints towards the complexity that, on a surface reading, may seem to take their rocks and craggy pathways for granted, but are really far off the beaten track compared to more regular film settings.

Published by Celluloid Wicker Man, 29/06/15

Echoes & Imprints: Towards a Sebaldian Cinema

This is an edited transcript of a talk given at Norwich Castle on Tuesday the 27th of August, 2019. My thanks to Dr Nick Warr and Philippa Comber for their help.

Considering the wealth of photography on the walls of the *Line of Sight* exhibition housed next door (*an exhibition detailing many photographs taken by the author for his novels*), it's unsurprising that the work of W.G. Sebald is deeply connected with another visual medium: cinema.

This may seem an unusual statement to make at first considering the lack discussion by the writer regarding the medium, at least in the public realm. I believe, however, that the link is not only perceivable but, more importantly, that such an influence was a two-way street. For the writer was greatly indebted, clearly passionate even, about the medium, and his writing appears to be the result of an immersion in the visual form as much as the more obvious literary one.

Equally, a number of filmmakers have been touched by Sebald's work since his untimely death and so the relationship between the two is unusually complex.

There's no doubt as to the power of Sebald's prose, which is a stark mixture of meandering travelogue, historical archaeology and melancholic observation, matched in atmosphere by the grainy photographs and seemingly inconsequential ephemera that litter his pages. But today, I'm going to talk about Sebald from three angles, all related to cinema rather than literature or photography.

The first is to look at cinema as an influence on Sebald's writing, his relationship to cinema and even his own shadow career as a would-be screenwriter. Moving on from this, the second section will look at Sebald's influence on cinema with the writer being its subject, looking in particular at documentaries about the writer and how making cinema about his work affected the way in which filmmakers approached the medium. And, finally, I will conclude by looking at the potential of a Sebaldian cinema itself; a cinema arguably influenced by his atmospheres but which uses them to create new work.

First, we go back to days before Sebald's rise in the literary pantheon had taken place and to his life as an early career academic; a time filled with cinema visits and scriptwriting.

Sebald and Cinema

Though he rarely mentioned it in his work, other accounts of Sebald's life show it to be one littered with cinema. Philippa Comber recounts meeting Sebald in her book *Ariadne's Thread* (2014). She recalls an early meeting with the writer:

> And so it was that on a warm Saturday evening at the end of August, arrangements were made for a group of us to meet at the Noverre Cinema for a showing of Polanski's 1979 movie, *Tess*.

Later on, she details a number of cinema visits, one particularly apt recounting a screening of Fritz Lang's *M* (1931); apt for it was chosen for the day's entertainment over seeing a Cubism lecture held right here at Norwich Castle. As she writes, 'Max came round again this evening. We went along to Cinema City to see Fritz Lang's *M*, opting for this rather than the lecture on cubism at the Castle Museum.'

Cinema was clearly important to Sebald, more important than is suggested in his novels and in the handful of interviews and essays of his that survive. Once aware of his leaning towards cinema, however, we can begin to see its effect on his prose.

As Nimrod Matin has argued, Sebald's prose, even leaving aside the presence of actual images, could itself be seen as a cinematic rendering of the written form, one argued by Matin to be a response to the equally solid-image prose of Franz Kafka. He writes:

> Its direct effect is a metaphysical shift of time, space and agency, which in turn creates the conditions for the image to become meaningful. Since this movement is a paradigm for writing, it can be seen as an embryonic definition of the cinematographic medium: writing through the setting-in-motion of images so as to enable their becoming meaningful.

This admittedly high-minded idea plays heavily into another: that of French post-structuralist Gilles Deleuze, who argued that cinema shifted from images of movement to images of time after the Second World War. He argued that its emphasis on images and scenes seemed to go directly against cinema, only showing things necessary to a narrative. Time was mapped earnestly rather than figuratively.

Sebald's writing is certainly closer to time-image cinema than narrative cinema but, considering the films that can be connected to him, this is unsurprising.

Sebald himself actually taught a module on early German cinema at the University of East Anglia alongside Professor Thomas Elsaesser, creating a list of suggestions for relevant texts for his students, including films by Robert Wiener, Paul Wegener, F.W. Murnau and Fritz Lang.

Out of all the films that Comber mentions in her book, however, the one that seems truly pivotal to Sebald is, in hindsight of the labyrinths of his own writing, not surprising (and another time-image film). She details it as follows:

> Going to the cinema with Max was a treat. Not long before this, when talking about films, it emerged that there was one that had always held a particular fascination for both of us. This was Alain Resnais' *Last Year in Marienbad*. Its appeal lay as much in the hypnotic quality of the cinematography and soundtrack as the enigma at the core of its narrative. Maybe this predilection dated us; but then, we were children of the sixties – of the Continental sixties.

Alain Resnais and Alain Robbe-Grillet's *Last Year in Marienbad* (1961) is in itself a premonition of some of Sebald's themes.

The film features the melancholia of a European retreat and the unreliability, perhaps even failure, of memory as the protagonist tries to solve the riddle of whether he originally met, and perhaps loved, a woman he meets in a luxurious spa retreat in Marienbad.

Of course, in typical Sebaldian fashion, the film was not actually shot in Marienbad at all but in a spa just outside of Munich (a common cinematic sleight-of-hand that Sebald echoed in his own mischievous photography).

Reading Sebald's work, in particular the Somerleyton segment of *The Rings of Saturn* (1996), reminds of the way Robbe-Grillet treats background characters. As in many films by Robbe-Grillet as director, and to a certain extent in his novels, conversations between main characters render the rest of the world frozen, bodies turning to mannequins as the sheer weight of history within the wider story unfolds.

The links go further still when considering Robbe-Grillet's edited publication of the script as a self-proclaimed *ciné-roman* in which the edited dialogue is interspersed with still photographs from the film. The document, in spite of being a film script and collection of film stills, was meant to be *read*.

So far, so Sebaldian.

There are several references to cinema in Sebald's own work, at least in what has been translated into English. In one of his essays, *Kafka Goes to the Movies,* he mentions the Wim Wenders film *Kings of the Road* (1976).

Part of the German New Wave of cinema that arose in the 1970s, alongside work by the likes of Werner Herzog, Rainer Werner Fassbinder and Volker Schlöndorff, Wenders's film highlights a particularly German take on the road movie, seeming at least in part related to what we could term Sebaldian. The narrative is meandering and melancholy, following two men travelling in an anti-road movie of sorts, recounting their various meetings with strangers on the way.

Equally, in Sebald's *The Emigrants* (1996), the narrator sits in the cinema and has a revelation of sorts whilst watching Werner Herzog's *The Enigma of Kaspar Hauser* (1974), while in *Vertigo* (1990), the references to a certain Dr K touch upon a character from Henrik Galeen's film *The Student of Prague* (1926).

Heavily influenced by Wenders's sometime collaborator Peter Handke (the writer of a stage adaptation of *Kaspar*), it's unsurprising to find some of the films Sebald mentioned loosely connected with the writer. Being a noted admirer of Handke's work, in particular *Repetition* (1986), Sebald's sensibilities are clearly enmeshed in the same visual needs of the cinema around him, and certainly in a Germanic culture that actively sought to exorcise its recent past. As in a great deal of German literature, German New Wave cinema sought to find a new language outside of the previous, war-tainted culture.

Handke, like so many from the group of artists who, in the post-war years, sought to escape their previous cultural baggage, made films as well as writing scripts and novels. Though rarely discussed or even publicised due to the copyright problems and the strict rules of archives, it's unsurprising, then, to find Sebald's early ventures into creative writing take the form, not of experimental novels or poetry, but (like Handke) scripts. Film scripts to be exact.

The first script Comber details regards the life of philosopher Immanuel Kant, called *And Now the Night Descends – Scenes from the Life and Death and Immanuel Kant*.

The script, which was completed and exists in its entirety, came close to actually being produced, allowing for a possible glimpse of an alternative history of Sebald. She describes it as follows:

> There was good news from Jan Franksen, Max's media contact in Berlin. It seemed that the TV station, Sender Freies Berlin, had contrived to secure a hefty sum for the 'Kant Project' – one and a half million marks, he thought. And whilst the studio was proposing to start filming next year, Max remained sceptical: he'd believe it when he saw it…

She further details the angle of the script, hinting at what it might have been like: a typically experimental biography project seeming not unlike films from the same era such as Peter Watkins's *Edvard Munch* (1974), Straub-Huillet's *The Chronicle of Anna Magdalena Bach* (1968), or Herzog's *Kasper Hauser*.

As she writes:

> the use of images was the ideal way to represent the life and works of thinkers of the past. (The same held for his use of images in a book: instead of 'instructing' the reader how or what to think, pictures spoke for themselves.)… Rather than trace Kant's development as a philosopher, or treat his metaphysics in any abstract sense, Max chose to introduce the reader/viewer to a human being of fragile constitution and marked eccentricity.

Alongside this is a less finalised script regarding the life of Ludwig Wittgenstein, though neither project was ultimately realised.

The plan for a chronologically jumbled collection of tableaux from the Wittgenstein's life sounds remarkably like Derek Jarman's later film project, so there was undoubtedly potential in such work.

Yet, the sheer fact of their existence shows that Sebald was cinematically literate, passionate about the medium and that it was an important creative pillar to what would eventually become his novels. In another life, perhaps he could have followed the path of Handke, whose films and novels sit on a vaguely similar plain, at least in mainland Europe.

Perhaps, then, this explains the contents of our next section of discussion; namely, films about the writer and how his work influenced cinema when he himself became the subject matter.

Sebald in Cinema

With the writer's place in the literary world growing exponentially after his death, it's unsurprising to find Sebald become a subject of interest for filmmakers. In many ways, especially due to his use of visuals to break up his prose, his work is ripe for documentary cinema.

The first films to mention Sebald are sadly ones that I can tell little about due to their scarcity. Having spoken to Comber at a recent BBC recording about her friend, film being one of the key connections about which we spoke, films by a director called Thomas Honickel came up in conversation.

Honickel is perhaps best known for his documentary on Fritz Lang's Dr Mabuse film series, *Mabuse in Mind* (1985), appropriately one of the films Sebald taught on his module on German cinema.

In 2007, Honickel made two separate films about the writer, *W.G. Sebald: Der Ausgewanderte* and *Sebald. Orte* (*both uploaded to YouTube since the time of this paper*). The former, which was translated into English, with the subtitle *The Emigrant*, documented his life and included interviews with his previous colleagues, while the latter followed in the footsteps of his books' various narrators.

The most successful film about Sebald to date, critically and in terms of recreating the atmospheres of his work, came in 2012 in the form of Grant Gee's *Patience (After Sebald)*. Simultaneously following the route from *The Rings of Saturn* – recreating many of its original photographic images on grainy black-and-white 16mm – and assessing Sebald's literary standing with a variety of talking-head interviews, the film represents a pivotal moment in appreciation for the writer's work. But, more importantly, *Patience* shows how Sebald's literary vision could be transposed with ease into cinema.

Interestingly, *Patience* as a project came about not as an exploration of *The Rings of Saturn*, but because of interest in *Austerlitz*. As Gee suggested in an interview with Book Forum, the film's title was a reference to that book:

> We went through about three major attempts and different proposals about how to do a film about Sebald. When we came up with the title *Patience*, it was because in the book *Austerlitz* there's a key

scene in which the Sebaldian narrator comes across the Austerlitz character, sees him from behind in a room, and he has a stack of black-and-white photographs. The narrator says he can see Austerlitz dealing them out in a sequence like he's playing a game of Patience, which is like Solitaire in the States.

I was lucky enough to talk to Grant about his project, alongside the film's composer James Leyland Kirby – alias The Caretaker – and, interestingly, Gee clearly saw the cinematic potential in Sebald's prose.

This was Gee's initial thinking about a Sebald film project:

Reading the books for the first time, I had the feeling of a strong, strange, cinematic quality to a strand of Sebald's imagery. More so than even the photographs throughout the books, the written imagery just seemed to suggest grey, grainy, gently seething movie-camera images, a bit like Béla Tarr's shots. Given the subject matter of the books, this seething weirdness was fascinating. Then I was asked by producer Gareth Evans to propose an idea for a trans-media event called The Re-Enchantment; all about artistic examination of place, and the idea crystallised to use the route walked in *The Rings of Saturn* for the form of a film.

Gee's recreation of Sebald's world is startling, a mirror image of the book that manages to use the structure of *The Rings of Saturn* to assess the writer who created it.

It's an innovative use of the original novel, one which reminds of a similar experiment exploring the work of that other East Anglian ghost walker, M.R. James. His haunted short story 'Oh, Whistle, and I'll Come to You, M'Lad' was similarly inverted by Jonathan Miller and turned into a film for BBC *Omnibus* in 1968 that psychologised the thinking behind the story's original writer. The two films also compare in that they both use the East Anglian coastline, including several shared locations (namely the crumbling coastline of Dunwich).

Perhaps the strongest aspect of Gee's film, and certainly why it ultimately is the strongest of Sebaldian films made so far, is the musical collaboration with The Caretaker. In a similar fashion to Sebald, The Caretaker took existing older recordings and played through their crackle until they disintegrated.

Named as part of the hauntology genre in recent years by Mark Fisher, The Caretaker's soundtrack for *Patience* highlighted its memory-ridden aesthetic. When I asked about the relationship between his and Sebald's work, Kirby suggested the following:

> Grant Gee got in touch with me and proposed the idea that he'd love for me to score this film for him based around old recordings of Schubert he'd sourced. After reading the book I could see why Grant approached me, certainly if you look at the graininess of the images in the book. There's a specific quality to that which could be compared to some of The Caretaker work I'd done up to that point. I wanted to stay true to the source material and looked for specific loops and also textures which I felt would work.

Both Gee and Kirby suggested that the use of Schubert's *Die Winterreise* and its various crackly recordings was because it had personal meaning to Sebald, Gee recalling that he'd learned that the music was played at Sebald's funeral.

He could not confirm this for certain, but the point is that the film was produced with a concern for every aspect of the production, recognising that a subject such as Sebald would benefit from being addressed through a common creative language; one filled with memory, disintegration and melancholy. Arguably, these are all central components and echoes when considering the potential for a Sebaldian cinema.

Gee also had the advantage of enlisting an array of knowledgeable speakers to litter his documentary with observations. The sheer diversity of background in the speakers, in particular the presence of people from the visual arts such as artists Tacita Dean and Jeremy Millar, the theatre director Katie Mitchell and the filmmaker Chris Petit, shows Sebald's influence to be essentially a multimedia one.

Dean is a particularly poignant inclusion, considering the presence of her 2007 film *Michael Hamburger* in the exhibition (until recently) housed in the Sainsbury Centre; a Sebaldian meditation on the space and ephemera surrounding the man featured for his ghostly coincidences in *The Rings of Saturn*. Dean's relationship with Sebald's work is complex. Suffice to say, some of these coincidences have manifested in the cinematic medium and, most importantly, through the analogue practices that Dean defiantly still works within to this day.

Gee's film was by no means the last explicitly Sebald-themed project, and was followed a few years later by a little seen film by Stan Neumann. *Austerlitz* (2015) was never properly distributed in the UK, surprising considering it was here where Sebald's literary success was jump-started, but it's available to watch online.

The French film deliberately blurs the line between documentary and fiction, featuring well-known Leos Carax regular Denis Lavant. The film documents, simultaneously, the discovery of Sebald's book and Sebald's overall narrative. Though less successful than Gee's film in recreating the atmosphere of Sebald's book, the film is certainly an interesting inclusion in the slowly growing canon of Sebaldian cinema.

Of course, for a more specific film looking at *Austerlitz*, the shorter film put together by Richard West and Source Photographic Review is also worthy of discussion. The film is barely half an hour in length but features in-depth, detailed exploration of the work, and revisits locations of the photographs Sebald used throughout *Austerlitz*, conducted by Professor Jonathan Long, author of *W.G. Sebald: Image, Archive, Modernity*.

In these films, we get a sense of Sebald's gravitational pull and his keen eye for the most bizarre synchronicities. Simply dealing with his work, his life and his various themes often results in filmmakers being forced to adopt similar ideas in order to do their subject justice.

In the final segment of this discussion, then, we will move on to films that take this Sebaldian mindset and wander further from the source of interest here; namely, films that are Sebaldian without actually being about the writer.

Sebaldian Cinema

What can we really call Sebaldian cinema? It seems a little too easy to suggest the previous films as being somehow uniquely Sebaldian when the writer was their subject. Instead, I argue that a number of films and filmmakers have tapped into the same vein of ghostly history and melancholy place-sketching as Sebald.

Sticking with the theme of *Austerlitz*, we come to another film of the same name. Ukrainian director Sergei Loznitsa has become relatively successful in recent years for similarly themed work, in particular addressing the legacy and the complexity of ghosts from the Second World War.

In his 2016 film *Austerlitz*, he turns his critical eye to what is often described today as 'dark tourism' and the troubling tension that has come from popularised, touristic visits to the remains of concentration camps. Though not connected to Sebald's book, Loznitsa named the film in Sebald's honour, most probably due to dealing with similar themes.

Loznitsa's film, in stark black and white, details the simple actions of tourists taking photos of extermination equipment with iPhones, going on disturbingly Tower-of-London-esque guided tours, and capturing selfies with the gates of Auschwitz and their motto *Arbeit macht frei*, hashtagged naturally.

In more calming, less critical work, we can see some Sebaldian potential in the work of filmmaker Ben Rivers. Filming on 16mm film, as so many filmmakers here do – Sebaldian cinema being distinctly analogue – his memory-drenched images of landscape and solitude bear more than a passing resemblance to both the photographs in Sebald's books and the general atmosphere of the prose they are placed within.

In *Two Years at Sea* (2011), Rivers shows the same keen eye for eccentric characters, capturing the life of Jake, a hermit who lives a Thoreau-esque life in the forests of Scotland. He could be a figure straight out of Sebald's *The Emigrants* or *Vertigo*.

Rivers also grapples with a common question raised by Sebald's work: namely, the blurred line between the real and the fictional. He turns the very process of filmmaking in upon itself, fitting narratives into the capture of other film projects, in particular his Paul Bowles-inspired project *The Two Eyes Are Not Brothers* (2015) in which his narrative occurs in the midst of the filming of someone else's real film. If any filmmaker comes close to recreating Sebald's slippery, almost auto-fictional elements, it is Rivers.

Looking at more narrative-based cinema, its most successful Sebaldian exploration is arguably in Andrew Haigh's *45 Years* (2015), a film that surprisingly swept the awards season on both sides of the Atlantic.

Its Sebaldian narrative of restless memories manifesting may perhaps owe as much to its original source material by David Constantine being distinctly Sebaldian as the choices in the film itself.

With its tale of a lost love reasserting itself as a painfully destructive ghost in the East Anglian countryside, breaking apart the relationship between Tom Courtenay and Charlotte Rampling, the film is essentially a romantic tragedy fitted into the mould of the Henry Selwyn segment of *The Emigrants*. Such is the likeness between the film and the story, even down to the location of Switzerland housing the lost loved one and the outer Norwich landscape being the realm of the haunting, that *45 Years* is really as close to a big-budget adaptation of a Sebald novel as we are likely to see.

I could go on to list filmmakers whose imagery draws likenesses to Sebald – I will mention here the filmmaker Guido van der Werve and his film *Nummer Zestien* (2015) in passing – but the point would often be moot, as the writer's mentality has crept quietly into a great deal of culture and many different forms.

Finally, then, and perhaps naïvely, there are the short films of my own, argued as being Sebaldian specifically because they were designed by my own admission to be so.

Shot on Super-8 stock that is older than me, I've often sought the Sebaldian disintegration in image and theme, going so far as to track several East Anglian locations touched by the writer and equally taking the themes of his prose one step further into strange and wyrd realms.

To conclude, I will screen my own short film *Heavy Water* (2016), reacting to the friction found on the Suffolk coastline between Sizewell and Dunwich. It's the same friction tapped into in *The Rings of Saturn*; where the past destruction of the lost town of Dunwich and the implied, unconscious future destruction hinted at by the looming structure of Sizewell Nuclear Power Station possesses an unusually eerie quality.

In conclusion, I hope this presentation has shown how Sebald was influenced, fluent, and perhaps even indebted to cinema as a medium. It's there in his past and it's there in his prose. I also hope that, in showing how Sebald as a subject augmented the medium, the potential for an actual Sebaldian cinema was initially opened. But most of all, I hope that such a potential is, in the future, realised further;

whether in new films or perhaps, if we are lucky, in adaptations of the writer's own scripts that already exist, currently gathering dust in archives, carefully protected by the guard dogs of copyright.

Once the work of this visually adept, detailed and powerful writer is taken into the mind's eye, his gaze cannot be easily switched off; his filter upon the world retains its startling ability to cut through the haze, and the potential of it, in our increasing age of circular history and calamity, has never promised so much that is necessary to all creative forms, film or otherwise.

Published by Celluloid Wicker Man, 03/09/19

Ghostly Remembrance in *45 Years*

On finishing W.G. Sebald's novel *The Emigrants* (1992), it felt
as if some loose connection to a recent film or book was left
hanging mid-air. The narrative of Sebald's novel is split into
the stories of four émigrés, all seemingly interconnected by
a multitude of strange images but chiefly by their fleeing
from Nazi Germany.

The connection didn't seem to be so much in relation to
the book's latter three narratives, but to the first and shortest
segment looking into the life of the husband of one of
Sebald's landlords in 1970s Norfolk, Dr Henry Selwyn. The
portrayal of Selwyn is a tragic one: a distanced, eccentric
man who appears to have been acutely estranged from his
wife for unnamed reasons.

It was only upon re-watching Andrew Haigh's recent
film *45 Years* (2015) that the connection clicked: this was the
film whose themes, not say to atmosphere, were astonishingly
parallel to Sebald's narrative.

Suffice to say, *45 Years* also concerns an elderly couple,
Kate and Geoff (Charlotte Rampling and Tom Courtenay),
whose upcoming forty-fifth anniversary, not to say their
pleasant retirement in Norfolk, is shattered by the revelation
that the body of Geoff's first love (who died in a hiking
accident in the Swiss Alps some years previous) has finally
been freed from the tomb of ice preserving her body.

The drama unfolds as Geoff's previous feelings reawaken with the discovery, questioning the ageing of both the body and emotions, but also dragging down Kate, whose life is all but in tatters by the end of the film.

Haigh described *45 Years* as a ghost story, stating in an interview with *The Film Stage* that it 'was all kind of trying to make it feel like we're watching a ghost story unfold'. The same feeling is present in Sebald's narrative.

Dr Henry Selwyn is himself haunted. The shadow of a man he lost in a strikingly similar accident walking in the Swiss Alps is hinted at being the rupture that led to the distance between Selwyn and his wife. The character tells Sebald's narrator of a short stay in Berne before the outbreak of the First World War, and the loss of his friend Johannes Naegeli.

'Even the separation from Elli,' he wrote, 'whom I had met at Christmas in Berne and married after the war, did not cause me remotely as much pain as the separation from Naegeli.' Selwyn even suggests that Naegeli, in spite of being dead, 'seems closer whenever he comes to my mind' than his wife Elli who 'has come to seem a stranger to me over the years'.

Naegeli, according to Selwyn, 'had fallen into a crevasse in the Aare glacier'. This highlights the relationship between the two works. Though the pain started for Selwyn when saying farewell to Naegeli at a train station at Meriningen, rather than witnessing the full accident as Geoff did, the impact appears to be the same.

Perhaps a slight difference (apart from the angle of relationship) is the place in time where the two stories sit. While *45 Years* charts the initial breakdown directly after such a revelation, Selwyn's story plays as one potential future that Geoff has waiting for him after the conclusion of the film.

Geoff's behaviour deteriorates rapidly upon receiving the news of his lover's retrieved body. He mimics the behaviour of Selwyn, who lives as a hermit, largely in the garden of the Norfolk house. The fact that both feature the Norfolk landscape, too, heightens the resemblance; the landscape being a flat, endless vista suitable for literary and screen hauntings of all kinds. It's also, after all, a landscape that is littered with enough debris from the past to bring out the most melancholic of Sebald's thoughts and writing, even when dealing with subjects that appear to have little to no connection with the county.

Selwyn's story ends in the ultimate tragedy: suicide. Sebald, however, does not let the haunting end with his death, but meets the inorganic demon of this episode while on holiday in Switzerland. Travelling from Zürich to Lausanne, he finds a newspaper detailing the recovery of Naegeli's body which 'had been released by the Oberarr glacier, seventy-two years later'.

It's a detail which he fails to spot until the train itself is actually crossing the Aare Bridge. This melancholic synchronicity again is reminiscent of *45 Years*, whose whole narrative is one of timing; the movement of the ice releasing the ghost only days before an (already interrupted) anniversary of a delicate relationship.

As Sebald finally writes when talking about Selwyn, 'they are forever returning to us, the dead. At times they come back from the ice more than seven decades later and are found at the edge of the moraine, a few polished bones and a pair of hobnailed boots.'

Published by Celluloid Wicker Man, 01/02/16

Larkin's Spirit in *Requiem for a Village*

> I thought it would last my time –
> The sense that, beyond the town,
> There would always be fields and farms,
> Where the village louts could climb
> Such trees as were not cut down;
> I knew there'd be false alarms
> – 'Going, Going', Philip Larkin

Above is the opening stanza of Philip Larkin's 1972 poem 'Going, Going'. The poem captures the sense of a world being lost, and is deeply concerned with the disappearance of rural ways of life in particular.

Four years after Larkin published 'Going, Going', filmmaker David Gladwell made the first of his two feature films, *Requiem for a Village* (1974), which is one of the few British films of the same period to channel Larkin's frustration over the issue.

What was being lost to both Larkin and Gladwell was the enclosed nature of the English village and, in the era of the 1970s, this was a steady but constant evolution that had been unfolding since the end of the Second World War: the threat of the bulldozers and the rise of the brutalist New Towns concerned both artists.

Neither, I argue, was gripped by nostalgia for some golden age of innocence, but instead they were concerned with the direction of their present; condemning the replacement of small-scale community with the dramatic increase of housing, roads and general interconnectivity required for a vastly growing population.

The inevitability of this conclusion means that both the poem and the film have an air of melancholy in their representations of rural life, as well as a sense of extremity when depicting the oncoming presence of suburban and urban life. They are both deeply paranoid works, though such a characteristic doesn't negate the negative impact of some of the changes seen:

> And that will be England gone,
> The shadows, the meadows, the lanes,
> The guildhalls, the carved choirs.
> There'll be books; it will linger on
> In galleries; but all that remains
> For us will be concrete and tyres.

Larkin is concerned with the encroachment of concrete upon his beloved villages, whereas Gladwell is more interested in building a collection of images to show both types of places before their clashing. For Gladwell, there is an ironic likeness between the people from each landscape. He is less fusty than Larkin on this point.

On saying this, however, Gladwell does present the coming of suburbia as being a powerful enough threat to literally waken the dead, the deceased villagers rising out of their graves à la Stanley Spencer. They are, however, rising to attend a worried village meeting rather than due to some transcendent calling. Compare this scene (the film's most famous and visually stunning moment) with the several segments from 'Going, Going', and Larkin could quite easily be seen as one of Gladwell's disgruntled villagers.

For Gladwell, Larkin's tragedy has already happened. The meeting of the people in the town seems deeply ironic as motorcycle gangs from nearby towns, thanks to the new roads, terrorise the area. The threat has already arrived, but their actions were already mimicked by local people anyway (specifically violence and sexual assault). Gladwell's vision refuses the uniquely positive vision conjured by Larkin. The director's vision is arguably closer to the brutality found in Ronald Blythe's *Akenfield* (1969), though it's worth noting that Peter Hall's 1974 film version drops the hardship for an equal Larkin-ish nostalgia.

Requiem for a Village becomes one of the artefacts that Larkin talks about in his poem, a reminder that a certain breed of English life 'will linger on' but only in artwork and 'in galleries', though hardly even in the latter any more. Spencer's paintings, for example, have long since been problematised by the reactionaries that increasingly inhabit the art world and are determined to nanny the viewer of any given painting with the usual finger-wagging sensibilities. The threat of being covered or hidden away in the archives to appease such bad actors ever lingers.

As 'Going, Going' progresses, Larkin's seething rage builds to the point where it clouds his vision with a pessimism that becomes sardonic. Clearly the new development of the landscape had a stark effect on the ageing poet, who seemed to be at the epicentre of an evolving and changing topography (though, in reality, he wasn't).

The closest Gladwell comes to sharing this anger is in the portrayal of the motorbike gang, a common rebellious symbol in cinema post-*The Wild One* (1953) and *Easy Rider* (1969). Interestingly, it's the ease between the estates they come from and the village in question that Gladwell seems to question. Roads are Gladwell's real enemy, and he has a morbid fascination with them.

Compare this to a pulp film such as Don Sharp's *Psychomania* (1973) and the difference becomes clear. While the portrayal and actions of bikers entering rural locales is very similar in both films, the key difference is that the bikers in the pulp film search out a rural locale as a sanctuary from the stuffy confines of a 1970s urban environment (they choose to hang around a stone circle over the newly brutalist Henley-on-Thames, quite understandably) but often release their frustration upon their fellow urban dwellers when back in the concrete streets.

In *Requiem for a Village*, the bikers also search out a rural plateau to escape their bland suburbia, and release their inhibitions within the countryside, where the rules seem intangible. The isolated fields, meadows and country lanes are open ground for their carnal desires.

While 'Going, Going' and *Requiem for a Village* channel very similar ideas and themes, one final difference is worth noting between the two works. Larkin's poem was one of the last he would write, predicting a future that was yet to fully finalise (it's telling that the poem's title implies an unrealised 'gone'; Larkin's prediction had yet to come true).

Gladwell, on the other hand, sees rural life already in the past tense. It's something to question the memory of, certainly, but also something to cherish. The position of tense is the key difference between the works. While both reflect a strange moment in 1970s British culture, they summarise a surreal supposition of how landscape should conform; one that never really existed in quite the way they mourn for but one still worth remembering, especially as most remnants of it have been obliterated in the years since passed, whether it was as they remembered it or not.

Published by Celluloid Wicker Man, 27/04/15

Place and Youth in *A Portrait of Ga*

In making a short film about her mother, Scottish poet and experimental filmmaker Margaret Tait also explored the interesting relationship between place and youth. In *A Portrait of Ga* (1952) – a four-minute short film shot on 16mm with a voice-over by the filmmaker – a fragment of biography becomes a joyous portrait of both place and the filmmaker's mother.

Known as Ga, a name that the film suggests was gifted to her by her grandchildren, Tait's mother is shown throughout the film to engage in the everyday rituals of walking along paths, climbing up grassy knolls, eating sweets, smoking cigarettes and dancing. Yet the effectiveness of the film is the placement of all these actions within a wider landscape. In emphasising the ordinary in quiet detail, Tait imbues the film's collection of moments with a higher sense of purpose. *A Portrait* is, at the very least, a monument erected to small, everyday moments.

The calm simplicity of Tait's work makes deeper readings needless, but there's certainly an impression of wider ineffability surrounding these rituals. As Tait herself suggested when discussing why she made the film, it was more to do with a personal interest in creating a maternal portrait. 'My mother seemed a good subject for a portrait,' she admitted, 'she was there, and I thought it offered a chance to do a sort of "abstract film", in the sense that it didn't have what you might call "the grammar of film".'

Tait suggests that the editing of the film is mostly ungrammatical, with what appears to be little actual post-editing, and only in-camera cuts connecting the occasional moment of shared colour (a reoccurring theme for the artist).

There's logic to its place-memory, the film reel collating bits and bobs of Ga's life and her home on the Orkney Islands with the same randomness of recollection. In other words, the shooting seems momentary, instinctive and personal rather than academic or tied to narrative concerns.

Perhaps because of the inherent Scottishness of the film and its subject, *A Portrait* – and Ga herself, for that matter – brings to mind the writing of Nan Shepherd. Shepherd writes of a fluency of walking pace that's gained from regularly exploring more mountainous paths (or at least paths less travelled). This chimes with Tait's film.

Shepherd writes in her book *The Living Mountain* of this fluency of foot. 'Eye and foot acquire in rough walking a co-ordination that makes one distinctly aware of where the next step is to fall,' she suggests, 'even while watching sky and land.' In a similar fashion, *A Portrait*'s opening shot shows Ga walking and ascending a roadside hill towards the camera with total dexterity; earnestly walking beyond the ease of the tarmac path in order to pick a flower, to sit in the grass and have a smoke.

The film continues in a similar fashion, with virtually every shot of Ga outside showcasing her hopping and jumping around scraggy patches and fields with youthful exuberance. Part of the film's charm is its sense of total abandon. She embodies with ease Shepherd's most famous phrase, 'It is a grand thing, to get to live.'

Place plays its role in this abandon, just as much as the unwrapping of a boiled sweet does in another segment of the film. There's even a hint of childish rebellion through such a playful relationship with the landscape. Ga, when on obviously easier terrain such as a road, starts to skip and break into little runs as a fading rainbow hangs over the hills. She even dances when back in the confines of her own garden; that is, when she is not digging and tending her plants.

The sense that the place has imbued her with a defiantly youthful bearing is perhaps less to do with Tait's editing (or lack of) and more to do with her subject. But her capture of it is still warming and masterfully subtle.

Author Ali Smith has written of *A Portrait*'s wonder, and her thoughts tie well with Shepherd's vivacious sense of aliveness in the landscape. 'A long-shot of her mother,' Smith describes, 'from behind, almost running almost dancing along a rural road beneath a greyed-out rainbow is, in that miraculous Tait way, so placed, so unquaint and so natural, as to leave its viewer renewed and knowing again what it is, simply to be alive.'

How appropriate it is to finish the film with Ga yet again climbing another grassy hill, this time in windier weather; leaving the viewer as renewed as a spry Scottish grandmother finding childlike exuberance in facing down the breeze on an Orkney hillside.

Published by Celluloid Wicker Man, 04/07/16

Derek Jarman's Avebury

One of Derek Jarman's first short Super-8 films was the haunting *A Journey to Avebury*. Early evidence that Jarman was interested in the genii loci of English landscapes, his walk through the Wiltshire landscape (taken after the intense stint of work on the sets for Ken Russell's *The Devils* (1971)) had a greater influence on him than the singular short film suggests.

The ancient landscape generated a whole range of minimalist paintings by Jarman, very much in the abstract tradition of Paul Nash and others, as well as the more popular short film (arguably famed for its posthumously applied soundtrack by cult musicians Coil, as well as for its social-media-friendly esoteric imagery, now very much in vogue). Jarman has always been a quiet landscapist as well as the gay pagan punk that the galleries like to characterise him as.

Having painted landscapes since leaving school, it could be said that this silent creeping of landscape into Jarman's work, later manifesting in his garden at Prospect Cottage in Dungeness, stems from his earlier exploration of the landscapes of Avebury. He seems to have been possessed for a time by the fields and stones of the little village.

A Journey to Avebury is sometimes treated as the overall output of this dreamy summer period, but Jarman produced roughly a painting a year of Avebury during the early years of the 1970s, recreating the same landscape while experimenting with the area's natural and manmade landforms through colour and line.

In paintings such as *Landscape with a blue pool* (1967), *Landscape* and *Landscape II* (years unknown, though undoubtedly between 1967 and 1970), Jarman reduced landscapes to a blank colour – either the colour of the canvas itself as in the latter two, or painting it one flat colour as in the former – and filled it with abstract landforms, horizontal lines creating the perspective of distance and the gradient of the land.

These were then contrasted with occasional, more overt presences such as the blue pool and rocks in *Landscape with a blue pool* or a ritualised person seemingly sat under a totem in *Landscape II*. He referred to these as 'eye-tricking imagery'. The latter is especially interesting in that the vertical lines feel like totemic objects rather than trees or other such natural features.

They are paintings fluent in esoteric ambiguity.

Jarman was clearly interested in re-mythologising such landscapes, finding quiet power in the typical English vista. It's no wonder he felt such a connection to Avebury when he eventually visited.

In the Avebury series of paintings, Jarman uses the same technique to form landscapes but is reacting to an overtly enchanted place. The natural obtrusion of Avebury's many menhir fits Jarman's minimal form, ironically mimicking their real relationship to the eye; their strangeness in the landscape renders the fields around them unusually blank. The grass is undeniably Avebury's canvas and not its main feature.

In these paintings, totemic poles cast their shadows on the canvas grass, accompanied by a variety of stones sitting upon planes created by horizontal lines. In a sense, Jarman does not present the landscape as it is but in abstraction, bunching up West Kennet Avenue and the like into a neat projection.

With the stones placed at random in the paintings, it would not be surprising to find them taken as models from his Super-8 footage. He certainly didn't paint them in situ.

In *A Journey to Avebury*, many shots consist solely of one stone, mostly taken around the main ring of the village. *Avebury Series No. 2* and *No. 4* (1973) have a sense of these objects being lifted from the landscape and realigned, collage-fashion, in a memory-scape of Jarman's own making.

Like *A Journey to Avebury*, the series feels like a false memory of the place. It's a fragmented, imagined Avebury. These are the bare bones of the place stained on Jarman's retina, retained in the mind and then reassembled. It's the equivalent of an incredibly neat and tidy scrapbook; something that Jarman would keep more earnestly about his own garden in Dungeness, later published variously as pretty coffee-table books.

Interestingly, the painting Jarman put most of the Avebury menhir into is not officially part of the series but instead a 1973 painting called *Sand Base*. The fact that it's painted in the same style and in the same year as *Avebury Series No.4* suggests that it's still part of the same general movement of work, even if not officially so. But there's something different about the stones in this work.

Whereas the stones in previous paintings generally have the same texture, the stones here are split into two forms. One lead stone is full of detail like the leader of a cult, while the other follower stones are painted in oily black. Some stones on the painting even feel observed with a bird's-eye view, the black rocks only defined by the shadows they cast upon the ground.

There's an unusual sense of a community created in the painting through a hierarchy of stone; as if we are witness to some ceremony that human eyes were not meant to see as the sun dipped under the horizon.

Published by Celluloid Wicker Man, 20/02/17

Derek Jarman's Garden

Sometimes I find myself staring idly at pictures of a garden. The garden is far from normal, resembling instead an alien world. Within its hazy border is a strange array of plants, shingle, driftwood sculptures, metallic debris of all sorts, a cabin painted black with tar, a nuclear power station on the horizon and, most importantly, no fence. It just goes on as far as the eye can see.

The garden is, of course, the shingly vista that surrounds Derek Jarman's Prospect Cottage in Dungeness. I find it fascinating, not so much from a horticultural point of view, but in what it says about the artist himself. It's as if Jarman left behind the most intimate of self-portraits when he passed away on the 19th of February 1994.

Jarman's garden represents an unusual rebellion, which ultimately informs us as much about its attendant's creative thinking as his gardening ability. In between the beauty and the quietude, there's something that connects his undeniably English eccentricity with a genuine radicalism; two things which seem poles apart in 2019.

Though born in Middlesex, Jarman's life was often spent on the move. After attending boarding school in Dorset, he eventually went to King's College and then Slade School of Fine Art in the 1960s. Though initially a painter – a preoccupation that would never leave him – Jarman quickly found his way into the film industry via set design and, eventually, Super-8 films.

He made his first fully fledged feature, *Sebastiane*, in 1976. From then on, Jarman courted controversy with an array of increasingly dazzling but provocative films; visceral in a way that I feel people who obsess over Jarman's garden today don't really engage with. Diagnosed as HIV positive in late 1986, he became a figurehead for gay rights activism; work that comfortably sat alongside his filmmaking, writing, painting, and, of course, work on the garden itself.

If Jarman's body of work is considered in its entirety, a sense of opposing aspects becomes palpable. His early paintings, often of landscapes such as Avebury in Wiltshire, share calmness with some of Paul Nash's eerily empty anti-pastoral works. Yet, it was his loudly urban feature films that gained Jarman notoriety, and he was constantly brought out to defend his radical reimagining of cinema within an increasingly hostile society. This was, after all, an era represented by Mary Whitehouse as much as Margaret Thatcher. Provocation became an art for Jarman, but a very natural one.

Jarman's radical vision extended all the way back to the likes of William Blake, John Dee and Gerrard Winstanley; the radicals, mystics and outcasts of English history. His own era, on the other hand, looked inwards, and pessimistically so. The world was solely a free market. Our projected national identity was little else but a retread of fantasies, a faux benevolence to the world that handily discarded the violence that underpinned it.

Jarman saw through this simplistic identity, often skewering it in his films (though I equally doubt he would have time for today's self-styled, self-serving culture of radical activists and artists; so inane in just about everything they do, politically or creatively).

Even if it acknowledged the collapse of liberal optimism, Jarman's radicalism never in itself seemed indulgently pessimistic. In *The Last of England* (1987), a film that views Thatcher's Britain as a dystopian bombsite run by thugs, there's something about its imagery that feels rebellious in a celebratory way, a cathartic release of rage. He was never high on his own fumes like the current creative generation.

When Tilda Swinton, adorned in a regal wedding dress, screams as flames lick the Dungeness horizon, it feels oddly optimistic; rage could not be extinguished by the blanket of neoliberalism.

Equally, dealing with the inherent homophobia of the times, his 1992 film, *The Garden,* used kitsch elements of gay culture to celebrate and defend its communities from the violence that it faced. And in *Blue* (1993), Jarman still finds beauty as the whole world literally disintegrates into the blind cobalt of his illness. The film, much like his journals, resists wallowing in the obvious sadness of the situation and bounces right off it. He is biting, enraged, witty, even playful about his own pain.

He is never less than radical.

In hindsight, Jarman's death felt like the end of something, in cinematic terms at least. Right from his controversial debut, Jarman bookended the revitalisation of British cinema. In the late 1970s, when it was (for some) virtually deceased, Jarman paved the way for what could loosely be called the British Film Institute film (for better and for worse).

Whether in subsequent work by Peter Greenaway, Terence Davies, John Akomfrah or Sally Potter, Jarman's inspiration changed the landscape of cinema and left it fertile for a new wave of filmmaking, unafraid to push the boundaries, even if sometimes falling into the more recognisable back-patting indulgence and self-aggrandising that characterises the same creative realm today.

He was a gardener of the cinematic landscape as much as his own shingly dwelling, making violent interventions into the ground in the hope of allowing something vibrant to flourish once more, in a future he would not see. What grew was mostly magnificent.

With Jarman's death in 1994, that wave of creativity seemed to come to an end, or at least the support that such radical filmmaking had briefly garnered dried up. Greenaway followed the money abroad and began making more theatrical film projects. Davies, in spite of his array of dazzling Liverpool-based films, ran into more and more financial difficulty, a state only now being reversed. Akomfrah moved to the gallery and Potter, despite the brilliant *Orlando* in 1992, made only one other feature film in the 1990s, fading subsequently into the realm of comfortable arthouse bland.

Jarman's spirit lives on in work by the likes of Isaac Julien, Andrew Kötting, Clio Barnard and Francis Lee to name but a few, though the commercial conditions for making independent cinema have barely improved in the last quarter century, and it is impossible to discuss some of these filmmakers without accepting the peaks or troughs in the quality of their work, usually caused by financial difficulty more than anything else.

Jarman's passing represents so much to so many different people, and yet there's something in his loss that feels like an endpoint for a certain form of British cultural daring. This was a period when figures like Jarman invested time in striving towards the unknown; that saw the country, like his garden, without needless barriers, erected out of malice or mere grandstanding uselessness.

Jarman himself was, for example, scathing about Kenneth Branagh's *Peter's Friends*, and later in the 1990s, England would soon be swallowed by a cinema of affluent myths, a tyranny of *Four Weddings* visual chintz; where the capital was the only city on the map, and even then only in highly edited fragments. A new cultural landscape of socially pedestrian, conformist fantasy would come to dominate, and even those who had previously documented and explored things outside of this world (Ken Loach, Mike Leigh et al) faded into the comfort zone of their own bland iteration of politics and echo chambers.

We still live in the shadow of this unadventurous cinema, where the radicals have a hymn sheet to sing from, if only to satisfy strangers on social media and their deranged, pervasive need to have every facet of their own socio-political views childishly reflected back at them note for note. Jarman would have had none of it.

The director's voice is much missed but his radical spirit is certainly a blueprint for how to respond to the age of boring culture and simplistic politics. He knew that the answer was always rebellion, loud or quiet, upset or in agreement; pottering about in his overalls in the garden or causing chaos in the cinema.

I imagine him now looking out beyond the plants and rusted metal of Prospect Cottage, a vision which he knew would just roll on over the sea and beyond, no matter how many fences he might have erected on its ever-shifting shoreline.

Published by The Quietus, 19/02/19

Back-to-the-Land in *Nuts in May*

Though far lighter in tone than many other works by Mike Leigh, the director's 1976 episode of the BBC's *Play for Today*, *Nuts in May*, surprisingly asks more pertinent and still relevant questions than many of his more overtly political and visceral social-realist works. This is arguably because of the effective framing around its very particular landscape and the tension found between countryside and class.

First broadcast during a particularly snowy January, *Nuts in May* must have seemed alien with its sunny jaunts and green chalk-land exploration of Dorset. But, alongside this sense of a revitalised spring (also implied by the unusual title taken from the nursery rhyme of the same name) is a portrayal of the slow disintegration of social barriers initiated by the journey into some sense of the wild. Assumptions regarding the natural landscape being purely for refreshment and healing turn out to be far from reality.

The play follows a pair of middle-class suburbanites, Keith (Roger Sloman) and Candice-Marie (Alison Steadman), as they take a break from their typical day-to-day monotony by replacing it with equal monotony disguised as a fun exploration of rural Dorset. They pack their Morris Minor to the brim and pay in advance to camp in an initially tranquil site. With expert precision and walking pace, Keith leads Candice-Marie through a range of breathless tourist activities; from looking for fossils in a quarry and walking bracingly along the Jurassic Coast to the Durdle Door, followed by a whistle-stop visit to Corfe Castle.

All is not well in the sanctuary of their holiday, however, as various problems arise with the pair's camping neighbours; first with the radio-playing Ray (Anthony O'Donnell), then a loud pair of Brummies starting illegal fires to cook sausages with. After several confrontations and a minor breakdown, Keith and Candice-Marie are forced to leave the site and find a new plot to spend the rest of their holiday, though not before Keith, the arbiter of sanctimonious rules and regulations, has been humiliated by a policeman. Blocking his rear-view mirror with overloaded miscellanea of holiday necessities was his downfall.

One of the narratives that *Nuts in May* exposes as questionable, perhaps even more so in hindsight, is the simplistic idea of the rural landscape healing wounds caused by the toil and bustle of urban life. It's the ultimate send-up, in foreshadow, of the *Guardian*'s never-ending obsession with wild swimming, and the vast library of books published about the wellness possibilities of nature and the countryside.

As Keith especially finds out, it actually turns into the reverse by unleashing more primitive and rule-breaking aspects of the human condition, traits often reserved and assumed as being part of an urban environment.

Even if it's clear that all the main characters are from inner-city areas, their baggage of cooked-up social pressure is ironically unleashed rather than quelled by the Dorset landscape.

Many landscape-infused works from the same period touch upon this in some way. Jonathan Miller's M.R. James adaptation, *Whistle and I'll Come to You* (1968) for the BBC's *Omnibus*, finds a parallel of suburban enlightenment and academia falling apart as it underestimates the East Anglian landscape and its impossibly old menaces.

Another *Play for Today* episode, *Robin Redbreast* (1970), directed by James MacTaggart and written by John Bowen, finds an equal Oxbridge urbanite falling foul of a rural village's old ways and violent, ritualistic adherence to a landscape-based pagan belief system.

Nuts in May does something slightly different to even these strange examples, however, for the unfolding drama and descent into eventual violence comes from the overall anarchy that the rural realm unleashes. Keith's measured and meticulous adherence to the rules finds little purchase when confronted with the Brummies' illegal fire-building. His reasoning with them fails, ultimately culminating in the release of his own pressured violence, swinging for them psychotically (and appropriately armed with the branch of a tree).

Imagining the same scene in an urban environment highlights just how much the rural realm shifts the sensibilities of the characters. It's the same pressure unleashed in Ben Wheatley's *Sightseers* (2012), though the increasingly violent pair in that film take it to absurd, psychotic territory; a sort of Michael Myers exercise sponsored by National Trust gift shops and English Heritage afternoon teas. It's also a far less socially astute film, in that it's mostly made in homage to Leigh's film more than anything else.

The rural fails to provide Keith and Candice-Marie with a slightly pleasanter canvas to enact their repetitive habits upon as they (or at least Keith) clearly hoped. Instead, it forces them to confront the repression of their puritanical lives, realising that the grass is not greener. People are the real makers of place, grey or green.

This was a growing theme in literature of the twentieth century, too. In writing by the likes of Edward Thomas, George Ewart Evans and J.A. Baker, the sheer indifference and toil of rural life, rather than the sponge-like purpose of a land supposed to soak up urban angst, was quietly questioned. French writing arguably understood this even better and earlier, thanks largely to Maupassant, Pagnol and Zola.

Equally, these ideas had been gradually taking hold in British cinema at almost the exact same time as Leigh's play. In David Gladwell's *Requiem for a Village* (1976), the same truth that Keith had clearly been blind to, that violence is more readily conjured when urbanites enter the rural realm (either as victims or as antagonists), is palpable.

In Kevin Brownlow and Andrew Mollo's *Winstanley* (1976), too, the sheer toil and fight to work the rural pastures is laid all too bare. Keith has also reversed the journey and desires of the main character from Peter Hall's adaptation of Ronald Blythe's *Akenfield* (1974), the character there actually wishing to escape his rural life for something more urban rather than vice versa.

Keith, of course, learns these lessons the hard way, descending into violence and eventually humiliation. It's equally apt that, when finally finding a new site to stay for the rest of the holiday, he's forced to finally break his own belief in the rules and climb over a barbed-wire fence to avail himself of the woods. Though the hardship of rural life was all too present in cinema and television of this period, *Nuts in May* is one of the first examples to properly address the psychosis unleashed in a domestic sense; whereby even a tranquil coastal holiday can remove the social inhibitions keeping us one step away from murdering the next person to cause us some petty annoyance.

Perhaps what makes *Nuts in May* truly special is that it was suggesting all of this in a period when such ideas were still being romanticised, especially by the suburban middle-classes keen to indulge their growing New Age fetishes; again, something that hasn't really changed.

The Back-to-the-Land movement that became vogue in the era is a surreal backdrop to Leigh's film, and gives it even more bite. *Nuts in May* was, after all, broadcast in the first year of *The Good Life* (1975–77). With that series being the poster-boy for such 'grow your own' self-sufficiency movements, *Nuts in May* feels like a strange parallel narrative where, instead of giving up the stressful job and attempting a simpler life in Surbiton, as happens to Tom (Richard Briers) in the series, we see what happens if he'd simply decided to take a holiday with Barbara (Felicity Kendal) to Dorset instead.

Even more fittingly, Dorset is the same coast that saw Reggie Perrin (Leonard Rossiter) of the series *The Fall and Rise of Reggie Perrin* (1976–79) at the beginning of each episode have a minor breakdown; finding the only escape from suburban tedium to be a failed suicide attempt on that same stretch of Jurassic Coast rather than a holiday.

Keith is a distant cousin of both Tom and Reggie, one who made the wrong decision and is ultimately stuck with the solitude of his rule-keeping. Alighting over the fenced boundaries to answer nature's only calling left, Keith is really a sympathetic fallen idol of sorts, albeit one who sings awful folk songs and insists on chewing food seventy-two times before swallowing.

He and his rules are barely functioning in the landscape by the end of the play, the sort of Perrin exercise of wandering naked into the sea being only conceivably a step away from his barbaric earlier efforts with the tree branch.

As Keith aptly suggests when Candice-Marie worries about the opinion of ghosts returning to find the coastline's abundance of litter, 'They'd find it difficult to comprehend all the changes that have taken place in the world.'

He's admitting more here than he perhaps realises.

Published by the British Film Institute, 22/12/16

Shifting Times and Places
in *Red Shift*

The year 1978 was an unusually successful one for the BBC single drama strand *Play for Today*. The slot featured a number of groundbreaking dramas including David Hare's *Licking Hitler*, David Edgar's *Destiny*, and Jim Allen's *The Spongers* to name only three.

One of the less discussed plays from that year is, however, just as effective as those groundbreaking dramas: John Mackenzie's adaptation of Alan Garner's fantastical work *Red Shift*. Mixing a melancholy, time-spanning tale with elements of psychological drama, the play is just as thought-provoking today as it was when first broadcast on the 17th of January 1978.

Staying true to Garner's 1973 novel, *Red Shift* follows the lives of three young men all interconnected by their troubled personas and the location of Mow Cop in Cheshire. Tom (Stephen Petcher) is an unsettled young man in the 1970s trying to hold onto his dwindling relationship with Jan (Lesley Dunlop) while strange visions befall him. Jan moves to London, and so they meet sporadically at Crewe station. From there they venture into the surrounding countryside and to a ruined tower, finding an unusual stone in the ground there, before their relationship begins to collapse.

In the English Civil War, Thomas (Charles Bolton) is holed up in a church near Mow Cop with his wife Madge (Myra Frances), hiding with others from Royalist soldiers who are after the concealed rebel John Fowler (James Hazeldine). Thomas is equally plagued by visions after finding the same strange stone hidden underground.

In the Roman period, a soldier called Macey (Andrew Byatt) is also suffering from unusual fits. The axe-head he uses on his weapon induces a berserker quality when he attacks and is said to be derived from a stone fallen from the stars. He and his unit are cut off from the main army and so take refuge on the hillside of Mow Cop, where they capture a young girl (Veronica Quilligan) and begin to turn upon one another.

Like most of Garner's work, place is key to the narrative and possesses temporal qualities. Time shifts and folds in upon itself, repeating and building like layers of stone and soil. In the novel, a paragraph break leads to a new period in time. Mackenzie, on the other hand, uses simple cuts to create this feeling of layered time and cascading years. It's an incredibly subtle shift, made effective by the fixed constant of the location, Mow Cop's castle tower never changing in spite of many years between the scenes.

Mackenzie manages brilliantly to retain the links built by Garner in his novel, connecting geography and history together through the palimpsest of the three protagonists' psychology. All three elements work to create strata that shift in time but always return to the location and to the stone which connects the three men.

Most famous for his novels set in Alderley Edge, few writers have developed such a complex and specific relationship to a place as Garner has. Due to the immense detail in his work, often built on genuine places and history, this has made his books ripe for adaptations.

Just under a decade before *Red Shift*, Garner's *The Owl Service* was adapted by Peter Plummer for Granada, while the themes that went into *Red Shift* were explored in an episode of the BBC documentary series *One Pair of Eyes* called 'Alan Garner – All Systems Go' (1972). Filmed when Garner was writing the book, the episode is worth noting as it reveals some of the genuine emotional trauma that the writer underwent himself when younger, later transplanted into the novel and film.

Red Shift is itself an excellent example of Garner's casual mixture of fantasy, psychology and an unusual avant-garde sensibility. Perhaps this is brought over to the screen from the novel's experiments with form and voice, but, like many other dramas in the *Play for Today* slot, such a sense of daring in content and visuals feels the norm.

There's something endlessly alluring and unusual about *Red Shift*, however, that makes it stand out from its peers, not least for its maturity in not telling the viewer what to expect or feel. The land is fixed, time is passing and, as in many of Garner's best works, the ancient and the otherworldly sit side by side.

Published by the British Film Institute, 17/01/18

Wire and Grass Landscapes

At the recent *Alchemical Landscape* conference in Cambridge, there was some interesting discussion of the landscape seen in the opening segment of Alan Clarke and David Rudkin's *Play for Today* episode, *Penda's Fen* (1974).

The point of the discussion was to show the subversive nature of these opening titles in regard to its melding of two potentially differing realities of English landscape. On the one hand, the typical pastoral qualities of the Malvern Hills; on the other, an encroaching urbanity represented by wire-mesh fences and a scarred, injured hand.

Though the general consensus of the two landscapes representing a binary was correct in regard to the world of Clarke's film, as well as the reasoning behind Rudkin's imbuing the landscape with such a binary in the first place, I began to question whether it actually reflected the genuine reality of the English landscape. On deeper reflection, I found it to be too simplistic to transplant such a binary onto the reality of everyday landscapes, and I sought to understand why I thought this.

When watching *Penda's Fen* again recently, it was only the hand itself in the opening segment which seemed to hint at a binary of landscape, where there was a manmade danger festering in the fenland of Pinvin. The hand is scarred and injured; perhaps the hand of the man killed by unknown technological forces conjured by the military of the narrative. But other than that, I *liked* this landscape, wire and all.

The aesthetic of mesh wire over a much greener natural landscape not only seemed perfectly normal to me but also naturally beautiful; this was not some privileged position of venturing into complicated landscapes and not having to deal with the realities of their possible ugliness, but an acceptance that the vast majority of landscapes I've been surrounded by have been filtered by wire and mesh fences.

There's no clash for me between the two, as this is how landscape has so often been packaged and experienced for me. Rarely has there been one of a pure rural or urban binary, even when venturing on holidays to cities such as London or Bilbao, or rural retreats to Norfolk, Suffolk and Dorset. There always seemed to be a wire fence or a concrete edifice next to the fields and fens.

Pondering why this seemed normal and not strictly subversive personally (though it no doubt *is* in the wider post-nature writing boom), it seemed to draw back to two things: where I come from and what I watched when younger.

It feels doubly poignant a point that Clarke came from Wallasey: the town where I'm from and a place littered with probably more wire fences than actual landscapes. The Wirral's own blurred binary between urban and rural means that it seems topographically schizoid, filled with wire, edgelands and rural zones, all, of course, variously fenced off.

However, more important are my first encounters with landscape in the television series *Doctor Who* (1963–89). The sheer pleasure of such wire-and-grass landscapes comes from numerous episodes rendering such places fantastical in my childhood vision of the world.

The series is replete with a huge range of edgeland spaces that, unsurprisingly, I ended up reimagining upon The Wirral landscape with ease. *Penda's Fen*'s wire and grass was a deliberate contrast; *Doctor Who*'s, by comparison, was accidental, and joyfully so.

The first instance I can recall came in the Jon Pertwee story 'The Green Death', broadcast in 1973. It tells of an oil company secretly polluting a Welsh coal mine and accidently creating a species of giant maggot. It also, incidentally, foretells a ruinous doom created by AI inventing the internet and polluting the world via globalisation. But these aspects are beside the point, as it has several moments of beautiful wire-and-grass landscapes.

The oil factory of the episode, Global Chemicals, has its plant filmed at the old RCA International building in Gwent, which was sadly demolished in 2008. The director, Michael E. Briant, makes the most of this landscape, a strangely commercial area not unlike a modern retail estate, fenced off with wire-mesh fences and turfed with neatly trimmed, yellowing grass.

The scene that still distinctly sits with me occurs some way into the story, where The Doctor has to break into the building in order to steal cutting equipment. While a group of hippies lead an anti-oil protest outside the building as a distraction, The Doctor uses a van with a remote extension lift to get himself over the fence and into the plant.

The landscape shots here are undoubtedly beautiful, and I have long and strangely detailed memories of desiring to simply sit with my back against this wire fence, relaxing on the grass while looking at the plant. The Doctor, of course, cannot indulge in this pleasure and has to run into the facility, where he sets off a security detector, itself built into the grass. This is not some nasty, makeshift landscape: this is a perfectly augmented zone designed for both industrial use and a veneer of aesthetic pleasure. But the veneer works for me more than most Areas of Outstanding Natural Beauty. I am totally sold on it.

There were many similar landscapes on The Wirral while growing up in the 1990s, even at my primary school, which itself had wire mesh fences around its fields. I would spend oddly long lunchtimes sitting against these fences, pretending to be Jon Pertwee but never quite managing to get up and enter Global Chemicals because of the sheer pleasure brought about by relaxing against a wire fence on a field.

The second example that comes readily to mind is also from a Jon Pertwee story, though there are plenty of others that hold a similar affection for me ('Robot' (1974) and 'The Android Invasion' (1975) being just two). In 'The Claws of Axos' (1971), an alien parasite lands in Dungeness by its power station (though called Nuton in the story), ready for a takeover as it starts its nutrition cycle to feed off the planet; starting with Derek Jarman's garden, of course.

Already, suggesting that a power station is present automatically tells of the sort of wiry landscapes that are on show, even if they are somewhat hidden by the freak snowstorms experienced by the crew during its filming (and written into the story last minute).

The point to raise here is the pleasure of feeling both proximity and distance from a power station's landscape; a feeling I felt again only recently when making a film about the beautiful, detritus-filled landscape of Sizewell in Suffolk.

In the story, the station becomes more and more of a dangerous place; one to retreat from in order to remain safe, as the alien takes over and attempts to drain its power and blow it up.

I used to enjoy transplanting the feeling I encountered in this story onto a place called Burton Mere on the Deeside of The Wirral. Though a nature reserve, its landscape provided so many wire-and-grass possibilities as to be worth visiting just to explore them. I was never a very good twitcher, instead accompanying my father to just enjoy the place while he searched in vain for a stubbornly camera-shy bittern.

From its grassy hillside and wire fence preventing access to a railway, Deeside power station could be seen in the distance. On wintry afternoons, it was just like being in 'The Claws of Axos'. These views were not about contrasts or binaries, but about grafts and amalgamations; the mixing of things to create a third, a compound rather than a mixture in chemistry terms.

Thinking back to *Penda's Fen*, to the arguments of the presentation and the general criticisms levelled at those who venture into more questionable landscapes (the natural kickback against psychogeography in particular), I realised (thankfully) that I was not engaging in a privileged journey into subversive landscapes whose problems (social, ecological, etc.) I did not have to deal with. On the contrary, I still, at the time of writing, have to deal with them today.

Instead, when engaging with these landscapes, I am traversing back into my own past; a sort of landscape nostalgia that brings great joy and pleasure. It just so happens that, unlike the typical landscapes that induce nostalgia in people (the rural idylls of Albion et al), mine happen to be the forgotten landscapes of television pulp; those wonderful places of wire and grass, growing together like ivy upon a trellis in a quaint but practical English garden.

Published by Celluloid Wicker Man, 01/08/16

Acknowledgements

My thanks must firstly go to Gary Budden at Influx Press. When the publisher went on hiatus it felt like being left out in the wilderness and, as I often reiterate in the thanks for my various books, I doubt I would be published without them. Thank you for the constant support. Thanks as well to Gary and Dan Coxon for the precise editing this book has undergone.

A great deal of the work featured in this volume has come from other sites, newspapers and magazines whose editors I owe a debt of thanks, not least as the commissions (and desire to take risks, which my work more often than not is in the clickbait age) are what keep me afloat. My thanks in particular to Sam, James and Kieron at the British Film Institute, Adam at *Little White Lies*, Jeff and Diva at *Caught By The River*, Jonny at Literary Hub, Alex at *The Daily Telegraph*, Thomas at *Port Magazine*, Tim at *Private Motor Club*, Mónica at *The Nightjar*, Luke and John at *The Quietus*, Hugh at the BBC, and Robyn and Torquil at BBC Radio 3 for their various support over the years.

Several of the photos featured in this book were taken during a period when sponsored by Polaroid who kindly provided a new camera and stock. Many thanks to them for such a privilege.

My thanks for friendship and general niceness over the last ten years to John Atkinson, Kit Caless, Ramsey Campbell,

Claire Catterall, Darren Charles, Jeremy Cooper, Mark Cousins, Jon Dear, Adèle Emmas, Lauren Elkin, Gareth Evans, Iain Forsyth and Jane Pollard, Mark Gatiss, Soma Ghosh, Simon Hollis, Justin Hopper, Clive Judd, Andrew Kötting, Deborah Levy, John McGrath, Robert Macfarlane, Andrew Male, Drew Mulholland, Benjamin Myers, Andy Paciorek, Jim Peters, Chris Petit, John Reppion, Gareth Rees, Ben Rivers, Georgina Rodgers (plus Oreo and Olive), Ellen Rogers, Holly Rogers, John Rogers, Paddy Rogers, Paul Scraton, Iain Sinclair, Richard Skelton, Katy Soar, Catherine Spooner, Matthew Sweet, Harriet Thorpe, Carrie Thompson, and Robert Valentine.

Thanks to Janet and Keith for being there for me when it mattered.

Thanks to Nan for our Monday afternoon phone calls.

And finally thanks to Laura who kept me grounded with love and support during the long and difficult process of editing this monstrous body of work.

Selected Bibliography

N.B. Publication years are based on editions quoted from, not the original publication year.

Antonioni, M., 1961. *La notte* [film]. Silver Films / Nepi Films.

Arendt, H., 2007. *Reflections on Literature and Culture.* Stanford University Press.

Ballard, J.G., 2010. *The Complete Short Stories: Vol 1.* Fourth Estate.

Ballard, J.G., 2008. *Concrete Island*. Harper Perennial.

Ballard, J.G., 2008. Crash. Harper Perennial.

Bernhard, T., 2013. *Concrete* [trans. David McLintok]. Faber & Faber.

Bernhard, T., 2006. *Gargoyles* [trans. Richard and Clara Winston]. Vintage International.

Bernhard, T., 2019. *Wittgenstein's Nephew* [trans. David McLinktock]. Faber & Faber.

Biggs, B, & Tookey, H., 2009. *Malcolm Lowry from the Merseyside*. Liverpool University Press.

Borges, J.L., 1999. *Collected Fictions* [trans. Andrew Hurley]. Penguin.

Brookner, A., 1984. *Hotel Du Lac*. Longman.

Burgess, A., 2013. *A Clockwork Orange*. Penguin.

Carter, A., 1995. *The Bloody Chamber and Other Stories*. Vintage.

Cole, T., 2016. *Known and Strange Things: Essays*. Faber & Faber.

Comber, P., 2014. *Ariadne's Thread: In Memory of W.G. Sebald*. Propolis.

Cortázar, J., 2013. *Blow-Up*. Pantheon.

Cox, M., 1983. *M.R. James: An Informal Portrait*. Oxford University Press.

Debord, G., 2002. *Society of the Spectacle* [trans. Freddy Perlman]. Black & Red.

Deleuze, G., 2008. *Proust and Signs* [trans. Richard Howard]. Continuum.

Dunn, C., 1995. *A Pleasant Terror: the Life and Ghosts of M.R. James* [film]. Seventh House Films.

Duras, M., 1981. *Agatha and the Limitless Readings* [film]. INA.

Duras, M., 2013. *L'amour* [trans. Kazim Ali & Libby Murphy]. Open Letter.

Duras, M., 1994. *Yann Andrea Steiner* [trans. Barbara Bray]. Hodder & Stroughton.

Fisher, M., 2011. *Patience (After Sebald): under the sign of Saturn* [Sight & Sound]. British Film Institute.

Flood, A., 2019. *Angela Carter's "carnival" London home receives blue plaque* [the Guardian]. Guardian Media Group.

Garner, A., 2002. *The Owl Service*. Harper Collins.

Garner, A., 2010. *The Voice That Thunders*. Harvill Press.

Garner, A., 2010. *The Weirdstone of Brisingamen*. Harper Collins.

Gatiss, M., 2013. *M.R. James: Ghost Writer* [film]. BBC.

Giddens, A., 2007. *Desert the Island Mentality* [the Guardian]. Guardian Media Group.

Godard, J.L., 1967. *Two or Three Things I Know About Her* [film]. Argos Films.

Hill, S., 2010. *M.R. James's dark world* [The Spectator]. The Spectator (1828) Ltd.

Hitchcock, A., 1960. *Psycho* [film]. Shamely Productions.

Hubert, R., 2011. *Grant Gee on Sebald and Cinema* [Book Forum]. 1865 Publications LLC.

James, M.R., 2007. *Collected Ghost Stories (Tales of Mystery & The Supernatural)*. Wordsworth Editions.

Larios, P., 2013. *Walser in Berlin* [Interview with Tacita Dean]. Frieze.

Larkin, P., 2003. *Collected Poems*. Faber & Faber.

Leigh, M., 1976. *Play for Today: Nuts in May* [film]. BBC.

Lovecraft, H.P., 2007. *The Whisperer in Darkness: Collected Stories Vol. 1*. Wordsworth Editions.

Lowry, M., 2000. *Under the Volcano*. Penguin.

Macfarlane, R., 2012. *Robert Macfarlane's Untrue Island: the voices of Orford Ness* [the Guardian]. Guardian Media Group.

Machen, A., 2006. *The Secret Glory*. Aehypan.

Machen, A., 2004. *The Terror and Other Tales*. Chaosium.

Martin, N., 2004. *Sebald Goes to the Movies: Reading Kafka as Cinematography*. Edinburgh University Press.

Perec, G., 2010. *An Attempt to Exhaust a Place in Paris* [trans. Marc Lowenthal]. Wakefield Press.

Perec, G., 2008. *Species of Space and Other Pieces* [trans. John Sturrock]. Penguin.

Pinter, H., 2005. *Various Voices: Prose, Poetry, Politics 1948-2005*. Faber & Faber.

Pixley, A., 2005. *Programme Notes – The Quatermass Experiment*. BBC
Pringle, D., 1987. *J.G. Ballard* [Interzone]. N/A.

Proust, M., 2004. *In Search of Lost Time – Swann's Way* [trans. Lydia Davis]. Penguin.

Radax, F., 1970. *Thomas Bernhard – Drei Tag* [film]. WDR.

Schruers, F., 1995. *That Strange, Sad Light* [Los Angeles Times]. Nant Capital.

Sebald, W.G., 2015. *A Place in the Country* [trans. Jo Catling]. Modern Library.

Sebald, W.G., 2012. *Across the Land and the Water: Selected Poems 1964-2001* [trans. Iain Galbraith]. Penguin.

Sebald, W.G., 2011. *Austerlitz* [trans. Anthea Bell]. Penguin.

Sebald, W.G., 2002. *The Emigrants* [trans. Michael Hulse]. Vintage Books.

Sebald, W.G., 2002. *The Rings of Saturn* [trans. Michael Hulse]. Vintage Books.

Shepherd, N., 2011. *The Living Mountain*. Canongate.

Smith, A., 2012. *Ali Smith on Margaret Tait*. Scottish Poetry Library.

Solnit, R., 2014. *Wanderlust: A History of Walking*. Granta.

Stifter, A., 2008. *The Bachelors* [trans. David Bryer]. Pushkin Press.

Stifter, A., 2008. *Rock Crystal* [trans. Elizabeth Mayer & Marianne Moore]. New York Review Books Classics.

Spark, M., 2006. *The Ballad of Peckham Rye*. Penguin.

Tait, M., 2008. *A Portrait of Ga* [Moving Image Archive]. National Library of Scotland.

Varda, A., 1962. *Cléo from 5 to 7* [film]. Ciné-tamaris.

Wakefield, H.R., 1982. *The Best Ghost Stories of H. Russell Wakefield*. Academy Chicago Publishing.

Wakefield, H.R., 1935. *Ghost Stories*. Florin Books, Jonathan Cape.

Walser, R., 2013. *The Walk* [trans. Christopher Middleton]. Serpent's Tail.

Williams, N., 2009. *Harold Pinter* – Part One: The Room [film]. BBC

Adam Scovell is a writer and filmmaker from Merseyside, now living in London. He completed his PhD in Music at Goldsmiths University in 2018, and now writes regularly for the BBC, the BFI and many other outlets. He is the author of *Folk Horror: Hours Dreadful and Things Strange* (2017, Auteur), alongside three novels all published by Influx Press.

Influx Press is an award-winning independent publisher based in London, committed to publishing innovative and challenging literature from across the UK and beyond.

www.influxpress.com
@Influxpress